Simon Clarke

SECOND EDITION

in company

PRE-INTERMEDIATE STUDENT'S BOOK WITH CD-ROM

MACMILLAN

SECOND EDITION STUDENT'S BOOK:

- **15 TOPIC UNITS** focusing on current business issues and everyday skills

- **5 SPEAKING SKILLS UNITS** focusing on functional business English language

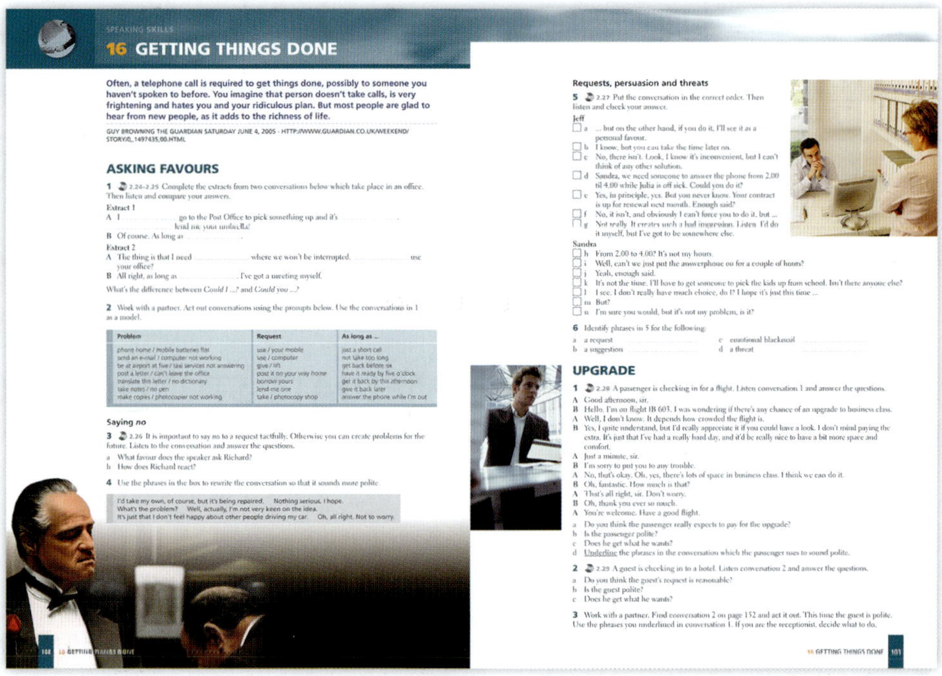

▶ **15 LANGUAGE LINKS** consolidating grammar and extending vocabulary from the Topic Units

▶ Phrase Bank for summary and revision

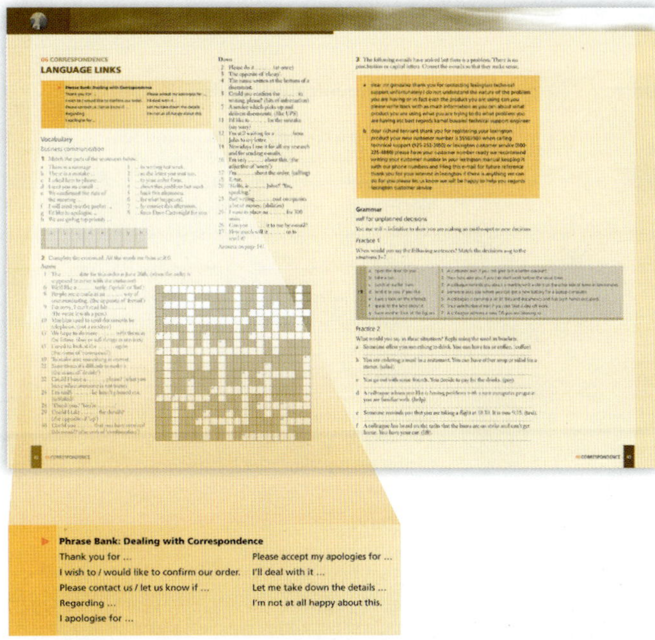

▶ **5 CASE STUDIES** reflecting real-life business scenarios

▶ **BACK-OF-BOOK MATERIAL:**

- Case Studies Glossary
- Listening Scripts with useful phrases from the Language Links Phrase Banks in bold
- Additional material for communicative activities

SELF-STUDY CD-ROM:

- Extra listening activities
- Interactive grammar and vocabulary activities
- Interactive glossary
- Downloadable Student's Book audio
- Downloadable Student's Book Phrase Banks

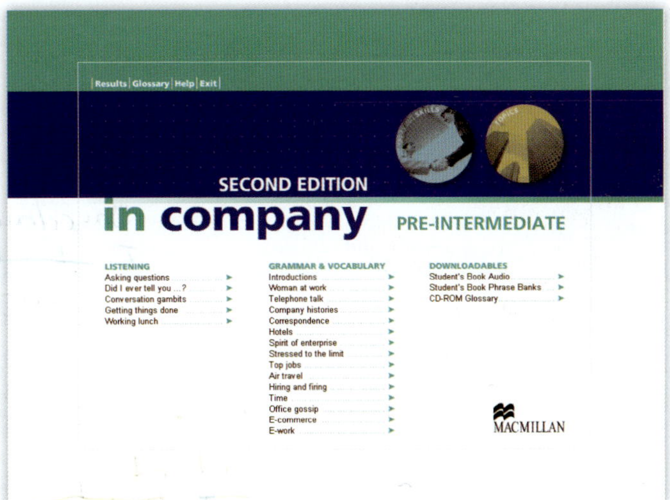

WEBSITE:

Course updates, regular e-lessons and supplementary material available at: **www.businessenglishonline.net**

CONTENTS

Unit	Communication skills	Reading and listening texts	Language links
01 **Introductions** p6	Making a presentation about yourself Asking for personal information Discussing social networking sites Discussing ideas for start-ups	**Reading** Description of Facebook Facebook page **Listening** Introductions at a training course Company profile	**Vocabulary** Describing your work, Computers and the Internet **Grammar** Present Simple, Present Continuous **Phrase bank** Describing your work
02 **Woman at work** p13	Discussing blogs Asking about work routines Completing a questionnaire on exercise Discussing exercise and ways to relax	**Reading** Blog description of a typical day Article about exercise and lifestyle **Listening** Conversation about someone's new job	**Vocabulary** Discussing and expressing opinion, Jobs **Grammar** Expressing frequency **Phrase bank** Discussing ideas
03 **Telephone talk** p19	Using telephone skills Discussing telephone frustrations Telephoning for information	**Reading** Article about telephone skills **Listening** Different ways of saying numbers Apologising on the phone Conversation about an order	**Vocabulary** Telephone language, Numbers **Grammar** Indirect questions **Phrase bank** Telephoning
04 **Asking questions** p26	Making conversation with new people Talking about other people	**Listening** Conversations with new people	
Case Study: Internet Access p28	Discussing policies for Internet use at work	**Reading** Article about Internet use at work **Listening** Explanation of company's Internet use policy	
05 **Company histories** p30	Completing a quiz about the history of the Internet Discussing personal experience of the Internet Making a presentation about a company's history	**Reading** Timeline describing history of Nintendo Article about the birth of the Internet **Listening** Documentary on the history of the Internet	**Vocabulary** Time expressions, Business verbs **Grammar** Past Simple **Phrase bank** Talking about the past
06 **Correspondence** p37	Discussing the importance of grammar Making on-the-spot decisions Giving and receiving details about an important order Complaining about errors in an order	**Reading** Article about grammar in business correspondence E-mails about an order **Listening** Telephone conversation about an important order	**Vocabulary** Business communication, Punctuation and spelling **Grammar** *will* for unplanned decisions **Phrase bank** Dealing with correspondence
07 **Hotels** p44	Making and responding to special requests Discussing hotel rooms Making comparisons Discussing the pros and cons of different office locations	**Reading** Comments about hotels Article about Yotels **Listening** Conversation at airport check-in Conversation at hotel reception	**Vocabulary** Travel and accommodation **Grammar** Comparatives and superlatives **Phrase bank** Travel and accommodation
08 **Did I ever tell you ...?** p52	Telling an anecdote Using *did* for emphasis	**Listening** An anecdote about a journey	
Case Study: Cristal Malvern p54	Discussing how to deal with a major problem	**Reading** Article about a company's troubles **Listening** Interview with company representatives	
09 **Spirit of enterprise** p56	Describing change in a country or company Completing a report about a company Exchanging information about a company	**Reading** Articles about two successful companies Business Briefing: Inditex **Listening** Radio programme about entrepreneurs	**Vocabulary** Business achievements, Language to describe change **Grammar** Present Perfect **Phrase bank** Talking about business achievements
10 **Stressed to the limit** p63	Discussing the causes of stress Comparing different jobs Asking about someone's responsibilities and duties at work Writing a consultant's report on a company	**Reading** Article about stress at work **Listening** People talking about stress at work	**Vocabulary** Stress at work, Health **Grammar** *have to / don't have to, should / shouldn't* **Phrase bank** Talking about your health
11 **Top jobs** p70	Finding out more information about someone Writing a report	**Reading** Time line describing history of Nokia Report about someone's career **Listening** Documentary about the founders of YouTube Phone call from a headhunter	**Vocabulary** Money, Company news **Grammar** Present Perfect for unfinished past, *for* and *since* **Phrase bank** Money and company background

Unit	Communication skills	Reading and listening texts	Language links
12 **Conversation gambits** p77	Introducing yourself and starting a conversation Choosing safe topics of conversation Ending a conversation	**Reading** Article about conversation strategies **Listening** People meeting by chance	
Case Study: **Staff Appraisal** p80	Deciding what staff appraisal scheme to implement	**Reading** Blogs discussing staff appraisal **Listening** Explanation of staff appraisal scheme	
13 **Air travel** p82	Discussing the dos and don'ts of business travel Negotiating skills	**Reading** Article about comfortable air travel Article about cut-price business travel **Listening** Conversations at check-in	**Vocabulary** Negotiating, Air travel **Grammar** Conditionals with *will* **Phrase bank** Air travel
14 **Hiring and firing** p88	Discussing when sacking is justified Writing a letter of application Asking for clarification Discussing labour laws and industrial action	**Reading** Article about someone being fired CV **Listening** People talking about applying for a new job Job interview	**Vocabulary** Asking for clarification, Procedures **Grammar** The passive **Phrase bank** Asking for clarification
15 **Time** p95	Discussing time management Asking and answering about time management techniques Talking about decisions and plans	**Reading** Article about working without clocks **Listening** A conversation about a delayed project A talk on time management	**Vocabulary** Time collocations, Working conditions **Grammar** *going to*, *going to* vs *will* **Phrase bank** Presentations, talking about time
16 **Getting things done** p102	Asking for favours Saying 'no' tactfully Using polite language	**Listening** A conversation with a refused request Conversations to persuade, promise and threaten People making special requests	
Case Study: **Company Structure** p104	Discussing how to restructure a company	**Reading** Article about company structure	
17 **Office gossip** p106	Reporting gossip Discussing the pros and cons of gossip at work Discussing office policy about gossip	**Reading** Article about a company banning gossip Posts on a forum about office gossip **Listening** Conversation about company gossip Radio interview about the importance of gossip at work	**Vocabulary** Office chat Relationships at work **Grammar** Reported speech, *say* and *tell* **Phrase bank** Social chat
18 **E-commerce** p113	Discussing purchase decisions Discussing advantages and disadvantages Discussing marketing e-commerce to the over-sixties	**Reading** Survey about the future of the Internet **Listening** Radio interview about the pros and cons of e-commerce	**Vocabulary** Discussing advantages and disadvantages, Shopping and the Internet **Grammar** *will* for future predictions **Phrase bank** Advantages and disadvantages
19 **E-work** p120	Talking about hypothetical situations Discussing the advantages and disadvantages of teleworking Discussing company policy about teleworking	**Reading** Article about the rise of e-workers Article about working from home **Listening** Conversation about working from home People talking about their experiences of telework	**Vocabulary** Teleworking, Explaining things **Grammar** Conditionals (future reference) **Phrase bank** Explaining things
20 **Working lunch** p127	Describing food Describing different roles in a job Using the correct business etiquette	**Reading** Article about business etiquette in Japan **Listening** Conversation at a restaurant Explanation of job roles	
Case Study: **Linux** p130	Discussing and evaluating different operating systems	**Reading** Article about Siemens adopting a new OS	
Additional material p132			
Listening scripts p143			
Case Studies Glossary p155			

01 INTRODUCTIONS

It may be a welcome break from the daily grind, but according to one in three US workers, their most recent employer-provided training was a waste of time.

FROM WWW.MANAGEMENT-ISSUES.COM

THE TRAINING COURSE

1 Match the words (a–k) to their definitions (1–11).

a payroll
b quality control
c retail chain
d personnel
e hiring and firing
f recruitment
g temporary employment agency
h management training
i market research
j personal assessment
k unique selling point

1 paying people
2 all the people employed by a company
3 a company that supplies workers for short periods
4 making sure there are no mistakes
5 finding out what people think about products and services
6 employing and dismissing people
7 evaluation of how well people are doing their jobs
8 a group of shops with the same name
9 finding people for jobs
10 the thing that makes a product or service different
11 courses in the skills of leading people

a ☐ b ☐ c ☐ d ☐ e ☐ f ☐ g ☐ h ☐ i ☐ j ☐ k ☐

2 Which words in 1 do you associate with the topic of Human Resources?

3 1.01 Listen to the start of the first session in a Human Resources training course. Which words in 1 are mentioned?

4 Listen again and complete the chart.

	From	Job	Home
Jan Werner	Norway		
Silvia Fortuni		Director of Staff Training	
Jean-Christophe Marchal			

Jan Werner

Silvia Fortuni

Jean-Christophe Marchal

5 Complete the phrases. Then listen again and check your answers.

a My .... Jan Werner. I .... Metronet Fibre. Our .... is fibre optics.
b Our head office is in Prague. That's where ...., but at the moment, …
c I work .... our headquarters in Barcelona.
d My role .... to personnel.
e I .... for recruitment and training in the European area.
f I have a .... in the HR department of Aqualux.
g I'm mainly .... staff training.
h I have five .... working in the HR field.

> ▶ **social networking** /ˈsəʊʃ(ə)l ˌnetwɜːkɪŋ/ *noun* meeting and talking to people informally

6 Prepare and give a mini-presentation introducing yourself to the rest of your class and/or your teacher. Use the phrases in 5 to help.

Discussion

7 Work in groups and talk about training courses. Do you ever go on training courses? What kind? Do you think they are useful?

SOCIAL NETWORKING

1 Work in pairs and discuss the questions. Then read the text to see if you are correct.

a What is Facebook?
b What can you put on your Facebook site?
c What must you have in order to join Facebook?
d What is the main purpose of Facebook?
e Can you choose who has access to your information?

About Facebook

FACEBOOK is a website that connects people with friends and others who work, study and live around them. People use Facebook to keep up with friends, upload an unlimited number of photos, share links and videos, and learn more about the people they meet.

Anyone can join Facebook

All that's needed to join Facebook is a valid e-mail address. To connect with co-workers or classmates, use your school or work e-mail address to register. Once you register, join a regional network to connect with the people in your area.

Discover the people around you

Facebook is made up of many networks, each based around a company, region, or school. Join the networks that reflect your real-life communities to learn more about the people who work, live, or study around you.

Keep it private

At Facebook, we believe that people should have control over how they share their information and who can see it. People can only see the profiles of confirmed friends and the people in their networks. You can use our privacy settings at any time to control who can see what on Facebook.

Mark Zuckeburg, the founder of Facebook
Source: www.facebook.com/about.php

2 Find the words and phrases in the text which mean the following:

a To maintain contact with. keep up with
b References to pages on the Internet. website
c People you have contact with at work. ....
d Groups of people which physically exist. community
e Options in a computer program which limit access to information. private settings

3 Jean-Christophe Marchal has a page on Facebook. Look at his page and answer the questions.

a What is Jean-Christophe doing at the moment? Sleeping
b Is he married? Yes
c When is his birthday?
d Where does he live?
e What things does he enjoy doing?
f What are his interests?
g What are his favourite TV shows?
h What do his friends say about him?

facebook

Profile edit **Friends • Networks • Inbox** home account privacy logout

Search •

Photos
Notes
Groups
Events
Posted items

Jean-Christophe Marchal **Profile •**

Jean-Christophe is:	sleeping
Networks:	None
Relationship Status:	Married
Birthday:	May 24, 1962

▼ Information

Contact Info

e-mail:	jc_marshal@aqualuxcom.fr
Skype:	jc_marshal
Mobile:	674647487
Land Phone:	756757575
Current Address:	7, Rue Richard-Lenoir, 93100 Montreuil-sous-Bois.

Personal Info

Activities:	Cycling, writing, reading and socialising.
Interests:	Video games, theatre, wine.
Favorite Music:	Coldplay.
Favorite TV Shows:	CSI, Nip Tuck, Prison Break.

Education and Work

Education Info	
College:	University of Ghent
High School:	Ecole Européenne de Bruxelles
Work Info	
Employer:	Aqualux
Time Period:	January 2008 – Present
Location:	Paris, France

The Wall

Displaying the only 2 wall posts. See All.
[Write something on your own Wall …]
Julia Maguire (no network) wrote at 9:46pm on July 28th, 2007:
You're putting on weight!

4 Now ask a partner or your teacher the same questions.
What are you doing at the moment?

Discussion

5 Work in groups and talk about social networking sites. Do you know of any other social networking sites like Facebook? Have you joined any? Do you think these sites are useful for people in business? What problems do you think there might be with using these sites?

Name of Company: Cobra Beer.

Founder: Karan Bilimoria

Exports: To more than a) .... countries worldwide.

Established in: 19 b) ....

Countries where Cobra is produced: the UK, c) ....

Product: d) .... with a lower level of e) ...., aimed at people eating Indian food. It has a premium strength of f) ....%.

Annual turnover: g) ....

Growth rate: h) ....% in last ten years.

Retail outlets: Cobra Beer is stocked in over i) .... restaurants and in most major supermarkets and off-licence chains in the UK. It is also sold in nearly j) .... pubs and clubs.

Location: Headquarters in Fulham, south-west k) .... Subsidiaries in l) ....

COMPANY PROFILE

1 1.02 Listen to an extract from a radio programme. The speaker is talking about a company. Complete the details in the company profile on the left.

2 Listen again and complete the phrases below.

a This month, we .... at the retail food trade.
b Cobra .... to more than 45 countries worldwide, and now with subsidiaries in India, South Africa and the US, ...
c ... it .... a mainstream, global beer brand.
d Cobra Beer .... a turnover of £75 million a year, ...
e The company .... rapidly, with a growth rate of 42% in the last ten years.
f The company headquarters .... in Fulham, in south-west London, but it now .... subsidiaries in India, South Africa and the US.
g ... it .... operations to meet the demand for Cobra in the European and worldwide market.

3 Match the sentences (a–g) in 2 to the descriptions.

a Present Simple to describe a stable situation: b, d, f
b Present Continuous to describe a current situation or activity: ....
c Present Continuous to describe a situation of change: ....

4 Write questions for these answers.

a Cobra Beer. What's the company's name?
b Karan Bilimoria.
c Beer.
d It doesn't have as much gas as normal beer and goes very well with Indian food.
e Yes, to over 45 countries.
f In Fulham in south-west London.
g £75 million.
h 42% over the last ten years.

5 Combine the verbs in A with the words in B to make as many different combinations as possible.

A extend have hire make run set up
B a company an idea operations previous experience a profit staff a turnover a website

make a profit

Collocations

6 Use the collocations in 5 to complete the sentences below. You may need to change the form of the verb.

a Our investors are happy because we are making a profit.
b We .... so that people can get information about our products online.
c They use a recruiting agency to ....
d Giovanni Bianchi .... which his family owns in Milan.
e He has the right qualifications for the job, but .... he ....?
f He .... for a new business, but I don't think it will work.

7 Choose three collocations from 6 and write your own example sentences.

Word building

8 The words in brackets are all important business words. Use the correct form of each to complete the sentences.

a His new business is a great .... (successful)
b We have good ideas, but we need to convince our .... (investment)
c As the market grows, they are increasing .... (product)
d It's a very .... business. (profit)
e Every day I read the .... newspapers. (finance)
f We are looking for new .... to provide us with the parts. (supply)
g Our online marketing led to amazing .... in sales. (grow)
h It's very important to .... if you want to survive in the IT market. (innovation)

YOUR START-UP

1 Work with a partner. Discuss your ideas for your own start-up (a new company). It can be either serious or humorous. Complete the 'your start-up' column in the table below. Then change partner and ask questions to complete the 'your partner's start-up' column.

	Your start-up	Your partner's start-up
Name of company		
Product or service		
USP (Unique Selling Point)		
Location		
Markets		
Competition		

2 Use the framework below to write a description of your new partner's company.

(name of company) .... is a
(type of company) ....
The main activity of the company is ....
Its USP is ....
The company is based in ....
but has offices in ....
Its main markets are ....
and its main competitor is ....

01 INTRODUCTIONS

LANGUAGE LINKS

> **Phrase Bank: Describing your work**
> I work for IBM/a pharmaceutical company.
> I work in a bank/an office/London.
> My job involves ...
> My role is to ...
> I have a post as head of marketing/in the marketing department.
> I am responsible for accounts.
> I have (five years of) experience in sales.
> We are based in ...
> Our headquarters are in ...

Vocabulary

Companies & the Internet

Complete the sentences using the words in the box.

employs experience franchises headquarters Internet involved investment profit responsible turnover website

a The company .... over 2,000 workers in Europe, located in four different factories.
b McDonalds has .... all over the world.
c My department is .... for marketing and sales in Eastern Europe.
d Our company .... provides information about our services and products, but we don't sell anything online.
e We need more .... to finance our expansion in China.
f The .... of Nestlé are in Geneva.
g He has an MBA but does he have any previous .... in sales?
h For the company to survive, our .... needs to grow by 20% this year.
i In my opinion, the BBC has one of the best websites on the ....
j They make a .... of $4.20 on each book they sell without any discounts.
k The company is mainly .... with food and drink products but also has other lines.

The Internet & computers

Complete the crossword.

Across

2 We are designing a new .... at the moment.
3 Please add our site to your .... of favourites.
5 If you give me your address, I can send you an ....
7 A .... with no cable is much more comfortable to use.
9 It's like the Internet but the pages are only accessible inside the company.
10 We pay them to include a .... to our website on their page.
11 How much do you pay for your Internet .... per month?
14 Our system is infected by a ....
16 I don't have much time to .... the Internet at work.

Down

1 I'll send you the document as an e-mail ....
4 Don't get so close to the .... It's bad for your eyes.
6 You can .... music and pictures from our site.
8 Nowadays I buy all my CDs and books ....
12 .... here for further information.
13 I'm looking for a web .... with information about share prices.
15 In order to .... the web in comfort you need a good computer.

Answers on page 132.

Grammar

Present Simple

Affirmative		Negative	
I You We They	work	I You We They	don't work
He She It	works	He She It	doesn't work

Interrogative		
Do Don't	I you we they	work?
Does Doesn't	he she it	work?

You use the Present Simple to talk about

- routine actions and habits.
  I go to work by bus.
  He ***works*** *late on Tuesdays.*
- ongoing situations we see as stable.
  We ***live*** *in London.*
  They ***employ*** *over 250 people.*

Present Continuous

Affirmative	
I'm (am)	
You**'re (are)** We**'re (are)** They**'re (are)**	**working**
He**'s (is)** She**'s (is)** It**'s (is)**	

Negative	
I'm not	
You **aren't** We **aren't** They **aren't**	**working**
He **isn't** She **isn't** It **isn't**	

Interrogative		
Am Aren't	I	
Are Aren't	you we they	working?
Is Isn't	he she it	

You use the Present Continuous to talk about

- activities happening at the moment of speaking.
  He's ***wearing*** *a grey suit, a white shirt and a blue tie.*
  Don't interrupt me, please. I'm ***trying*** *to concentrate.*
  'What ***are*** *you* ***doing****?' 'I'm* ***preparing*** *this month's sales figures.'*
- activities or situations you see as temporary.
  We're ***using*** *this office until the new one is ready.*
  I'm ***working*** *from home for a few days so don't phone me at the office.*
- situations which are changing.
  The economic situation ***is getting*** *better.*
  Our company share price ***is*** *steadily* ***improving****.*

You often use the Present Continuous with time expressions: *at the moment, this week/month/year* etc.
We ***are having*** *a lot of problems with our suppliers at the moment.*
I'm ***doing*** *a course this month, but it's not very interesting.*

Practice 1

Complete the sentences using the verbs in the box in the correct form – Present Simple or Present Continuous. Use each verb twice.

do	get	live	sell	think	work

a Normally, I am in the office in the afternoon, but this month I .... a course.
b In the winter, the reps .... more than in the summer.
c Our most important market is the Far East. We .... business with several companies there.
d Our new product line .... very well this year.
e Our boss .... very long hours.
f He .... of changing his job because he's not very happy.
g 'What's your address?' 'I .... in a hotel until we find a nice flat.'
h In June, the weather .... hot there, so take some cool clothes.
i He .... his job is really interesting.
j It .... hotter. We need to get some air conditioning for this office.
k At present, we .... on new products and services for the future.
l During the week, he .... in his city flat and at the weekend he goes to the country.

Practice 2

Write questions about the information which is missing.

a The company makes money by …
  How does the company make money?
b Our business is expanding because …
  Why ....
c They are setting up a business in …
  Where ....
d We are looking for $ …
  How much ....
e He has previous experience in the … business.
  What kind ....
f Their unique selling point is …
  What ....
g My company employs … people.
  How many ....
h The manager of the company is …
  Who ....
i They are talking to … about further investment.
  Who ....

TOPICS

02 WOMAN AT WORK

The failure of Fortune 500 companies to add women to their corporate leadership in the last three years highlights a startling gap between rhetoric and reality.

CATALYST CENSUS OF WOMEN CORPORATE OFFICERS AND TOP EARNERS OF THE FORTUNE 500

TOP EARNERS

1 Look at the quotation above. What do you know about Fortune 500? Why is the writer not happy?

2 Complete the statistics about the USA using the numbers in the box. Compare your answers with a partner.

6.4%	16.4%	46.4%	1.6%	14.7%

a .... of all workers are women.
b .... of corporate officers in the Fortune 500 are women.
c Women represent .... of top earners.
d .... of individuals serving on Boards of Directors are women.
e However, only .... of CEOs in the Fortune 500 are women.

Discussion

3 Look at page 132 to check the statistics in 2. Then discuss the questions.
a Is the situation similar in your country?
b Do you think this situation will change in the future?

4 Read the blog of a leading executive on a corporate website and answer the questions.
a What time does Sally McDermott start work in the morning?
b What time does she normally get to the office?
c Does she ever smoke?
d Why does she use the phone so much?
e How often does she have to work at the weekend?

5 How old do you think Sally McDermott is? How typical is her life?

- **Fortune 500** /ˌfɔː(r)tʃən faɪv ˈhʌndrəd/ the 500 largest companies in the US
- **Board of Directors** /ˌbɔːd əv dəˈrektəz/ *noun* a group of people who control a company
- **CEO** /ˌsiː iː ˈəʊ/ *noun* the most senior manager in the company

Definitions from Macmillan Essential Dictionary and Macmillan English Dictionary

A day in the life of Sally McDermott

We are a major telecom with operations in most of Europe and in Latin America. The career of our International Operations Manager, Sally McDermott, includes periods of work in Portugal, Paris, and London, and a post with British Telecom. She speaks Spanish, French and Russian as well as English.

People often ask me how I manage to combine a successful career with family life. The secret is that I don't need much sleep! Five hours is usually enough. So by 5.30 I'm up and at my laptop, working on business and e-mails from the previous day. Socially, my day begins with breakfast at 8.00, together with my husband, Derek, and my 15-year-old daughter, Katie.

I go to work in a taxi which picks me up at 8.30 every day. On the way to work I look through the daily papers. I enjoy having this time to myself and switch off my mobile. It normally takes us about 20 minutes to get to the office. My office is a beautiful room with fantastic views on the top floor of our headquarters. When I arrive, my secretary joins me and we go through any correspondence and plan the day. I make decisions about appointments and organise meetings. I'm giving up smoking, but I find it difficult. By 9.30, I feel like a cigarette! I never have one of course, as apart from anything else, these days smoking in the office is not allowed, even for me.

I keep going by drinking a lot of coffee and mineral water. I usually have a working lunch in a nearby restaurant. I try not to eat too much and never drink any alcohol. Then in the afternoon, it's nearly always back to the office and more meetings. When I'm not in a meeting, I'm constantly on the phone. I use the phone whenever possible because it's nearly always quicker than using e-mail. Even if I'm in the office, I prefer to use my mobile. I don't know why, it's just a habit I suppose. I hardly ever send text messages, except to my daughter – it's just too time-consuming.

I like to pick Katie up from school when I can, but most days I work until at least 8.00 and then there is sometimes a business dinner to go to. Weekends are sacred and pretty much reserved for my family. I don't often have to work but occasionally something comes up which I just can't avoid. All in all, it's hard work but I enjoy my job. That is just as well, because at this stage in life, if something isn't fun, I don't do it!

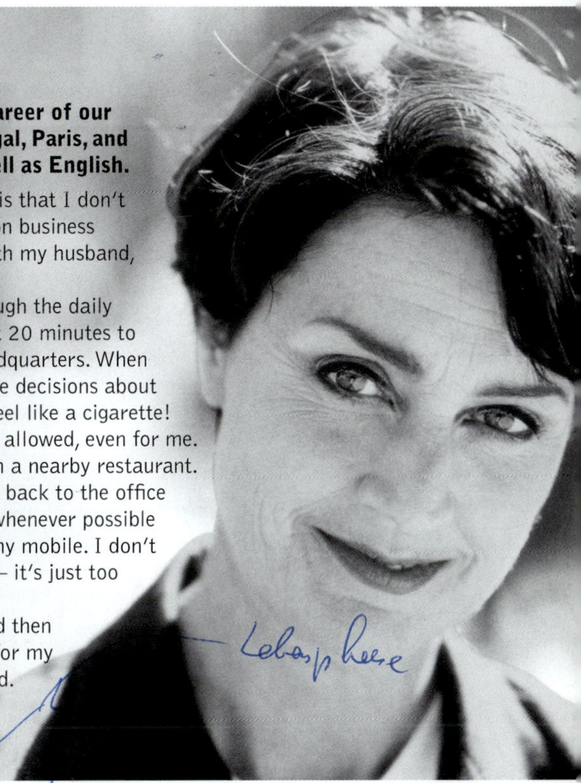

6 Underline all the phrases in the blog which say how often something happens. The first one has been done for you.

7 Underline the correct option.

a In most cases, Adverbs of Frequency (*sometimes*, *often*, *never*, etc.) go **before/after** the main verb.
b Adverbs of Frequency go **before/after** the verb *to be*.

Expressing frequency

8 Add a frequency expression to each sentence so that it is true for you.

always every day every week hardly ever never not often
often once a month sometimes twice a year usually

a I go to work by car.
b I get home late.
c I work at the weekend.
d I have a holiday.
e I feel bored with my job.
f My boss gives me a hard time.
g My computer crashes.
h I find time to relax and enjoy myself.
i I have arguments with people at work.
j I read the financial papers.

9 Complete the 'Action' and 'You' columns in the chart below. Then ask questions to complete the 'Your partner' column.

	Action	You	Your partner
	eat out	*once a week*	
How often do you ...?			
Do you ... much?			
Do you ever ... ?			

BLOGS

1 Discuss these questions with a partner.

a What is a blog? What different types of blogs are there? Do you ever read them?
b How can blogs be useful in business? Do you know any famous corporate blogs?

2 1.03 Listen to two people talking about blogs. Are their ideas similar to yours in 1?

3 Listen again. As you listen, number the phrases below in the order you hear them.

a ☐ What do you think about … ?
b ☐ For example, from a (business) point of view …
c ☐ Yes, you're probably right, but …
d ☐ Okay, but …
e ☐ Maybe, but …
f ☐ Do you really think … ?
g ☐ I'm not sure about that.
h ☐ What do you mean?

4 Form two groups.

Group A: Think of arguments in favour of blogs and make notes. Look at page 133 for ideas.
Group B: Think of arguments against blogs. Look at page 139 for ideas.

5 Find a partner from the other group in 4 and have a discussion where you defend your arguments for/against blogs. Use each phrase in 3 at least once.

WHAT'S IN A JOB?

1 1.04 Two friends meet and talk about someone's new job. Listen to their conversation and answer the questions.

a What is the relationship between Eddie (the man) and Fiona (the person with the new job)?

b How does Eddie feel about the new job?

2 Complete the dialogue using the questions in the box.

> Does it involve long hours?
> Does it mean a lot of travelling?
> Does she enjoy it?
> Does she have to work weekends?
> How much holiday does she get?
> What does it involve?
> What's she doing?

A Hi, Eddie. How are you?
B Oh hello, Jennie. I'm fine. And you?
A Fine, thanks. How's Fiona?
B Oh, she's okay. She's got a new job.
A Really, that's good.
B Well, yes. I suppose so, but I'm worried she's working too hard.
A Oh dear. a) *Does it involve long hours?*
B Officially 40 hours, but she often works late. We don't see her at home much.
A b) ....
B It's the same company – you know – educational software – but she's now Regional Marketing Manager for western Europe.
A Sounds impressive. c) ....
B Apart from being in charge of the sales reps, she's also involved in new product development and the whole marketing strategy of the company.
A d) ....
B It seems to. At least a couple of trips a month.
A I see.
B I don't mind that. It's the weekends that cause problems.
A e) ....
B Not every weekend, but we can never make plans.
A Oh dear. f) ....
B It's not bad. Three weeks a year. But that's a long way off.
A You're being a bit negative. g) ....
B It's hard work, but I think she enjoys the challenge.
A But you're not very happy.
B I'm happy for her. The money's good, and it's great for her career, but there is a downside.
A: Well, it's always difficult at the beginning. Anyway, give her my regards. Why don't we go for a drink sometime?
B Okay, I will, and yes, I'd like that.

3 Work with a partner. Ask questions as in 2 to complete your chart.

Speaker A: Look at the chart on page 135.
Speaker B: Look at the chart on page 142.

4 Ask your partner similar questions about their job or the job of someone they know.

TAKING THINGS EASY

1 Do you take regular exercise? Do you think it's important? Work with a partner and complete the questionnaire below.

a	Taking exercise is the best solution for stress.	true ☐	false ☐
b	Sport is the key to a healthy and long life.	true ☐	false ☐
c	People who get up early suffer from stress.	true ☐	false ☐
d	People who have a sleep during the day live longer.	true ☐	false ☐
e	People in their 50s need to save their energy.	true ☐	false ☐
f	Brisk walks are the healthiest form of exercise.	true ☐	false ☐

2 Now read the article below to see if your answers are the same as the author's.

3 Underline three expressions in the article which mean *to relax* or *to rest*.

4 Choose the best title for the article.

a All work and no play makes Jack a dull boy
b Health risks for the over 50s
c Siesta or Marathon?
d .... (your own idea)

Discussion

5 Discuss the following questions with other people in the class.

a Do you agree with Professor Axt?
b What do you do to relax?
c Do you find it easy to relax?
d Do you do more or less exercise than you would like to? Do you do more or less exercise than you think is good for you? Why?

THEY SAY that a healthy body is a healthy mind, but according to a German expert it is lazy people who lead longer and healthier lives. Professor Peter Axt recommends avoiding strenuous activity like aerobics or working out in a gym. 'People who prefer to laze in a hammock instead of running a marathon or who take a midday nap instead of playing squash have a better chance of living into old age,' says this scientist. They are also less likely to suffer from professional stress.

He co-wrote **On the Joy of Laziness** with his daughter, who is also a doctor. In the book he advises people to 'waste half your time. Just enjoy lazing around.' Those who get up early in the morning usually feel stressed for the rest of the day, so his advice is to take it easy.

However, Professor Axt stresses that laziness is only one of the keys to a longer life. In fact, the subtitle of his book is **How best to use your energies**. He argues that if you are too fat, you need more energy to maintain body functions, and is in favour of moderate exercise like 'meditative' jogging or brisk walks to 'relax body and spirit at the same time'.

On the other hand, any exertion is not recommended, especially for middle-aged people who should be particularly careful about doing too much sport. Professor Axt believes we have only a limited amount of energy, and people who use up their supply more quickly live shorter lives. 'Research shows that people who run long distances into their 50s are using up energy they need for other purposes.'

02 WOMAN AT WORK

LANGUAGE LINKS

Phrase Bank: Discussing ideas

What do you think about … ?
For example, from a (business) point of view …
I don't think that …
Yes, you're probably right, but …
Do you really think … ?
I'm not sure about that.
What do you mean?

Vocabulary

Work & routines

1 Match the parts of the sentences below.

a Professor Axt thinks that lazing …
b Doing as little as possible is better …
c Lying about is the key …
d Take a midday break instead …
e He's in favour …
f Try to take …
g We only have a limited …
h If you get up early, you are likely to …

1 … around is good for you.
2 … of playing squash or going for a run.
3 … amount of energy.
4 … it easy this weekend.
5 … than going to the gym.
6 … to a long life.
7 … of moderate exercise like walking.
8 … feel stressed for the rest of the day.

a	b	c	d	e	f	g	h
1							

2 Write in the missing pairs of words below.

charge + hiring engineer + degree experience + qualifications get + off marketing + women ratio + to productive + day

a We only .... half an hour .... for lunch.
b You should get some practical .... as well as ....
c She's in .... of .... and firing.
d Why do .... departments have more .... than men?
e If you want to be an .... , you'll need a ....
f The .... of men to women is two .... one in my job.
g Nobody can be .... sixteen hours a ....

Do as an auxiliary

Complete the conversation using *do*, *does*, *don't* or *doesn't*.

A (a) .... you do a lot of exercise?
B Yes, I suppose I (b) .... Why do you ask?
A Well, it's better if you (c) .... , according to a German scientist.
B What (d) .... he say about it?
A He (e) .... say that exercise is bad for you exactly, but that if you do too much, you use up all your energy.
B That (f) .... make sense. Sport is good for you and makes you feel better.
A Yes, but according to him people who run a lot and play squash (g) .... usually live to an old age.
B Well, I (h) .... believe it. He probably just (i) .... like sport.

Jobs

Reorganise the letters to form words related to jobs. Then complete the sentences using the words.

contacaunt denistrep driteer litte nacharim nagream soipoint texecuvie

a She's the chief .... officer.
b He's the .... of the board.
c He doesn't work, he's ....
d The CEO is the top .... in the company.
e Her job .... is 'vice president'.
f It's hard to explain what I do, but I guess I'm a sort of department ....
g The financial director is a qualified ....
h The job title '....................' sounds more important than 'chairman'.

Phrasal verbs

Combine a verb from box A with a preposition from box B to complete each sentence below.

A

pick switch give go work use

B

through up off up up out

a Please can you .... your mobile phones before the presentation begins.
b After a long day at the office. I like to .... at the gym before I go home.
c I want to .... smoking because I know it's bad for my health.
d The taxi .... me .... every morning at half past nine.
e I don't want to .... all my energy doing strenuous exercise.
f She .... her correspondence with her secretary every morning.

Grammar

Expressing frequency

To say how often something happens you use:

- Adverbs of frequency

always	hardly ever	never	not often
often	sometimes	usually	

The adverb comes **before** the main verb:

I You We They He She	(don't/doesn't) **usually** (don't/doesn't) **often** **sometimes** **never**	drive(s) to work. go(es) out for lunch.

but **after** the verb 'to be'.

I You We They He She	**am** **are** **is**	(not) **usually** (not) **often** **sometimes** **never**	late. tired.

- Frequency expressions
  every day/week
  once/twice/three times a day/ week/month/ year etc.
  These expressions come **at the beginning** or **end** of the sentence.

I You We They He She	have (has) a break go (goes) on holiday	**every day.** **once** **twice** **three times** **four times**	**a day.** **a week.** **a month.** **a year.**

Every day **Once** **Twice** **Three times** **Four times**	**a day** **a week** **a month** **a year**	I you we they he she	have (has) a break. go (goes) on holiday.

Practice 1

Reorganise the words and phrases to make correct sentences.

a abroad times I a year travel four

b a on department meeting we always have Monday morning

c often he to Germany doesn't go

d manager the department usually leaves on Friday early

e I use the car never can't because drive I

f has the office canteen she always lunch in

g often they for work aren't late

h always Microsoft is the news in

i my every I change mobile year

j ever do you have parties office?

k often to how gym you the do go?

l you your do use much laptop?

Practice 2

Rewrite the question using question words *what, who, when* etc.

a Do you go to work by car? On foot?
How do you go to work?

b Do you use the phone a lot? Ever?

c Do you get to work at 8.30? 9.00?

d Does he do the housework because he likes it? Because he has to?

e Does he play squash every day? Every week?

f Does she go to work with her husband? A friend?

g Do you spend the morning making plans? Having meetings?

h Do you work 35 hours a week? Forty hours a week?

i Does it take you 20 minutes to read the newspaper? Half an hour?

j Do you work so hard because it's fun? Because you need the money?

TOPICS

03 TELEPHONE TALK

A Vodafone UK survey of more than 1,100 business people reveals that the telephone is still the dominant networking tool (59 per cent), but phone usage with clients has dropped by almost a third (30 per cent) in the space of a generation, with e-mail taking priority.

HTTP://WWW.COMPUTING.CO.UK

TELEPHONE NUMBERS

1 1.05–1.09 Listen to the extracts and write down the phone number.

a ……
b ……
c ……
d ……
e ……

2 Listen again and put the phrases in the order that you hear them.

a [1] Can I speak to Derek LaMotte, please?
b [ ] You have one message from 903586759 at 18.30 on April 1.
c [ ] Ring now on 0902386980. I'll repeat that for you. If you know the answer, phone us now on 0902386980.
d [ ] Can you give me the number of Budget Car Rental, please?
e [ ] No, I'm afraid you've got the wrong number.
f [ ] I'm sorry. Could you say that again a bit slower?

3 Underline phrases in the sentences in 2 that you think are useful to know.

4 Discuss the following questions with a partner.

a Do you find it easy to remember telephone numbers? How many do you know by memory?
b Write down five random telephone numbers and dictate them to your partner as fast as possible.

INDIRECT QUESTIONS

1 1.10 We use indirect questions to sound more polite. Complete the dialogue below. Then listen to see if you are correct.

A InterAir, can I help you?
B Yes, please. I'd like some information about a flight arriving from Munich.
A Yes. Do you ……
B The flight number? I'm not sure. I know it leaves Munich at 1730.
A Oh, yes, that's IA 345.
B Yes, that's it. Could …… gets in?
A Yes, the arrival time is 1910.
B 1910. Do you …… any delay?
A No, the flight is on time.
B Right, thank you very much.
A You're welcome. Goodbye.

2 Look at the prompts on page 132 and practise the conversation with a partner.

3 Look at the chart below. Then rephrase the questions using *Do you know …?* or *Could you tell me …?*

Do you know … **Could you tell me …**	how long it takes? where the airport is?
	if she got my message? if you'll finish the order on time?

a What time does the flight leave?
Could you tell me what time the flight leaves?
NOT ~~Could you tell me what time does the flight leave?~~

b Which terminal does it leave from?

c How far is the factory from the airport?

d How long is the meeting with Mr Fuentes?

e Which car hire company is it?

f Which models do they have available?

g Do I need an international driving licence?

h Where are we staying?

i Is it a nice place?

j How far is the hotel from the nearest town?

k Have they booked a meeting room?

4 Work with a partner.

Speaker B: Look at page 138.
Speaker A: Read the instructions below.
You are travelling on business in the UK. When you finish there, you are going straight to another country for a special sales conference. You expected to receive information about this trip from your office, but the hotel's Internet connection doesn't work, and you don't have access to your e-mail account. Ring your office to get the necessary information. Ask the questions in 3. Make a note of all the information.

TELEPHONE FRUSTRATION

1 Complete the list of possible telephone frustrations using verbs in the box.

call	get (x 4)	listen	play	put	repeat	return	take	transfer

a They .... irritating music when you're put on hold.
b You .... cut off in the middle of your call.
c People you call .... a long time to answer.
d They .... you on hold and forget about you.
e You .... an answer phone.
f They .... you to another person and you have to .... your enquiry.
g They don't .... properly to what you are saying.
h You continually .... an engaged tone when you .... someone.
i People don't .... your calls.
j You .... through to a voicemail system.

2 With a partner or your teacher, decide which of the problems in 1 are the five most frustrating. Then look on page 136 to see what the five most frustrating problems are according to a survey.

3 Answer the questions with a partner.

a What percentage of all sales enquiries do you think begin on the telephone?
1) 25% 2) 50% 3) 90%?
b For what type of companies might effective use of the telephone be especially important?
c How many calls do you estimate an average telephonist answers in a year?
1) 30,000 2) 300,000 3) 3,000,000
d What kinds of things do telephone receptionists need to be good at?

4 Now read the text. According to the author, what are the answers to the questions in 3?

5 According to the article, 'More business is lost through bad service than by poor product performance.' Do you agree?

Ringing in the Millions

In this age of the Internet, e-mail and electronic communication, the telephone continues to be one of the most important business tools. Ninety per cent of all sales enquiries begin on the telephone, so from the start, it is vital to project a company image which is friendly and professional. At the same time, poor and ineffective telephone behaviour can cost millions of dollars in terms of lost sales opportunities. For example, in the insurance business, failure to answer a call promptly and respond efficiently could result in a valuable policy going straight to the competition. The average telephonist can answer as many as 300,000 calls in a year, so in many companies, this is a vital role.

Although good receptionists have a certain amount of natural ability, companies need to train staff in specific skills of telephone use: transferring a call, placing a call on hold, dealing with angry callers, answering correspondence by phone, using a caller's name and taking messages correctly. Callers should not hear informal expressions like 'oh, she's just gone out' or 'sorry, he's not with us anymore'. Surveys show that customers want a prompt response from a real person (not a machine) who can take a decision, and so answering systems will often be a false economy.

More business is lost through poor service than by poor product performance, and the quality of a firm's response to a call is one of the chief factors in creating a perception of good or bad service.

Source: www.brendan.com

6 1.11–1.16 Listen to six extracts from telephone calls. Identify which skill listed in paragraph 2 of *Ringing in the Millions* is being used.

a placing calls on hold
b ....
c ....
d ....
e ....
f ....

7 Listen again and complete the missing phrases.

a **A** Can I have .... 305, please?
B I'm afraid the line .... Will you hold?
b **A** Could I ....? You need 50 units by Friday, and Mr Johansson can contact you on 943 694726.
B Yes, that's correct.
A Right, Mr Smith. I'll .... as soon as he's free.
c **A** … and it really isn't good enough.
B Yes, Mr Wright. I understand what you're saying and .... the error. As soon as Mr Downs is back, I'll ask him to get in contact with you. .... about this.
A Right, thank you. I realise it's not your fault.
d **A** Could I have the Sales Department, please?
B One moment, please. Just .... now.
e **A** Shonagh Clark speaking.
B Hello, I'm .... your letter of 12th June.
f **A** This is Jorgen Bode here. Could I speak to Jean Simmons, please?
B Oh, I'm sorry, Mr Bode, but Ms Simmons .... right now. Can I ask her to call you back? Or I can .... if it's urgent.

8 Discuss the following questions with a partner.

a Does your company have any policies on phone use? Does it provide training?
b Do you prefer to use a mobile or a landline?
c What functions does your phone have? Do you know how to use them all?

Telephone phrases

9 Match the following to make telephone expressions.

Could you …	put	a message?
	repeat	that?
	read	that back to me?
	give	me through to (Accounts)?
	take	me your name?

Could I …	leave	to Mr Wilson?
	speak	over that again?
	have	extension 103, please?
	check	that?
	go	a message?

I'm phoning …	to	your advertisement.
	about	an appointment.
	to	some information.
	for	confirm our meeting.
	about	see if you could attend a meeting on the 20th.

SALES CONTACTS

1 1.17 The sales team at ADH Graphics uses the form below to record the details of all phone calls with potential clients. Listen to the conversation and complete the form.

PHONE CONTACT FORM

ADH Graphics

DATE: Wednesday 14 May

CALL INITIATED BY: Client

CALL HANDLER: B.White

CLIENT: Bellstone & Smith

ADDRESS: (a) ~~15~~ 14 ...., Clapham Rd, London SW14

CONTACT: Mr Clarkson

POSITION: Head of (b) ....

TEL: (c) 0207895 ~~[illegible]~~ 4216

E-MAIL: clarkson.bellstone@lineone.com

NATURE OF BUSINESS: Elevator manufacturer

PURPOSE OF CALL: Wants estimate for printing a (d) Servic ~~manual~~ manuals of (e) 100 pages. Copies: (f) 20'000
Estimates also for (g) 10'000 and (h) 20'000 copies.
Size: (i) 85 in black and white. Cover in colour. Will supply material on disk or CD.

COMMENTS: They are updating all their manuals, so could give us more work if the price is right.

ACTION REQUIRED: Visit client with (j) ....

BY WHOM: B. White

DATE AND TIME: (k) Friday 06:00 May at 10 am.

Role-play

2 Work with a partner and practise telephoning for information and taking notes.
Speaker A: Look at page 135.
Speaker B: Look at page 133.

S a

03 TELEPHONE TALK

LANGUAGE LINKS

> **Phrase Bank: Telephoning**
> Can I speak to … ?
> Can you give me the number for … ?
> Can I/you take a message?
> Can I have extension … , please?
> This is … .
> The line is engaged.
> You've got the wrong number.
> I'm phoning about … .

Vocabulary

Numbers

Write the full form of the numbers and figures.

a 321 three hundred and twenty-one
b 69% ……………………
c 3,428 ……………………
d £3m ……………………
e $9.39 ……………………
f 24,678,902 ……………………

Telephone phrases

1 Put the conversation below in the correct order.

☐ Hello, ADH Graphics.
☐ Yes, please. Could you ask him to phone John Clarkson from Bellstone & Smith? He has the phone number.
☐ Just one moment … I'm sorry, there's no answer.
☐ Yes, of course. Could I just check your name? John Clark from Bellstone & Smith.
☐ Thank you. Goodbye.
☐ Oh, dear. I'm phoning for some information. It's quite urgent. Do you know where I can contact him?
☐ Oh, good morning. Could I speak to Peter White, please?
☐ No, sorry, I'm afraid I don't. Can I take a message?
☐ No, it's Clarkson. He knows what it's about.
☐ Oh, sorry, Mr Clarkson. I'll tell him as soon as he's available.

2 Complete the conversation using the words and phrases in the box.

> bad line call me Can I take a message?
> Could I speak to dialled the wrong number engaged
> hold put me through This is You're through

A Sales Department. Can I help you?
B Oh! I must have (a) …………………… . Can you (b) …………………… to Customer Services, please?
A I'm sorry, it's a (c) …………………… . Did you say Customer Services?
B Yes, that's right.
A Just one moment. I'm sorry, but the line is (d) …………………… . Do you want to (e) …………………… ?
B All right.
A (f) …………………… now.
B Hello. (g) …………………… the department manager, please?
C I'm afraid he's not in the office this morning. (h) …………………… ?
B Yes, please. (i) …………………… George Smith. Could you ask him to (j) …………………… ?
C Yes, of course. Goodbye.
B Bye.

3 Match the parts of the sentences below.

a Tell her it's Mr Jenkins. I'm returning …
b Typical! I got cut …
c I hate it when they put you …
d I keep getting an engaged …
e Could you say …
f Can you read that …

1 … on hold, and then forget about you.
2 … back to me, just to check?
3 … tone. Maybe his phone is off the hook.
4 … her call this morning.
5 … that again, please? I didn't understand.
6 … off in the middle of the call.

a	b	c	d	e	f

4 Match the words to their definitions.

☐ a telephone directory
☐ b engaged
☐ c dialling tone
☐ d reverse charge call
☐ e national call
☐ f off-peak call
☐ g wrong number
☐ h switchboard
☐ i extension number
☐ j cell phone
☐ k directory enquiries
☐ l operator

1 A continuous sound that means you can dial the number you want.
2 The equipment which distributes calls to the different departments and offices in a company.
3 A phone number you dial by mistake.
4 Busy – someone is using the line you want.
5 The number of each different phone in a company.
6 A call which is paid for by the person you are calling.
7 Also called a mobile phone.
8 A book with a list of telephone numbers.
9 A service you phone if you want to find a number.
10 A call to a different part of the country.
11 A person who helps you make a call.
12 A call made in the evening or at the weekend which has a lower charge.

5 Rewrite the following conversation to make it sound more polite.

Galaxy Computers Galaxy Computers. What do you want?
a Galaxy Computers. Can I help you?
Michael Jones I want to speak to Harris.
b Could I speak to Mr Harris, please?
Galaxy Computers Who are you?
c What is your Name please
Michael Jones Jones. ABC Industries.
d The Jones Company.
Galaxy Computers Who? What's your name again?
e ~~Repeat your name please~~. Can you say it again please
Michael Jones Michael Jones.
Galaxy Computers He's speaking to someone on his line. Want to wait?
f ~~Is it possible~~ Do you have time for waiting
Michael Jones No. Tell him I called, right?
g ~~I call No sorry~~. Tell him please, I called
Galaxy Computers No problem. Bye.
h ~~Yes I do.~~ Aye of course Goodbye
Could you say him I called please?

Grammar

Indirect Questions

Direct questions	Indirect questions		Differences
Where **are you** from?	Can you tell me	where **you are** from?	• Word order
How **is she**?		how **she is**?	• No *do* or *does*
Where **are we** meeting?	Can you remember	where **we're** meeting?	• *if* in *Yes/No* questions
Where **do you live**?	Could you tell me	where **you live**?	
How much money **does he earn**?		how much money **he earns**?	
Does he like football?	Do you know	**if he likes** football?	
Has he got my address?		**if he has got** my address?	

Practice 1

Reorganise the words to make indirect questions or statements.

a tell if got my me could you she message
Could you tell me if she got my message
b know be back will do when he you
c do long know takes you how it
Do you know how long it takes
d remember the what bus time can leaves you
e this know do what word you means
f know think he wants what you to do
g idea the is time I've no what

Practice 2

Change the direct questions into indirect questions.

a What time does the meeting begin?
Do you know ……
b How much is the hotel?
Could you tell me ……
c Why is he angry?
Do you know ……
d Is there a restaurant car on the train?
Can you tell me ……
e Where can I park the car?
Can you tell me ……
f Is the office near the town centre?
Can you remember ……

SPEAKING **SKILLS**

04 ASKING QUESTIONS

A gossip talks about others, a bore talks about himself – and a brilliant conversationalist talks about you.

ANONYMOUS

1 **1.18** Rick Van Looy and Florent Rondele meet in a hotel bar after dinner. Listen to Conversation 1 and answer the questions.

a What does Florent do?
b What does Rick do?
c Do they know each other?

1.19 Now listen to Conversation 2 and answer the questions.

a Where are the speakers?
b One of the speakers asks 'Does this belong to you?' What do you think 'this' is?
c Where are the speakers going?
d Why?

2 Listen again and complete the questions that are asked in the conversations.

	Question words	Auxiliary	Subject	Verb	etc.
a		Do	you	mind	if I join you?
b		Are	you		from around here, then?
c	What	do	you	do	do?
d		Do	you	mean	sports equipment?
e	How many stores	have	you	got?	
f	What line of business	are	you		in?
g		Do	you	know	it?
h		Are	you	opening	a store here, then?
i			you		something to drink?
j		Does	is	belong	to you ?
k		Have	you	got	the time?
l		Do			soon?
m		Do	you	know	Bangkok?
n			this		your first trip there?

3 How are questions b, h and n in 2 different to the others?

4 Write questions for the answers in **bold**.

a *Who do you work for?* **IBM.**
b .... **Berlin**. Our offices are in the city centre.
c .... **In the Royal**. It's a great hotel.
d .... **No**, only French.
e .... He's talking **to a client**.
f .... I'm an **accountant**.
g .... **Yes**, two boys aged seven and ten.
h .... **Portugal**. I was born in Lisbon.
i .... **Yes**, I am – in fact, this is my wife, Yuki.
j .... **No**, I don't. There's no golf course near where I live. I play squash.
k .... **Yes**. I met her last year at a conference in Vienna.

Answers on page 132.

5 Your company has sent you to an international meeting. It starts in five minutes. You don't know the person sitting next to you. Use the chart below to make conversation and to find out about them.

Questions word	Auxiliary	Subject	Verb	etc.
			live	
			work	here
	do		do	English
Where	does	you	doing	at the moment
What	are	your company	have	any other languages
How	has	he	got	your job
Why	do	she	like	this book
When	are	they	go	any children
How many employees	have		travel	to work
			studying	much in your work
			speak	

TALKING ABOUT OTHER PEOPLE

1 1.20 Look at the conversation below. Number the lines in the correct order. Then listen and check your answers.

- ☐ What's he like?
- ☐ Yes, isn't he Director of Business Development at Guinness?
- ☐ Do you know Jan Nowacki?
- ☐ The National Bank of Poland, that's interesting. Do you have any contact with him in your work?
- ☐ Not any longer. Now he's the Public Relations Manager at the National Bank of Poland.
- ☐ He's a nice chap. You'd like him.
- ☐ Not really, but I occasionally play golf with him.

2 Which parts of the conversation could you replace with the expressions below?

a Have you ever met ...Do you know...
b doesn't he work for ....
c bump into him at conferences ....
d I don't like him much really. ....
e I don't anymore. ....
f What do you think of him? ....
g You'd get on well. ....

3 Look at the table below which shows the jobs five people did before and what they do now. (One of them is retired.) Work with a partner. Using the conversation in 1 as a model, have conversations about the people. Add comments about them using the phrases in the box.

> He/She's a nice person. He/She's an interesting person. He/She's quite reserved.
> He/She's a good laugh. He/She's a bit arrogant. He/She's a bit dull.
> He/She always has the latest gossip.

	Before		Now	
Name	**Position**	**Company**	**Position**	**Company**
Pedro Amado	Managing Director	Edwards Shipping	Sales Director	Iberica Electric
Martina Ferlan	Managing Director	Health Group	President	Biological Co.
Frank Mangliochetti	Vice-President Finance	Dynamica	Chairman & CEO	Medical Plans
Cathy Cheung	Marketing Executive	Deltaco Dental Care	Marketing Manager	Deltaco Dental Care
Dennis Sexton	President	SpeedTrackSystems		

4 Now think about some people you know and have similar conversations about them.

INTERNET ACCESS

1 Discuss the questions in groups. Do you have free access to the Internet at work? Which of the four groups in the monster.co.uk survey below would you be in? Is this an important issue in your work?

Do you have / use Internet access at work?

39%		267 votes for	Yes, a high-speed access with more than 2 Mbit/s
37%		254 votes for	Yes, I use an always-on connection (e.g. DSL)
17%		117 votes for	No, I don't use the Internet at work
5%		40 votes for	Yes, but with a modem only (narrow band)
Total:		**678 votes**	

2 Read the article and answer the questions.

a Why did Hywel Jenkins hire an IT expert?
b What kind of websites were the workers visiting?
c What was the position of the union representative? Do you think it is reasonable?
d What kind of things does Mr Fisher think companies should do to prevent these situations from happening?

Office Workers Dismissed for Spending Two Hours a Day on eBay

Nine office workers have been dismissed by a Town Council in South Wales after it was discovered that they were spending up to two hours a day on eBay. The workers' internet habit was discovered when an IT expert was hired by the council to investigate the amount of time its staff were spending on the Internet. The Head of Financial Services at Neath Port Talbot Council, Hywel Jenkins, said: 'The main reason for carrying out the investigations was the significant time staff were spending on the Internet. The investigation revealed that these Council employees were spending their time on shopping, entertainment and BBC/Sky-related websites.'

Union officials suggested that the Council should have set up its IT system to prevent workers accessing sites like eBay. Mark Fisher, a welfare officer with the union Unison, said: 'People get very involved in eBay, Sky Sports and their favourite football teams. It happens in many offices. Obviously we cannot justify people spending a couple of hours of working time looking at these sites, but temptation was put in their way.'

Mr Fisher emphasised the need for employers to take preventative measures. He said: 'We want the Council to make changes to its IT system to stop workers getting into this kind of trouble. We want firewalls installed to prevent staff accessing these sorts of websites at any time other than between the traditional lunch breaks between noon and 2pm. We are looking at how the system can be tightened up so these people won't get dismissed.'

Source: http://technology.timesonline.co.uk/tol/news/tech_and_web

3 Work in groups of four. You are going to take part in a meeting to decide on a policy for Internet use in your company. Each take a role: A, B, C or D.

A

The Human Resources Manager

You see one of your company's biggest problems is to recruit talented, well-qualified, young people. Potential employees of this type have been using computers and mobile phones since they were born. Digital communication is part of their lives. They will hesitate to work for an employer who prohibits Internet access. For example, a lot of companies block instant messaging because they see it as a distraction and a waste of time, but for many people now, instant messaging is a legitimate work tool that allows quick communication between colleagues and actually saves money.

B

The Company Boss

You are in favour of controlling access to the Internet and using filters to prevent users visiting non-authorised sites. You are not so worried about people downloading porn (although anyone who does this will be sacked!), but you suspect that employees waste a lot of time looking at things like eBay, mySpace, Facebook and worst of all, online gambling sites. You can see two problems. On one hand, if workers are using the Internet for personal use, then they are not doing anything useful during paid time. On the other hand, if they are doing this when they have finished all their tasks, it shows they have not been given enough work to do.

C

The IT Manager

This sounds like more work for you and you would prefer not to have to do it. You know that although it is possible to use filters to limit Internet access, there will be some technical problems. People will constantly be asking you to modify the system so that they can surf sites which are useful for their work. Another problem is that people will think they are being spied on and blame you for it. Also, in your work you use the Internet to investigate security issues in some 'underground' sites. These sites often have 'inappropriate' content which could get you into trouble.

D

The R&D Manager

You are against any use of filters because you are convinced that for your department unlimited access to the Internet is essential. You think it is sufficient to give every worker their own personal logon and then monitor their Internet use. You also think that you should give workers clear rules about what they can do and what they can't do. They should also be obliged to sign a document accepting these conditions. In other words, you believe it is important to treat people as adults and not like naughty children who cannot be trusted.

4 1.21 Caroline Wheeler is business development director at Pace Telecom, a business telecommunications company. The firm started in 1993 and has 35 employees who need e-mail and Internet access. Caroline explains how they put an e-mail and Internet policy in place. Listen and complete the missing information.

a The policy covers personal use, ..., ... between colleagues and what happens if the rules are broken.
b Every employee has to .... a copy of the policy.
c Employees are allowed to access the Internet for personal use during ....
d .... e-mails which are not related to work are not allowed.
e Employees must not look at .... websites and have to be careful what they ....
f They once had a problem when an employee was sending e-mails to her .... all day.

5 In 3 did you come to the same conclusions as Caroline?

TOPICS

05 COMPANY HISTORIES

Computer and video game companies play an ever-increasing role in our nation's growing economy. These companies and their colleagues across the nation are making entertainment software one of the fastest-growing industries in the United States.

MICHAEL GALLAGHER, CEO OF THE ESA.

1 Read the quotation above. How important do you think this industry is in the world economy? Is it important in your country? Do you personally consume these products?

2 1.22 What do you know about Nintendo? Listen to a short history of the company and answer the questions.

a What was the first product of the company?
b How important is the video games business?
c What company is one of Nintendo's biggest competitors?
d What are the names of some of the products mentioned?

3 Read the history of Nintendo below. Complete the text using the words and phrases in the box. Then listen again to check your answers.

advertising competitor console innovation manufacture
mass-produced partnership playing cards sales trade

NINTENDO is one of the best-known brands in the world and a leader in interactive video entertainment - a multi-billion dollar industry. The company has a history which dates back to the nineteenth century.

1889 Fusajiro Yamauchi **founds** a small company to manufacture traditional (a) ....

1953 The company **manufactures** the first (b) .... plastic playing cards in Japan.

1963 The company **changes** its name to Nintendo Co. Ltd. and starts to (c) .... games in addition to playing cards.

1965 Boss Hiroshi Yamauchi **hires** Gunpei Yokoi - the engineer behind many of the company's most successful products.

1975 Nintendo **forms** a (d) .... with Mitsubishi Electric to take advantage of their micro-processor technology..

1983 Nintendo **develops** a (e) .... for use at home, the NES.

1989 Nintendo **launches** Game Boy – the first console you could carry around in your pocket. The package **includes** Tetris – one of the most addictive games of all time.

1990 Nintendo sales **represent** 10% of the (f) .... deficit between Japan and the USA.

1994 Sony **releases** the Playstation, which **works** as a CD player as well as a console. Nintendo **faces** a major new (g) .... and sales **suffer** badly.

2001 Nintendo launches a sophisticated new console, the GameCube. Sales are poor but at the same time in the USA, the 'GameBoy Advanced' **dominates** the handheld market.

2004 With the disappointing (h) .... of GameCube and the success of GameBoy Advanced, Nintendo **decides** to concentrate on the portable market and release a new handheld console – the Nintendo DS (Dual Screen). The DS is popular but has to compete against Sony's new handheld, the PSP.

2006 Things **look** bad for Nintendo, but once again, a brilliant (i) .... **saves** them from disaster – the 'Wii'. Its most brilliant feature is a 'wand' which allows players to physically move while they play a game of tennis on screen – there are no complicated controls and anyone can play with it. With a clever (j) .... campaign (aimed at adult gamers) in a very short time it **achieves** higher levels of sales than all its competitors.

Past Simple: regular verbs

4 All the verbs in **bold** in 3 have regular forms in the Past Simple: infinitive + *-ed* / *-d*.

suffer → *suffered*
release → *released*

The pronunciation of *-ed* can be /d/, /t/, or /ɪd/. Write the Past Simple of the verbs in **bold** in 3 in the table below, according to their pronunciation.

Group 1	Group 2	Group 3
/d/	/t/	/ɪd/
manufactured	developed	founded
....	....	....
....	....	....
....	....	....
....	....	....
....	....	....

5 Listen again to the history of Nintendo. Check your answers in 4.

6 Write five questions about Nintendo's history. Use the Past Simple.
When did the company change its name?

7 Ask your partner the questions in 6.

WHO REALLY INVENTED THE INTERNET?

1 1.23 You are going to listen to a radio documentary on the history of the Internet. First, do the quiz below. Then listen to see if you are correct.

THE INTERNET QUIZ

a In which year did Leonard Kleinrock connect the first two computers?
1 1969
2 1975
3 1983

b What was the first message sent on the Internet?
1 'hello'
2 'lo'
3 'log in'

c What did the first version of the Internet connect?
1 military installations
2 government buildings
3 universities

d In which year was the first international computer connection made?
1 1969
2 1973
3 1983

e What is the 'universal language' of the Internet?
1 English
2 Java Script
3 TCP/IP

f What was the name of the first browser?
1 Netscape
2 Mosaic
3 Gopher

2 Listen again and number the events below in the correct order.

- ☐ Bob Kahn and Vincent Cerf invent software for connecting computers on the Internet.
- ☐ Professor Kleinrock connects two computers.
- ☐ Ray Tomlinson sends the first e-mail.
- ☐ The first net links four American universities.
- ☐ The first user-friendly Internet browser becomes available.
- ☐ The Advanced Research Projects Agency starts work on ARPANET.
- ☐ An 'official language' of the Internet is established.

3 Complete the article with the verbs in the box in the Past Simple. Some of them are irregular.

become	begin	call	connect (x 2)	crash	increase	invent	launch	make	reach	send	want

Birth of the Internet

How old is the Internet? It is difficult to fix a single date for the birth of any complex technology. In the case of the Internet people suggest different dates. It depends on what they understand the Internet to be.

We know that in 1965, the Advanced Research Projects Agency (ARPA) under the US Department of Defence (a) .... work on a system to connect computers. They (b) .... the project ARPANET.

On September 2nd, 1969, in a laboratory at the University of California Professor Leonard Kleinrock (c) .... the first two machines. At its simplest level, the Internet connects computers so for many people that day the Internet was born. The next month they sent the first message to a computer at Stanford University. The message was 'lo'. They (d) .... to send the words 'log in' but when they typed 'g' the system (e) .... So appropriately, this first word was a phonetic version of 'hello'.

By January 1970 ARPANET (f) .... computers in four American universities, and by the following year there were 23 in the system, connecting different universities and research institutes. In 1973 Ray Tomlinson (g) .... the first e-mail via ARPANET. In the same year the Net went international, connecting computers in England and Norway.

The ARPANET was a single network, but the next step was to connect different networks and to create an 'internetwork'. In 1974 Bob Kahn and Vincent Cerf (h) .... a software that allowed networks using different operating systems to connect to each other. The software, called TCP/IP, (i) .... the universal language of the Internet on January 1st, 1983. Many experts argue that this event was the real birth of the Internet because it (j) .... it possible to link different networks in one web.

More and more networks joined the system and the number of connected computers (k) .... dramatically: from 10,000 in 1984 to 100,000 in 1987. By the early 1990s the World Wide Web was the most popular way of browsing the web, and the network was accessible to anyone in the world with a computer. In 1992 the number of hosts (l) .... 1,000,000.

In 1993 two programers, Marc Andreessen and Eric Bina, (m) .... the first version of Mosaic. This was the first graphics-based browser of the type we all use today and made possible what many people now understand as the Internet – an easy means to browse websites, get information and spread news.

4 Listen again and check your answers.

Asking questions

5 In pairs, ask and answer questions about the history of the Internet using the word prompts.

a When / Professor Kleinrock / connect / first two computers?
b Where / they / send / first message?
c What / Ray Tomlinson / send / 1973?
d What / Bob Kahn and Vincent Cerf / invent?
e When / TCP/IP / become / official language?
f How much / the Internet / grow / between 1984 and 1987?

6 The questions in 5 use the following structure:

Question word	*did*	Subject	Infinitive	etc.
When	did	Professor Kleinrock	connect	two computers?

When you do not know the subject, you use the following structure:

	Who/What	Verb in past simple	etc.
~~Who did send the first e-mail?~~	Who	sent	the first e-mail?
~~What did happen yesterday?~~	What	happened	yesterday?

This usually only happens with *who* and *what*.

Questions with no subject

7 Look at the chart below and practise asking and answering questions like this.
Who did Sarah text? Jack. Who phoned Jack? Jane.

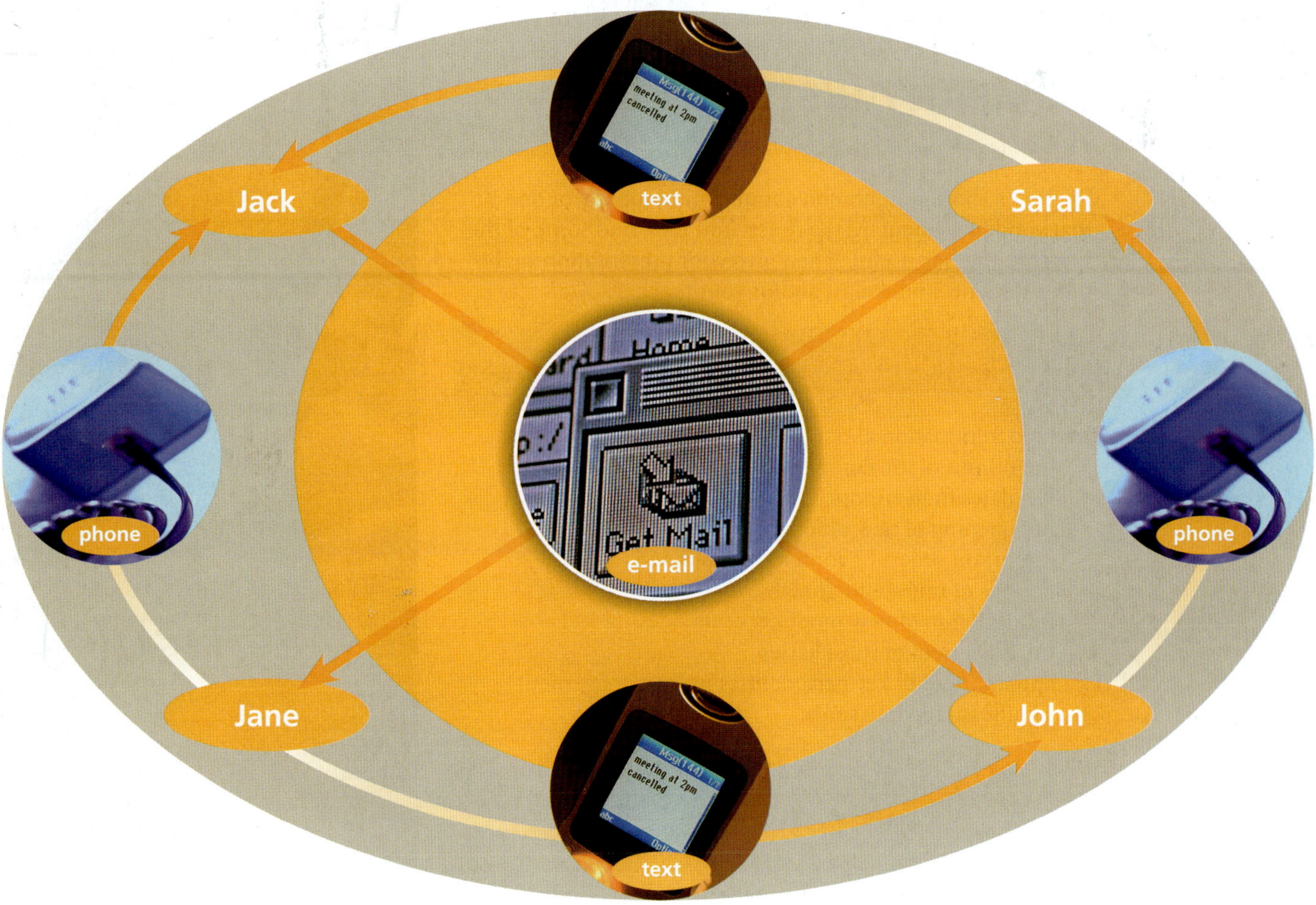

When was the last time you …?

8 Use the verbs on the left with the words and phrases on the right to ask your partner questions beginning *When was the last time you …?* Then ask follow-up questions. For example:

A *When was the last time you sent an e-mail?*
B *This morning.*
A *Who did you send it to?*
B *To a customer.*
A *What was it about?*

Use the phrases in the box, if you like.

I never do / have.	I really can't remember.	It was a long time ago.	I'm not sure.

Speaker A		Speaker B	
send	an interview	take	a car
find	a phone call	download	late for a meeting
travel	an e-mail	deal	a plane
make	on business	negotiate	to a useful meeting
take	something useful on the Internet	go	a PDA
go	on a course	buy	a new program
eat	on business	hire	with a complaint
have	a taxi	arrive	a deal

Discussion point

9 Work in groups and talk about the Internet.

a When was the first time you used the Internet?
b What did you use it for? Did it change your life in any way?
c What is more important for you – the Internet or your mobile phone?

COMPANY HISTORY

Fluency

Prepare a short presentation about your company or one that you know about. Make notes. You may find some of the words in the box useful. Then give your presentation to the other students in the class and/or your teacher.

achieve	begin	develop	establish	expand	found
increase	launch	manufacture	produce	reach	want

Include information about the following:

- the origins of the company, who founded it and when
- key dates in its history
- the opening of new offices or factories
- important orders or contracts it obtained
- periods of important growth
- introduction of new products or services
- establishment of subsidiaries
- appointment of key personalities in its management
- significant recent events

LANGUAGE LINKS

Phrase Bank: Talking about the past
When was the company founded?
How long ago did ... ?
When was the last time ... ?
Who founded the company/invented ... ?

Vocabulary

Business verbs

Complete the sentences below with an appropriate verb.

a His ambition is to ....becam.... the president of the company.
b The company plans to ~~introdus~~ launch .... a new product line.
c To make money, companies need to ....expaned.... quickly.
d A lot of dot.coms don't really ....sell.... anything.
e The present president didn't ....found.... the company, his father did.
f Our objective is to ....reached.... sales of $30 million this year.
g We want to ....make.... a new deal with our suppliers.
h The fastest way for the company to grow is to ....acquire.... smaller companies. (erwerben)
i Consultancies ....do.... services for other businesses.
j How much did your turnover ....reach.... last year?

Answers on page 132.

Grammar

Past Simple

Affirmative	
I	
You	
He	
She	**worked**
It	
We	
They	

Negative	
I	
You	
He	
She	**didn't work**
It	
We	
They	

Interrogative		
	I	
	you	
Did	he	
Didn't	she	work?
	it	
	we	
	they	

Formation: regular verbs
infinitive
- *work – **worked***

infinitive ending in *e*
- *like – **liked***

infinitive ending in consonant + *y*
- *hurry – **hurried***

one syllable verbs ending in one vowel + one consonant
- *stop – **stopped***
  (except verbs ending in *w* or *y*)
- *play – **played**, show – **showed***

two syllable verbs with the stress on the second syllable
- *prefER – **preferred**, admIT – **admitted***

two syllable words with the stress on the first syllable
- *VISit – **visited**, ENter – **entered***

Formation: irregular verbs
Many of the most common verbs are irregular.
*go – **went**, come – **came***

You use the Past Simple to express finished actions, events or situations.
*We moved to a new office last year.**
Before I got married I lived in Lisbon.
In my first job, I travelled a lot.
* You often use the Past Simple with expressions describing completed periods of time: *three weeks ago, last year, on Tuesday, in March, at Christmas*, etc.

Time expressions
To say when things happen in the past, you use:
- *in* + month / year – *in March, in 1987*
- *on* + day / date – *on Monday, on 5th December*
- *at* + time / special periods – *at 5.00, at Christmas*
- length of time + *ago* – *five minutes ago, a week ago*
- *when* + past situation / action – *when I was younger, when he arrived*

Practice 1

Write the Past Simple of the verbs below.

work	a) worked	marry	j) ....
stop	b) stopped	plan	k) ....
live	c)	reach	l) ....
start	d)	arrive	m) ....
use	e)	fit	n) ....
travel	f)	visit	o) ....
drop	g)	call	p) ....
carry	h)	increase	q) ....
tip	i)	like	r) ....

Practice 2

The 12 verbs below are some of the most common in English. They are all irregular. Write the Past Simple of each.

tell	a) told	make	g) ....
say	b)	do	h) ....
get	c)	go	i) ....
give	d)	come	j) ....
take	e)	write	k) ....
put	f)	have	l) ....

Practice 3

Complete the sentences with one of the words in the box or put 'X' when no word is necessary.

ago	at	for	in	on	when

a John started working here ...... Christmas and he spoke to me for the first time ten minutes ....

b I travelled a lot ...... last year.

c ...... Monday I had a meeting with Mr Leblanc.

d I sent them the fax ...... Monday.

e ...... I lived in London, I usually went away ...... the weekend.

f The delegation from Geneva arrived ...... three o'clock.

g I worked for IBM ...... three years.

h We had a really interesting business trip to Turkey ...... March.

i I had a meeting ...... 9.30 ...... the evening and eventually got to my hotel ...... two ...... the morning.

j When I woke up ...... yesterday morning, I didn't know where I was.

k Did Mr Heinkers phone ...... I was out?

Practice 4

The following facts are incorrect. Make the sentences negative. Then give the correct information.

a Bill Gates founded Oracle.
Bill Gates didn't found Oracle, he founded Microsoft.

b On October 4 1929, the Wall Street Crash started a worldwide economic boom.
......

c On March 25 1957, six European states signed the Treaty of Madrid, creating the EEC.
......

d On January 1 1999, eleven member states of the European Union adopted the pound as a common currency.
......

e Henry Ford manufactured the first mass-produced electronic components.
......

f In 2001, Napster had legal problems over people downloading books.
......

Answers on page 133.

Practice 5

Write questions about the missing information.

a I went to ...... on my last business trip.
Where did you go on your last business trip?

b He set up the company in ....
When ......

c They started selling ...... last year.
......

d At first, the product sold well because ....
......

e They made a profit by ....
......

f He worked for ICI for ...... years.
......

g I spoke to ...... at the conference.
......

h ...... invented the mobile phone.
......

i ...... people work in the Lille factory.
......

j I travelled from Munich to Berlin by ....
......

Practice 6

Complete the article using the verbs in the box in the Past Simple.

be (x 2)	become	begin	convert	develop	grow

Like many other aspects of the computer age, Yahoo! started as an idea, (a) ...... into a hobby and then (b) ...... a full-time passion. The two developers of Yahoo!, David Filo and Jerry Yang, (c) ...... Ph.D. students in electrical engineering at Stanford University when they (d) ...... working on Yahoo! in April 1994. At first it (e) ...... a way to keep track of their personal interests on the Internet. Later they (f) ...... their personal lists into a database designed to serve the needs of any user. They (g) ...... software to help them locate, identify and edit material stored on the Internet. Today, Yahoo! contains organised information on tens of thousands of computers linked to the Web.

06 CORRESPONDENCE

The use of e-mail continues to grow, but there are suggestions across the industry that its popularity will begin to decline quickly if measures aren't put in place to guarantee access, availability and security.

HTTP://MANAGEMENT.SILICON.COM/ITDIRECTOR/0,39024673,39123837,00.HTM

1 Read the following article from a business magazine and discuss the questions with a partner.

DOES grammar matter?

According to a report published recently, standards in written English are falling. This is because people see the e-mail as an informal way of communicating where the normal rules of grammar and punctuation do not apply. In a survey by MSN, two-thirds of those aged 18–24 said that they were more concerned about the content of their e-mails than grammatical correctness. Of older users, one in four also admitted they were not concerned about grammatical correctness in their messages.

Surprisingly, in the same survey most people said they were annoyed by errors in the e-mails they received. This was a bigger problem with conventional letters. In another survey bosses said they would not do business with companies whose correspondence had mistakes in it. Unbelievably, they thought it was worse than charging too much.

a Do you agree that e-mails are an informal way of communicating?
b If someone sends you a badly written e-mail, do you find it annoying? Are you more tolerant if you know they are not writing in their first language?
c Is there anything else about e-mails that annoys you e.g. not using a sensible title in the subject line, not including the original message when replying, etc.?
d Do you think the bosses in the survey were right? Why/Why not?

2 Read the following e-mails from a company called CiclosCiclone to a customer, David Holmbrook. Re-write the e-mails and correct the mistakes in punctuation and grammar. Also change anything which you do not think is appropriate in style. Then compare your e-mails with the versions on page 134. Underline any phrases which you think are useful for this type of e-mail.

In

Delete Reply Reply All Forward New Mailboxes Get Mail — From — Search Mailbox

CiclosCiclone

ORDER FORM

CUSTOMER:	David Holmbrook	
CUSTOMER ORDER NO:	15724	
DETAILS:	1 x item GH56	£19.50
	3 x items GH98	£48.00
	shipping:	£12.40
TOTAL		**£79.90**

In

Delete Reply Reply All Forward New Mailboxes Get Mail — From — Search Mailbox

Dear mr Holmbrook
Thanks for the order. I just wish to conferm that we have recieved your order details and we have started to process the order. If your item is not instock or if there are are any d1spach problems we will contact you within the next 24/36 hrs. Please contact us if you not have received you order within 7 days at orders@ciclosciclone.com so we can resolve the issues.
thankyou once again for your order.
Kind Regards.
CiclosCiclone (Despatch Team)

In

Delete Reply Reply All Forward New Mailboxes Get Mail — From — Search Mailbox

Hi there,
Re the modification thats not a problem the whole amounut for your order will be £84.85.
I look forward to hearing from you,
Best wishes
Diego Martin

In

Delete Reply Reply All Forward New Mailboxes Get Mail — From — Search Mailbox

Dear dave
We appoligise for the delay, but we have worked out the cost of your shipping amounts of the modified order it is going to cost you £6.99 more.
To activate this transaction we will need to re-take your card details by phone to process the payment manully. We will need the long number on the front of your card, the expire date, and the security code on the back of card.
Thank you for you patience and shopping with CiclosCiclone, I look forward to hearing from you,
Best wishes
Diego

In

Delete Reply Reply All Forward New Mailboxes Get Mail — From — Search Mailbox

ok Dave, will sort this out for you, and it shall be with you soon! Sorry again.
Best wishes
Diego

ON-THE-SPOT DECISIONS

1 1.24 Listen to the telephone conversation between Cathy Slater, the caller, and Jim Kutz, who answers the call. Answer the questions.

a Who does Cathy want to speak to?
b Why?
c Why did she send him a text message?
d What solution does Jim offer?
e What is Jim's e-mail address?

Taking decisions

2 Some situations require on-the-spot decisions. What did the speakers in 1 say? Circle the correct answers.

I'll send you **I'm going to send** **I'm sending**	a copy of the certificate.	
Don't worry,	**I'll deal** **I'm going to deal** **I'm dealing**	with the e-mail straight away.
You use *will* + infinitive to show that you are making an on-the-spot decision and to promise action.		

3 Complete the conversation below using *will* + infinitive of the verbs in the box.

fly	ring	send (x2)	write

A Have we got a decision from Jim about the Mason contract?
B No, don't worry, I ....
A I tried – there's no answer.
B Well, I ....
A You can't – our intranet is down.
B Never mind – I ....
A I don't think they have one.
B Well, in that case, I ....
A Oh, come on, that'll take far too long.
B So, we ....
A Oh, that's a bit expensive.

4 1.25 Listen and check your answer to 3.

5 Work with a partner.

Speaker B: Look at the chart on page 137.
Speaker A: Choose a problem from the table and tell Speaker B. Begin *I've got a problem ...* Speaker B will offer a solution and then tell you about a problem. React using one of the solutions below. Say *Don't worry, I'll ...*

A *I've got a problem, the battery in my mobile's flat.*
B *Don't worry, I'll lend you mine.*

Problems	Solutions
I've got a headache. We didn't get your fax. This report has lots of errors in it. I can't remember his phone number. I haven't booked my flight to Berlin. I need three copies of this proposal. I don't know anything about this company.	I'll take you to the airport. I'll fax the details to you instead. I'll show you how it works. I'll explain them to you. I'll call the IT technician. I'll phone you this afternoon. I'll change the ink cartridge.

Answers on page 139.

AN IMPORTANT ORDER

1 1.26 Listen to a telephone conversation about an order and answer the questions:

a Who does Elena Moretti want to speak to?
b What product does she want to order?
c What is the reference number?
d How many units does she want?
e What is the delivery date?
f Why is this order particularly important?

2 Work with a partner. Practise the conversation using the prompts.

A S-A-G / help?
B Yes / speak / John Bird?
A afraid / not / office / now / can / message?
B Oh, dear! / urgent order / we / five hydraulic pumps / June 22nd
A Just / minute / tell / name please?
B sorry / Elena Moretti / Stern Hydraulics / Switzerland
A Right / take down / details / get John / contact / say five units?
B Yes / reference / SG 94321
A SG 94321 / five units
B yes / right / important thing / delivery date / June 22nd
A not think / a problem
B good / for / new customer
A I see / when John comes / tell him immediately / confirm / order / by e-mail?
B yes / course / thanks / much
A you / welcome / goodbye
B goodbye

3 Fill the spaces to complete Elena Moretti's e-mail confirming the order..

In
Delete Reply Reply All Forward New Mailboxes Get Mail From Search Mailbox

Dear John,
Further to a) .... with your colleague this afternoon, I wish b) .... our order for c) .... hydraulic pumps (ref SG 94321), to arrive no later than d) .... Please let us know about about any problems processing this order. We are especially concerned about receiving the parts on time, as it is for an e) .... customer.
Best regards,
Elena Moretti

4 Later that day, John Bird phoned back. Work with a partner. Try to complete the conversation using the words and phrases in the box.

all the details	Could I speak to	good	help you	in touch
is that	it's quite	more business	phoning	worried	worry

John .... Elena Moretti, please?
Elena Speaking. .... John?
John Yes. Hello, Elena. I'm .... back about your order.
Elena Yes, ... urgent.
John Don't .... I've got .... in your e-mail. No problem.
Elena That's .... I was rather .... about it.
John Well, can I .... with anything else?
Elena No, but I hope we get .... from this customer.
John Yes, of course. Okay, I'll be .... Bye for now.
Elena Goodbye.

5 1.27 Now listen to the conversation in 4 to see if you are correct.

6 Later, Elena received this e-mail confirming her order. What is the mistake?

ORDER CONFIRMATION	
Date:	1 June
Order no:	DH010601
Received:	23 May
No. of units:	5
Delivery required:	7 July
Processed by:	John Bird

7 1.28 Elena phoned SAG to tell John Bird about the mistake. Number the lines of the conversation in the correct order. Then listen and check.

- ☐ S-A-G, can I help you?
- ☐ No, it's not your fault. Just ask John to phone me.
- ☐ Right, Elena, leave it with me. I'm terribly sorry about this.
- ☐ Oh, hello, Elena. I'm afraid John isn't here at the moment. Can I take a message?
- ☐ Yes, it says July 7th, but the agreed delivery date was June 22nd. It's really important.
- ☐ Yes, this is Elena Moretti from Stern Hydraulics. Could I speak to John Bird, please?
- ☐ Oh, dear. Can you give me the details?
- ☐ All right, then. Bye for now.
- ☐ Thank you. I'm not at all happy about this. A lot depends on this order.
- ☐ I see. Well, I'll tell him as soon as he comes in.
- ☐ Yes, he sent me an order confirmation – the reference is DH010601 – but the delivery date is wrong.
- ☐ Goodbye.

Answers on page 136.

8 When John Bird got back to the office, he tried to phone Elena but couldn't get through. He decided to send an e-mail. Write his e-mail using the prompts below.

answer / your e-mail / June 1st / checked / correspondence / you / right / apologise / mistake
spoken / production department / they / giving / order / top priority
as a result / confirm / delivery date / June 22nd
once again / please accept / apologies
best wishes
John Bird

Fluency

9 On June 22nd the parts didn't arrive. They didn't arrive until June 30th. Elena phoned John again. Work with a partner and act out the conversation.

Speaker B: Look at page 138.
Speaker A: You are Elena Moretti. You are furious with John Bird. The order arrived late and as a result you will get no more orders from your customer. SAG let you down and you think John Bird is responsible. You are also angry about the fact that he never returns your calls and always makes mistakes. Unless he offers you some compensation (such as heavy discounts on future orders), tell him you will take your business elsewhere.

06 CORRESPONDENCE

LANGUAGE LINKS

Phrase Bank: Dealing with correspondence

Thank you for …
I wish to / would like to confirm our order.
Please contact us / let us know if …
Regarding …
I apologise for …
Please accept my apologies for …
I'll deal with it …
Let me take down the details …
I'm not at all happy about this.

Vocabulary

Business communication

1 Match the parts of the sentences below.

a There is a message …
b There is a mistake …
c I asked him to phone …
d I sent you an e-mail …
e We confirmed the date of the meeting …
f I will send you the packet …
g I'd like to apologise …
h We are giving top priority …

1 … in writing last week.
2 … in the letter you sent me.
3 … to your order form.
4 … about this problem last week.
5 … back this afternoon.
6 … for what happened.
7 … by courier this afternoon.
8 … from Dave Cartwright for you.

a	b	c	d	e	f	g	h

2 Complete the crossword. All the words are from unit 6.

Across

1 The .... date for this order is June 26th. (when the order is supposed to arrive with the customer)
6 We'd like a .... reply. ('quick' or 'fast')
8 People see e-mails as an .... way of communicating. (the opposite of 'formal')
9 I'm sorry, I can't read his .... (He wrote it with a pen.)
10 Machine used to send documents by telephone. (not a modem)
13 We hope to do more .... with them in the future. (buy or sell things or services)
15 I need to look at the .... again. (the noun of 'correspond')
19 To make sure something is correct.
21 Sometimes it's difficult to make a .... (the noun of 'decide')
22 Could I leave a ...., please? (what you leave when someone is not there)
24 I'm really .... he hasn't phoned me. (irritated)
28 'Thank you.' 'You're ....'
29 Could I take .... the details? (the opposite of 'up')
30 Could you .... that you have received this e-mail? (the verb of 'confirmation')

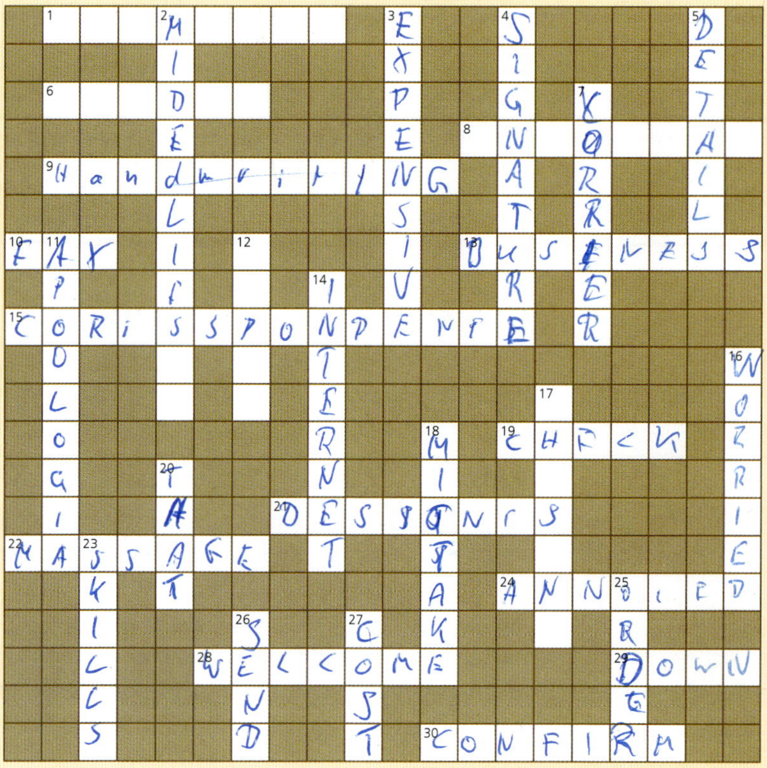

Down

2 Please do it .... (at once)
3 The opposite of 'cheap'.
4 The name written at the bottom of a document.
5 Could you confirm the .... in writing, please? (bits of information)
7 A service which picks up and delivers documents. (like UPS)
11 I'd like to .... for the mistake. (say sorry)
12 I'm still waiting for a .... from John to my letter.
14 Nowadays I use it for all my research and for sending e-mails.
16 I'm very .... about this. (the adjective of 'worry')
17 I'm .... about the order. (calling)
18 Error.
20 'Hello, is .... John?' 'Yes, speaking.'
23 Bad writing .... cost companies a lot of money. (abilities)
25 I want to place an .... for 300 units.
26 Can you .... it to me by e-mail?
27 How much will it .... us to send it?

Answers on page 141.

3 The following e-mails have arrived but there is a problem. There is no punctuation or capital letters. Correct the e-mails so that they make sense.

a dear mr gonzalez thank you for contacting lexington technical support unfortunately I do not understand the nature of the problem you are having or in fact even the product you are using can you please write back with as much information as you can about what product you are using what you are trying to do what problem you are having etc best regards kamal bouaissi technical support engineer

b dear richard tennant thank you for registering your lexington product your new customer number is 55563500 when calling technical support (925-253-3050) or lexington customer service (800-225-4880) please have your customer number ready we recommend writing your customer number in your lexington manual keeping it with our phone numbers and filing this e-mail for future reference thank you for your interest in lexington if there is anything we can do for you please let us know we will be happy to help you regards lexington customer service

Grammar

will for unplanned decisions

You use *will* + infinitive to show you are making an on-the-spot or new decision.

Practice 1

When would you say the following sentences? Match the decisions a–g to the situations 1–7.

I'll	a open the door for you.	1 A customer asks if you can give him a better discount.
	b take a taxi.	2 Your boss asks you if you can start work before the usual time.
	c catch an earlier train.	3 A colleague reminds you about a meeting with a client on the other side of town in ten minutes.
	d lend it to you, if you like.	4 Someone asks you where you can get a new battery for a laptop computer.
	e have a look on the Internet.	5 A colleague is carrying a lot of files and documents and has both hands occupied.
	f speak to the boss about it.	6 Your wife/husband asks if you can take a day off work.
	g have another look at the figures.	7 A colleague admires a new CD you are listening to.

Practice 2

What would you say in these situations? Reply using the word in brackets.

a Someone offers you something to drink. You can have tea or coffee. (coffee)

....

b You are ordering a meal in a restaurant. You can have either soup or salad for a starter. (salad)

....

c You go out with some friends. You decide to pay for the drinks. (pay)

....

d A colleague whom you like is having problems with a new computer program you are familiar with. (help)

....

e Someone reminds you that you are taking a flight at 10.30. It is now 9.15. (taxi).

....

f A colleague has heard on the radio that the buses are on strike and can't get home. You have your car. (lift).

....

TOPICS

07 HOTELS

In a survey by Carlson Hotels Worldwide, 72% of hotel-bound business travellers cited that the 'basic condition of rooms' frustrated them most, followed by uncomfortable beds (64%) and rooms that were not ready following a late arrival (64%). More than half of the respondents (53%) said they are more frustrated by a non-working television in their hotel room than by waiting in line to check in and out (47%).

HTTP://WWW.4HOTELIERS.COM/4HOTS_NSHW.PHP?MWI=3653

1 How often do you stay in hotels? Have you had any of the problems which frustrated travellers in the survey quoted above? What things about hotels do you like?

2 1.29 Listen to a conversation and answer the questions.

a Where does the conversation take place?
b What does the customer want?
c What is the customer going to do?

3 Complete the dialogue using the phrases in the box. Then listen again to check your answers.

booked in on the next flight	Can you recommend	could try the Travel Inn
like me to phone for you, sir	there's nothing before	was delayed, so I've missed

A Hello. My connecting flight, IB621, (a) .... the flight to Caracas.
B Yes, sir. I'm sorry about that. You're (b) ....
A Right, but it's not until eleven tonight, right?
B Yes. I'm afraid (c) ....
A That's nearly eight hours to wait. (d) .... a hotel I could try?
B You (e) .... It's not far from the terminal building.
A Thanks. I really need somewhere to sleep.
B Would you (f) .... ?
A No, that's okay. I need to stretch my legs anyway. Thanks very much.

4 Have you ever been in this situation? What did/would you do?

5 1.30 Listen to another conversation and answer the questions.

a Where does the conversation take place?
b What special request does the guest make? Does he get what he wants?
c What would the guest like sent to his room?
d Does the room have Internet access?

6 Listen again and complete the phrases. There is one word for each gap.

a Good afternoon. Do you have .... ?
b Well, actually I have a flight at 11 this evening so I'll ....
c .... to pay for a room by the hour?
d Well, never mind. I'll ....
e Is there Internet .... ?

7 Act out the dialogue with your teacher or a partner.

TIME TO KILL

1 Read these comments by business travellers about a type of hotel. What kind of hotel is it? Where do you think the hotel is?

Author	Topic
Chris Roberts, Boston, USA	posted – 17.05.10 Before my flight home I had a few hours to kill and I checked-in using the automatic service. The price was very reasonable and I was very impressed with the stylish interior of the rooms. I would recommend it to anyone who finds themselves waiting for a flight and doesn't have a problem with small spaces.
Stephanie, New Jersey, USA	posted – 12.37.35 Incredible what they can fit into seven square metres! A chance to shower and sleep off the jetlag after my overnight flight from New York. And good the other way, too. Many short-hop flights from continental Europe arrive in the UK late in the afternoon, leaving you stranded until the next day's flight to the U.S.
Sally Chatterley, Las Vegas, Nevada	posted – 10.15.02 This is great for airports where passengers have to change planes and perhaps wait for eight hours. It's certainly more comfortable than stretching out on a couch in the departure lounge. No windows but it's quiet and private, and within walking distance of the terminal building.

2 Find words and phrases in the comments which mean the same as the following:

a lying down stretching out

b had nothing to do for a few hours ....

c having to wait without anything to do ....

d the opposite of 'long-haul flights' ....

e not expensive ....

3 Complete the sentences with the words in 2.

a When I get home in the evening the only thing I want to do is .... on the sofa and watch TV.

b I don't like cheap .... They're uncomfortable and tiring.

c I like electronic gadgets like games consoles. They're good for when you ....

d Mobile phones are really useful when you are .... and need to contact someone.

e On the whole, the prices for food and drink in hotels are ....

4 Are the sentences in 3 true for you? If not, give reasons.

5 Now read about a hotel chain called *Yotel* on the next page and say whether the statements are true or false.

a	Yotel rooms are standard three-star hotel rooms.	true ☐	false ☐
b	You can't sit down in a Yotel room.	true ☐	false ☐
c	Yotel aims to provide a service for office workers.	true ☐	false ☐
d	Only the premium Yotel rooms have natural light.	true ☐	false ☐
e	Check-in is automated but there is room service available.	true ☐	false ☐
f	Yotel hopes that in any 24-hour period more guests will stay in the hotel than there are rooms.	true ☐	false ☐
g	You can rent Yotel rooms by the hour.	true ☐	false ☐
h	The creator of Yotel thinks that travellers like having reduced space.	true ☐	false ☐

Goodbye Minibar, Hello Miniroom

Simon Woodroffe, founder of YO! Sushi relaxes in his latest concept YOTEL at the '100% Design 2004' exhibition at London's Earl's Court.

THE 46 ROOMS at Yotel Gatwick manage to squeeze a bed, a pull-down desk, closet space, a shower and a flat-screen TV into just seven square metres (or ten square metres for the 'premium' class). The rooms have all the best features of first-class air cabins. The result is clean and stylish, like the interior of a luxury yacht.

The philosophy of Yotel is to provide luxury, but at an affordable price. To reduce costs, they use many of the features of budget flights such as online-only booking, self-service check-in, and a pricing policy which encourages early booking. The concept is really a Western adaptation of the Japanese 'capsule' hotel – ultra-cheap accommodation for office workers who sleep in coffin-like plastic modules stacked on top of each other. This is ideal for sites where space is limited, like airports and city centres.

Of course Yotel's rooms are bigger than the Japanese capsules. They are also more luxurious than the average three-star hotel room. Each soundproof cabin contains a sofa that converts into a double bed and leaves space for your suitcase underneath. A soft white-and-grey colour scheme and lots of glass and mirrors gives an impression of light and airiness. On the other hand, there is no natural light as the Premium 'cabins' have only a window onto the corridor and in Standard class there is no window at all.

Yotel want to become the iPod of the hotel industry. They are hoping that techie travellers won't mind booking into a small but well-designed box filled with electronic gadgets. There are 60 TV channels, 80 radio channels and 5,000 music tracks as well as wireless Internet to keep you entertained if you find it difficult to get to sleep. You can order food through the TV, and it is delivered promptly by the 'cabin crew' in takeaway boxes with wooden cutlery.

Any hotel in the world aims for 100% occupancy, but Yotel aims for better than 200% occupancy. There are travellers who stay the night, another group who check in for four or five hours' rest in the morning and finally the afternoon guests looking for a more comfortable place than the airport terminal to have a siesta. The standard room costs £55 for the night or £25 for a four-hour slot (the minimum). Premium costs £40 for four hours, £80 overnight.

If you have an early morning flight, a long wait between flights or an unexpected delay Yotel offers an attractive option. At first sight it may seem a little claustrophobic but its creator, Simon Woodroffe, believes that this is compensated for by the quality of the product. 'Ask a focus group if they would like to sleep in a ten-square-metre room with no natural light and you won't get many takers – walk into a Yotel room and you want it,' he says. Yotel has plans to open more Yotels at airports around the world. ■

6 Look at the ground plan of the Yotel rooms. There is a mistake in the article. What is it?

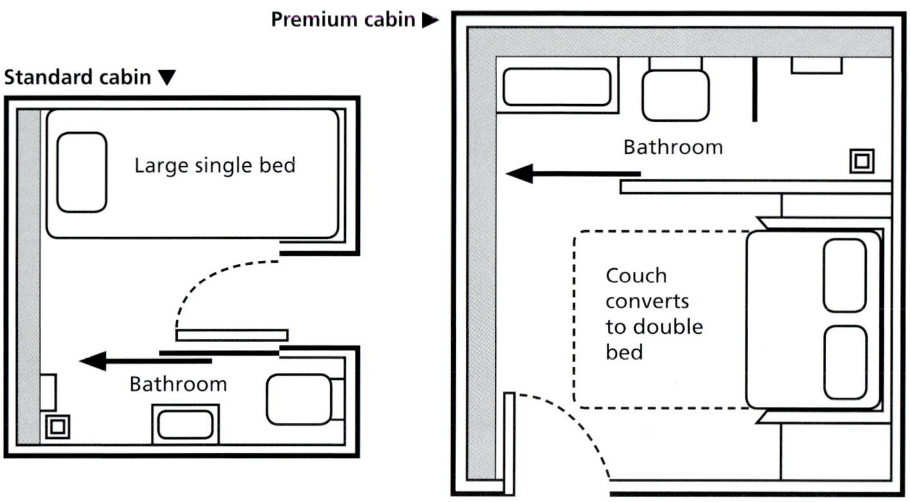

Discussion

7 Do you think you would want to stay in a Yotel room? Why/why not?

8 What features do you expect a good hotel to provide? Tick the features you expect. Add your own ideas to the list.

widescreen television	☒	bar	☐
wi-fi connection	☒	restaurant	☐
convenient location	☒	swimming pool	☐
parking	☒	fitness rooms	☐
minibar	☒	24-hour room service	☐
air conditioning	☒	massage service	☒
beautiful surroundings	☐	gym	☒
sauna	☒	meeting rooms	☒

COMPARATIVES

1 Look at this sentence from the article.

Of course, Yotel's rooms are bigger than the Japanese capsules.

Underline any other sentences in the article where things are compared.

2 Make as many sentences as you can comparing a Japanese capsule room, a Yotel room and an average three-star hotel room using the adjectives in the circle.

A Yotel room is smaller than a normal hotel room.
A capsule is more claustrophobic than a Yotel room.

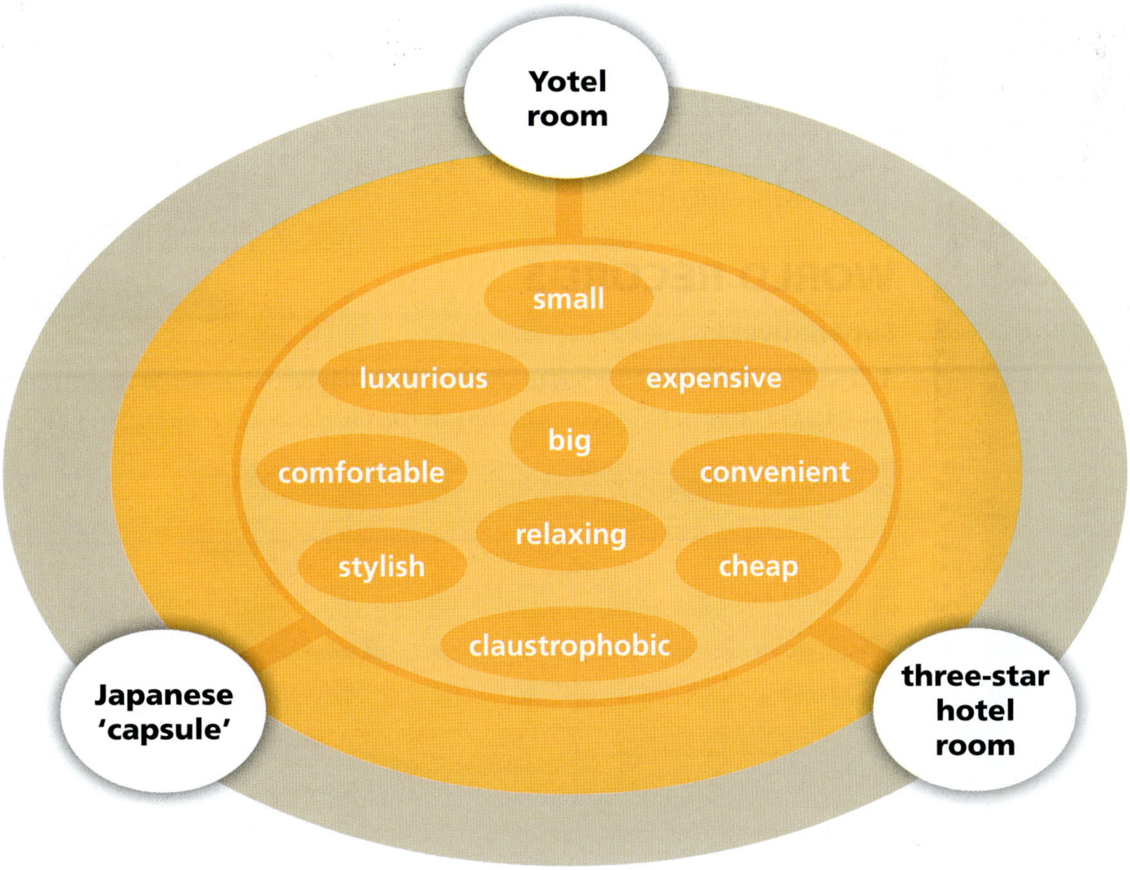

3 Now work with a partner and compare:

a three cities you both know.
b three different cars.

ROOM SERVICE

1 1.31 It is ten o'clock at night. A guest calls room service to ask for something. Complete the conversation below. Then listen and compare your answers.

Room Service	Room service. My name is Johan. Can I help you?
Guest	Yes, this is room 301. a) .... an early morning call, please?
Room Service	Certainly, sir. What time b) .... the call?
Guest	At half past six.
Room Service	6.30. No problem. c) .... breakfast sent up to your room?
Guest	No, thanks. I d) .... it in the dining room.
Room Service	The dining room doesn't open for breakfast until 7.30.
Guest	Oh, in that case I e) .... in my room. Just coffee and a croissant.
Room Service	Coffee and a croissant. f) ....?
Guest	No, that's all.
Room Service	Okay. g) ...., sir.
Guest	Thank you. Good night.

2 Practise the conversation in 1 with a partner.

Fluency

3 Work with a partner.

Speaker A: You are the room service clerk.
Speaker B: Phone room service to make requests for:

- something to eat
- someone to dry-clean a tie or a skirt
- someone to fix the air conditioning
- help with wifi connection
- tomorrow's weather forecast
- (your own request)

Now change roles.

Speaker B: You are the room service clerk.
Speaker A: See page 134.

WORLD RECORDS

Superlatives

1 Use the adjectives in the box to say how the hotels below are world record breakers.
The MGM Grand in Las Vegas is the largest hotel in the world. It has 6,276 rooms.

expensive   high   large   northern   old   southern   tall

Hotel	Location	Detail
MGM Grand	Las Vegas	6,276 rooms
Rose Tower	Dubai	72 floors
MGM Grand	Las Vegas	\$5,000 room/night
Lhasa Hotel	Lhasa	12,087 feet above sea level
Ny-Ålesund	Svalbard, Norway	78°55'N 11°56'E
Ushuaia	Ushuaia, Argentina	54°48'S 68°18'W
Hoshi Ryokan	Awazu, Japan	It opened in 717

Answers on page 142.

2 The room prices of four different big hotel chains vary from country to country. With a partner complete the information in the tables. Tell your partner about hotel prices like this.

In Frankfurt, the most expensive chain is Crowne Plaza. The cheapest chain is of the four is Accorhotels. The second-most expensive is Hilton International and the third in the list is Best Western.

Student A: Look at the information below.

Student B: Look at the information on page 140.

city	chain	price	city	chain	price
Amsterdam		272	London	Accorhotels	476
		238		Hilton International	408
		195		Crowne Plaza	329
		178		Best Western	188
Frankfurt	Crowne Plaza	494	New York		584
	Hilton International	330			457
	Best Western	157			268
	Accorhotels	152			260
Geneva		394	Paris	Crowne Plaza	420
		357		Accorhotels	381
		260		Hilton International	361
		148		Best Western	254

LOCATING AN OFFICE

Fluency

Your company is planning to open a European office and needs to choose the best location. Look at the information below and decide which cities are the most suitable.

Talk about the following:

- high / low population
- near to / far from an international airport
- high / low taxi fares
- high / low / expensive / cheap office rents
- expensive / cheap hotel rooms
- high / low / expensive / cheap apartment rents
- high / low cost of living
- expensive / cheap place to live

DATA	FRANKFURT	GENEVA	DUBLIN	BRUSSELS
Population	642,811	185,028	495,781	1,031,925
Distance – city centre to airport (km)	12	4	10	14
Average taxi fare to airport ($)	24–29	27–31	17–20	40–44
International conferences per year	27	161	42	189
City-centre office rents (US $/sq m)	630	540	936	447
Hotel rooms (€ mid range/top range)	110/270	140/360	140/290	110/230
Three-room apartment rents (€/month)	1431	1430	2545	1367

LANGUAGE LINKS

Phrase Bank: Travel & accommodation
I have a few hours to kill.
I'd like a chance to shower.
stretch out.
relax.
sleep off the jet lag.
They offer luxury at an affordable price.
The price was very reasonable.
I have an early morning flight.
an afternoon
an evening

Vocabulary

Hotel services

1 Number the lines of the dialogue in the correct order.

Receptionist
- ☐ Yes, sir. What would you like?
- ☐ Room service. Katherine speaking. Can I help you?
- ☐ Well, I'll have to ask in the kitchen to see if they have any foie gras. Would you like it with some toast?
- ☐ You're welcome, sir. Goodbye.
- ☐ Yes. Dry, medium or sweet?
- ☐ Right, sir. It will be with you in a few minutes.

Guest
- ☐ Hello, Katherine. This is room 208 here. I'm feeling a bit hungry. I'd like to order a snack.
- ☐ Thank you, Katherine.
- ☐ Oh, as dry as possible, please, and nicely chilled.
- ☐ Oh, I don't know. Perhaps a little foie gras?
- ☐ Yes, please. And I'd also like some champagne.

2 Complete the sentences using the correct form of the words in brackets.

a It can be difficult to find a decent hotel room at an .... price. (afford)
b If you call room service, they will .... meals to your room. (delivery)
c Although the room was small, it was perfectly .... (comfort)
d A lot of our revenue comes from food and drink but our rooms are more .... (profit)
e Hotel guests from the USA .... a standard room layout. (preference)
f You can .... old buildings into hotels but there is a limit to what you can do. (conversion)
g We have to meet our customers' .... (expect)
h Multinational companies often expand by taking over smaller .... (operate)

Grammar

Comparatives and superlatives

Adjective type	Adjective	Comparative	Superlative
1 syllable	rich cheap	rich**er** cheap**er**	**the** rich**est** **the** cheap**est**
1 syllable with 1 vowel + consonant	hot big	hot**ter** big**ger**	**the** hot**test** **the** big**gest**
2 syllables ending in *-y*	early heavy	earl**ier** heav**ier**	**the** earl**iest** **the** heav**iest**
2 syllables or more	economical interesting	**more** economical **more** interesting	**the most** economical **the most** interesting

You can often use the comparative form of adjectives with *than* to compare people, places and things.
- *Life is **easier than** in the past.*
- *The company is **more profitable** than its competitors.*

You can use *much*, *a lot*, *a bit* and *a little* to show if the differences are big or small.
- *Mexico City is **a lot bigger** than Rome*
- *London is **much more expensive** than Madrid.*

You can also use *not as … as* to show differences.
- *Travelling by train is **not as expensive as** by plane.*

You use the article *the* with the superlative form of the adjective.
- *Taking important decisions is **the hardest** part of management.*
- ***The most useful** aspect of the Internet is communication.*

You can use *second*, *third* etc. with superlatives.
- *Locally we are **the second largest** provider of Internet services.*

You can also use *less … than* and *the least* to show differences.
- *Life in the past was **less comfortable than** it is now.*
- *His company is **the least profitable** on the stock exchange.*

Practice 1

Rewrite the sentences using the opposite of the adjective.

a The Internet is faster than the post.
The post is slower than the Internet.
b Hotels are more expensive than motels.
Motels ....
c English is easier to learn than Chinese.
Chinese ....
d Trains are more comfortable than buses.
Buses ....
e People think that marketing is more interesting than accounting.
People think that accounting ....
f Flying is safer than driving.
Driving ....

g Small meetings are more efficient than large ones.
Large meetings ....
....

h This job is better paid than my last one.
My last job ....
....

i The economic situation is worse than it was four years ago.
Four years ago the economic situation ....
....

Practice 2

Complete the sentences with *as* or *than*.

a The job isn't as interesting .... I hoped.
b The journey was more expensive .... I expected.
c This office has more space .... the old one.
d I'm feeling more tired .... yesterday.
e Fords aren't as good .... Audis.

Practice 3

Complete the second sentence so that it means the same as the first sentence.

a It's easier to build hotels in the USA than in Europe.
It's not as difficult to build hotels in the USA as it is in Europe.
b A Maserati GT is more powerful than a Chevrolet.
A Chevrolet isn't ....
....
c A Chevrolet isn't as expensive as a Maserati.
A Maserati is ....
....
d Profitability is more important than turnover.
Turnover isn't ....
....
e Sales aren't as good as last year.
Sales are ....
....
f This computer is faster than the old one.
The old computer wasn't as ....
....
g It isn't as hot as yesterday.
Yesterday ....
....

Practice 4

Who are the richest people in the world today? Look at the table below and complete the sentences. Has the situation changed since the information was published?

2007	2008	Name	Net worth (billions) 2007	Net worth (billions) 2008	Date of Birth	Citizenship	Sources of wealth
2	**1**	Warren Buffett	$52.0	**$62.0**	1930	USA	Berkshire Hathaway
3	**2**	Carlos Slim Helú	$49.0	**$60.0**	1940	Mexico	Telmex, América Móvil
1	**3**	Bill Gates	$56.0	**$58.0**	1955	USA	Microsoft
5	**4**	Lakshmi Mittal	$32.0	**$45.0**	1950	India	Arcelor Mittal
14	**5**	Mukesh Ambani	$20.1	**$43.0**	1957	India	Reliance Industries
18	**6**	Anil Ambani	$18.2	**$42.0**	1959	India	Anil Dhirubhai Ambani Group
4	**7**	Ingvar Kamprad and family	$31.0	**$33.0**	1926	Sweden	IKEA
62	**8**	Kushal Pal Singh	$10.0	**$30.0**	1931	India	DLF Group
40	**9**	Oleg Deripaska	$13.3	**$28.0**	1968	Russia	Rusal
15	**10**	Karl Albrecht	$20.0	**$27.0**	1920	Germany	ALDI, Trader Joe's

Source: www.forbes.com/lists

In 2007 …
a Bill Gates was the .... person in the world.
b Carlos Slim Helú wasn't .... as Warren Buffett.
c Kushal Pal Singh was .... Oleg Deripaska.
d Warren Buffett was one of the .... people in the world.
e The .... of all these people was Karl Albrecht.

In 2008 …
a Warren Buffet was the .... person in the world.
b Carlos Slim Helú wasn't .... as Warren Buffett.
c Mukesh Ambani was just a bit .... than his brother.
d Bill Gates was still one of the .... people in the world.
e The .... of all these people was Karl Albrecht.
f Mukesh Ambani was more than twice .... as in 2007.
g The .... Indian was Lakshmi Mittal.
h All of the people in this list were .... in 2008 than in 2007.

08 DID I EVER TELL YOU ...?

The trouble with telling a good story is that it invariably reminds the other fellow of a bad one.

SID CAESAR

anecdote
/ˈænɪkˌdəʊt/ *noun*
a story that you tell people about something interesting or funny that has happened to you

Definition from Macmillan Essential Dictionary

1 1.32 Complete the anecdote below with suitable words. Then listen and compare your answers.

A Look at that car!
B Yes, very nice. It's a Porsche 911.
A Did I ever tell you about the time I had a a) .... in a Porsche?
B No, I don't think so.
A It was when I b) .... a student. I was c) .... in Europe and a man in a Porsche stopped. He took me all the way across Austria. We d) .... about 220 kilometres an hour all the way.
B What about the e) ....?
A Well, they f) .... us about four times, but this chap just showed them some identity card and they waved us on.
B Was he someone g) ...., then?
A I don't know, I didn't ask. I h) .... he was some sort of high-ranking official. He didn't talk much, but he did drive well.

2 1.33 Look at these sentences from the anecdote in 1.

It was when I was a student. I was hitch-hiking in Europe.

Make similar sentences using the prompts below. There are several alternatives. Then listen and compare your answers.

a while / live / Italy
b before / start / work / here
c after / leave / university
d when / work / ICL
e before / get / married
f just after / children / born
g look / job
h do / Masters / the States
i study / at Cambridge
j work / small company / north
k travel / Asia
l stay / Continental Hotel / Prague

3 1.34 The speaker ends the anecdote in 1 with a comment:

He didn't talk much, but he did drive well.
… *he did drive well* is similar to *he certainly drove well.*
Did adds emphasis to the verb *drive*. *Did* is stressed when you speak.

Make similar comments using the following prompts, then listen and compare your answers.

a we / have a good time / cost a fortune
b he / get the job / have to marry the boss's daughter
c we / get there in the end / sit on a bus all day
d I / get a good job / have to leave the country / find one
e she / make a success / business / her husband / leave her
f he / sell more than anyone else / have a heart attack

4 Complete the sentences below. Use *did* for emphasis.

a It was a good car, ……………………
b I enjoyed the meal, ……………………
c The conference wasn't very good, ……………………
d They managed to find a hotel, ……………………

5 Complete the sentences below so that they make sense.

a …………………… , but we did ask first.
b …………………… , but I did send him an e-mail.
c …………………… , but he did take her out to dinner.
d …………………… , but she did give him the job.

6 Work with a partner and each tell an anecdote based on the questions below. Help your partner by asking more questions.

Speaker A
Have you ever been stopped by the police when you were driving? Where were you going? Why did they stop you? Were they right or wrong? What was the outcome? Did it change your attitude either to driving or to the police, or did it confirm what you already thought?

Speaker B
Who was your least favourite teacher at school or lecturer at university? Why didn't you like them? Can you remember an incident that was typical of that person? Who was involved? What happened? What was the outcome? Did it change your point of view in any way or did it confirm what you already thought?

CASE STUDY

CRISTAL MALVERN

1 Discuss these questions in groups. Do you drink bottled mineral water? Why do you think mineral water is so popular now? How do people decide which brand of mineral water to drink?

2 Read a report in a newspaper about a local mineral water company. What happened? Why does the fact that the company's product is mineral water make the situation so difficult?

Local Community Rocked by Cristal Malvern Fire

A fire which broke out at Cristal Malvern bottling plant in the early hours of yesterday morning has completely destroyed the factory and offices of the mineral water company. According to company sources, for the moment the cause of the fire is unknown, although a problem with the plant's power supply is suspected. In a meeting this morning the workforce was informed that although the company will eventually rebuild the factory, redundancy notices will be served. Cristal Malvern is an established brand which has become popular due to its original and striking TV ads. The problem facing the company is that the bottling plant is located next to the spring which gives the mineral water its name. Ron White, a union spokesman, says the fire is a tragedy for the local community as Cristal Malvern is one of the area's main employers.

3 1.35 Listen to the television interview with Ron White, the union representative, and Peter Jones, the public relations officer of Cristal Malvern. Answer the questions.

a What kind of 'adjustment plan' do you think the company has?
b Why is it not possible to move to another location?
c What is the attitude of the union?
d What does Ron White say about the rumour that the company might have to close?

4 You are going to take part in the meeting to decide what to do about this situation. Each take a role: A, B, C or D.

A
The Managing Director
Your family has been connected with the company for over a hundred years, and although there are now other shareholders, you still have control. Apart from nostalgia and emotional reasons for re-building the plant, there are very good business reasons. Mineral water is now an important consumer product, sales have increased a lot over the last few years and your brand is one of the market leaders. In fact, the fire may be a 'blessing in disguise'. The insurance money and other subsidies available will cover most of the cost of modernising and building a modern plant. A new plant with modern processes will require fewer workers so some permanent redundancies will have to be negotiated. You feel a genuine concern and responsibility for the workforce. You have known many of them for years. Probably you can lose some people through early retirement but you hope to keep as many of the employees as possible. Apart from this worry, your major concern is to lose as few customers as possible while the factory is rebuilt.

B

The Union Representative

You have been with the company all your working life. You are worried that Cristal Malvern may disappear – that the company owners will take the insurance money and run! In fact you suspect that the fire might not have been an accident. The plant was very old and a big investment was required to continue production. On the other hand, you are quite sure that the brand has a good future because the mineral water has always sold very well. The other possibility is that the company management will make everybody redundant and then start up again as a new company. Perhaps they will sell the company to one of the big multinationals. Your hope is that you can negotiate a temporary redundancy for staff while the factory is being re-built, and then as many people as possible can return to work with the same salary and conditions as before.

C

The Plant Manager

You are the Managing Director's son/daughter. You recognise that the company could still be a viable business but you would prefer to do something else with the insurance money. You have little interest in reconstructing the business. Apart from anything else, you are bored with life in this quiet rural area. In any case, by the time you are ready to begin bottling again, it will be almost impossible to regain your market position. You can just see one problem after another and you are desperate to do something more interesting and exciting somewhere else. Try to convince your father that the best plan would be to sell up. You could probably get a good offer from one of the big food and drink multinationals.

D

The Marketing Manager

This situation is a real challenge for you. Your mission is to keep the brand alive while the problems of production are sorted out. You know that the idea of transporting the water to other plants is not viable due to the costs. However, your idea is to make a deal with other companies to distribute and sell their own water as Cristal Malvern with a slightly modified label where the origin of the spring water is in small print. You believe that most people will not notice the difference in taste. After all, water is water, and if people drink it from bottles rather than taps, it is really a triumph of marketers. You are optimistic about the future and believe it is a good opportunity for the company to modernise its production in order to meet an increasing demand. If you can survive the coming months, Cristal Malvern can grow, modernise and benefit from this disaster.

5 Read the newspaper article to find out what happened in a similar case in Spain and discuss the questions.

a Was this company's decision similar to what you decided in 4?
b Do you think the water really 'travelled' to the other bottling plants?
c In what ways is the mineral water business such an unusual one?

Insalus Water

In July 2003 the bottling plant of Insalus Water was destroyed by a fire. 18 months later the company has been able to renew its activity in a new installation, built at an estimated cost of 10 million euros. The company was able to continue its commercial activity during the period of reconstruction, but one of its biggest concerns was the situation of its workers. In the end less than 10% of the workforce was made redundant. The majority of the remaining employees agreed to be temporarily laid off, although those workers involved in sales and marketing continued in their posts while the new production facilities were built.

During the period of reconstruction, it was vital for the Insalus brand to maintain a market presence. It was able to do so by reaching agreements with other mineral water bottling companies in both Spain and France. The spring water "travelled" from the Lizartza site to these bottling plants for distribution. Although the situation had a negative influence on sales, with the new factory in operation, sales have quickly recovered and continue to grow. In fact, Insalus took the opportunity to modernise production and built two separate plants, one for glass bottles (suitable for 'sparkling' water), and the other for plastic (PET). The new processes make it possible to produce up to 30,000 bottles per hour.

09 SPIRIT OF ENTERPRISE

Don't explain how we're going to make money today. Tell me how we're going to make it in five years' time.

AMANCIO ORTEGA – FOUNDER AND PRESIDENT OF INDITEX

entrepreneur
/ˌɒntrəprəˈnɜː/ *noun*
someone who uses money to start businesses and make business deals

Definition from Macmillan Essential Dictionary

1 Read the extracts below then discuss the questions which follow.

I've always felt that going to business school was a substitute for being an entrepreneur, not a complement. Those who can, sell. Those who can't, sit in class.

Business consultant and writer Arnold Kling on http://gondwanaland.com/mlog/2005/11/23/learning-by-selling/

Born entrepreneurs can be taught how to become better businesspeople. But businesspeople cannot be taught how to become entrepreneurs.

Wil Schroter's Blog http://www.gobignetwork.com/wil/

Entrepreneurs are people who imagine things as they might be, not as they are, and have the drive to change the world. Those are qualities that business schools do not teach.

Founder of Body Shop Anita Roddick

a What is the word for 'entrepreneur' in your language? Give some examples of entrepreneurs who are famous in your country.
b Is it possible to teach someone to be an entrepreneur?
c What kind of skills and qualities do you think entrepreneurs need?
d Is it an advantage to go to university before you start a business? Which opinion above do you agree with most?

2 **1.36** Now listen to a radio programme where an author talks about a book on entrepreneurs. Answer the questions.

a Which of the opinions in 1 does the author most agree with?
b How many examples does he give of successful businesses?
c Which of the following does he say the entrepreneurs have in common?

- an MBA
- hiring good employees
- taking risks
- intelligence
- setting up efficient distribution networks
- working for someone else before setting up a business
- luck
- providing excellent customer service
- using television advertising
- hard work

3 Listen again and complete the phrases.

a Mike Clare, the founder of *Dreams*, and Michael Walsh of *Blackcircles.com* are both good examples of people who .... work when they .... school.
b They .... knowledge and skills while they .... for someone else, but each .... that his real mission in life was to be an entrepreneur.
c Both .... customer service a major selling point.
d .... successful at building up their networks.
e They .... incredibly hard to get where they are today.

4 Which of the sentences in 3 are examples of:

- the Past Simple ....
- the Present Perfect ....
- an event or stage in someone's life which is completely finished ....
- an achievement or event which is part of an ongoing situation ....

5 Work in pairs. One of you reads text A on this page and the other reads text B on page 58. Complete the chart below with information from your text.

	Dreams	Blackcircles.com
First job of founder		He worked in a garage.
Age when he started the company	He was 35.	
First business premises		
Main product		
Distribution network		
Customer services		
Recent developments		

6 Ask your partner questions to complete the information about the company you didn't read about.

7 Read the other text. Underline the examples of the Present Perfect in both texts.

A

Blackcircles.com

MICHAEL WELCH left school at 16 and started work in a garage as a car-tyre fitter. He quickly learnt about the car-tyre business and decided to set up his own mail-order company. He advertised in motoring magazines and sold high-performance specialist tyres. He knew very little about running a business so he took a college course to study aspects like financial management. His next step was to get a job with the tyre company Kwikfit where he got some experience, and was able to study his future competition. After a year there and still only 20, he decided it was time to go it alone.

His company, Blackcircles.com, allows customers to order tyres on the Internet and get them fitted within a day at one of its affiliated garages. Its low-cost, speedy service has proved to be a spectacular success. Welch started in an office with a single desk which he rescued from a rubbish bin. At the beginning he needed to find reliable garages to fit the tyres and spent a lot of his time approaching and checking fitters across the country. After six months, he took on his first employee to help and the business began to grow, despite some problems with his investing partners.

These days, Blackcircles.com is a thriving business and the company has built up a network of 970 franchise outlets. The company has set up a central call centre which phones every single customer to get feedback on the service. This way Welch can see how garages are performing and identify problems. 'We've spent time on the basics, making sure customers are getting the right service,' he says. Growth has been slower as a result, but he thinks this is a secret of his success. As it says on the company website, 'Since 2001, we have supplied and fitted tyres for thousands of satisfied customers, many of whom have bought tyres from Blackcircles.com again and again.' Recently the company has launched a specific web-based service for customers with fleets of cars and has added motorbike tyres to its range of over 20,000 tyres.

Source: http://www.startups.co.uk/6678842908076678039/black-circles.html

B

DREAMS

WHEN MIKE CLARE left college at 18 with a basic business diploma, he started working for a furniture shop in the beds department. Eventually, he became a manager, but when he was 35 and after 12 years working for someone else, he decided it was time to start his own business. He got a small loan and sold his car to raise some money, and found a small shop which was in a terrible state, but was cheap. He started the Sofabed Company in 1985 and within two years, he had three stores. After a while, he decided to concentrate only on beds because they take up less space and you can store more of them. He also found that beds were easier to sell because people are less concerned about the look of a bed than a sofa. He changed the name of the company to Dreams and has not looked back since.

Dreams has built its business on four main selling points: Choice, Price, Delivery and Comfort. This simple formula and Mike's enthusiasm have taken the business to over 150 superstores. Distribution has been the company's biggest challenge, and they now have a fleet of over 100 vans. They have also given a lot of special attention to customer service. When a Dreams driver delivers a bed, he puts on a special pair of slippers to avoid making a mess. 'The slippers cost us virtually nothing, but after a delivery it's all the customers can talk about,' explains Clare.

Dreams has established a reputation for quality and service and has won the Retailer of the Year prize three times. In 2005, it launched an online store and has recently opened its own bed factory. The company is still growing and it has branched out into the international market through franchising. Clare is optimistic about the future. 'It's not easy, and a lot of businesses do fail,' he admits. 'But it's not as complicated as a lot of people think either.'

Source: http://www.startups.co.uk/6678842908348533189/mike-clare.html

CHANGE

1 Label each graph with two verbs from the box which describe change.

go up	fall	remain stable	go down	increase	not change

2 Work in groups. Using the verbs in 1, describe what has happened recently in your country or region, and in the company you work for. Use the topics below to help you.

Interest rates ***have fallen*** *in the last six months.*
The number of people working in my team at work ***has increased*** *recently.*

in your country or region	**in your company**
house prices	number of staff
rate of inflation	revenues
unemployment	profits
economic growth	amount of work
taxes	
interest rates	
population	
traffic	

Has anything else important happened in your country, region or company?

3 Read the information below about a successful Spanish company, Inditex, and answer the questions.

a Who is the founder of the Inditex Group? ....
b Where and when did it start? ....
c What business is it in? ....
d What is the secret of its success? ....
e How many companies are there in the group? ....

BUSINESS BRIEFING

INDITEX

THE FOUNDER OF INDITEX, Amancio Ortega, has a catch phrase: Don't explain how we're going to make money today. Tell me how we're going to make it in five years' time. The Inditex Group's first Zara shop opened its doors in 1975 in La Coruña, Spain. Today, the Group's stores can be seen in places such as New York's 5th Avenue, Paris' Champs-Elysées, London's Regent Street, and Tokyo's Shibuya Shopping Quarters. Its unique management methods, based on innovation and flexibility, have turned Inditex into one of the world's largest fashion groups, made up of almost a hundred companies dealing with activities related to textile design, production and distribution. ■

Source: www.inditex.com/english/home.htm

4 Work with a partner.

Speaker B: Look at the instructions on page 134.
Speaker A: Look at the information in the table below. Work with your partner to complete the missing information and find out how Inditex has changed over the last four years.

Inditex	four years ago	now
Shops worldwide	....	3,131
New stores in year	322	....
Employees	....	69,240
Countries where the group operates	56	....
% of international sales	....	60%
Chains in group	six - Zara, Pull & Bear, Massimo Dutti, Bershka Stradivarius, Oysho	....
Turnover	....	€8,196 million
Net profits	€639 million	....
Headquarters	....	Arteixo, La Coruña

5 Complete the report using information from 4 and the verbs in the box in either the Past Simple or Present Perfect.

grow increase launch make move open reach

The recent history of Inditex is a tremendous success story. Over the last four years the group (a) .... enormously. It now operates in (b) .... countries, and the number of shops worldwide (c) .... from (d) .... to (e) .... In this time the group (f) .... (g) .... new chains, and (h) .... 329 new shops in Spain and 300 in the rest of the world. This year, net revenues (i) .... a level of (j) .... , and the group (k) .... profits of (l) .... All Inditex's activities are controlled from Arteixo, La Coruña, where the group recently (m) .... into new headquarters.

6 Write a similar report about the changes in a company you know about.

LANGUAGE LINKS

Phrase Bank: Talking about business achievements

He was still only twenty when he set up the business.
The company is still growing.
He left school at 16.
Eventually he became a manager.
They picked up skills and knowledge.
To set up a business, take risks and make money.
Customer service is a major selling point.
One thing they have in common is a capacity for hard work.

Vocabulary

Word-building

Complete the table below with the appropriate form.

verb	noun	adjective
acquire	acquisition	acquired
reject	....	rejected
grow	....	growing
....	success	....
....	....	beneficial
innovate	....	....
....	....	flexible
....	operation	operating
....	....	profitable
....	increase	....
....	fall	fallen/falling
install	....	installed

Grammar

Present Perfect

Affirmative		
I You We They	**'ve** **(have)**	**finished** the report
He She	**'s** **has**	

Negative		
I You We They	**haven't**	**finished** the report
He She	**hasn't**	

Interrogative		
Have **Haven't**	I you we they	**finished the report?**
Has **Hasn't**	he she	

Short answers

***Have** you **seen** John?*
*Yes, I **have**. / No, I **haven't**.*
***Has** Jane **sent** the letter?*
*Yes, she **has**. / No, she **hasn't**.*

The past participle of regular verbs is the same as the Past Simple, but with many common irregular verbs it is different:

- *go – went – **gone***
- *come – came – **come***
- *eat – ate – **eaten***

The tense you use to talk about past events depends on how you see them.

If you see actions and situations as part of a sequence of finished past events and situations (e.g. stages in your life, events in history, events in a narrative, etc.) you use the **Past Simple**.

- *I **studied** economics at university.*
- *His first wife **was** Argentinian.*
- *Her last job **was** with an engineering firm.*
- *Bill Gates **founded** Microsoft with a friend.*
- *Some people **made** a lot of money in the war.*
- *Suddenly he **stopped** talking and **left** the room.*

If past actions or situations are not related to other past events or time periods (they simply happened before now), you use the Present Perfect. Often it is because you are referring to recent events, or to contrast a present situation with the past.

- *I've **had** a fantastic idea!*
- *We've **developed** a new product for our range.*
- *Our turnover **has grown** by 10%.*
- *The photocopier **has broken** down.*

There is one important exception:

- *What **did** you **say**?* not ~~*What have you said*~~?

Practice 1

Write the past participles of the verbs below.

see	a)	write	i) ....
buy	b)	break	j) ....
sell	c)	set	k) ....
do	d)	read	l) ....
find	e)	fall	m) ....
come	f)	rise	n) ....
put	g)	meet	o) ....
take	h)	think	p) ....

Practice 2

Reorganise the words to make sentences in the Present Perfect.

a lost glasses I have my

....

b gone by 3% prices have up

....

c has stable economic remained growth

....

d prices last years have in fallen five the

....

e has 2,000 workers sacked Molinex

....

f company has the Mr Rodriguez left

....

g not a John week I have for seen

....

Practice 3

Write a sentence using the verbs in the box and the Present Perfect for the situations below.

arrive	be	break	change
give	lose	move	stop

a Half an hour ago, it was raining and now it isn't.
It's stopped raining.

b The photocopier doesn't work. Half an hour ago, it did.
.... down.

c Ten minutes ago, you called for a taxi. It's now outside the office.
The taxi ....

d Last year, your company was based on a site outside town. Now its offices are located in the centre of town.
.... into the centre of town.

e You can't find your notes for a presentation.
.... notes.

f You're giving a presentation. You did the same presentation last week and the week before.
This is the third time ....
....

g Philip Windish works for a company. A week ago, he worked for a different company.

....

h A friend comments that nowadays he never sees you.
.... very busy lately.

Practice 4

Match the questions to the answers.

a Where is my pen?
b Why are you looking so pleased with yourself?
c How is the new product line doing?
d Why are you looking for a new car?
e What's our share price today?
f Why are you looking so tired?
g Where's Jeremy?

1 It's gone up by four cents.
2 I've achieved my sales target for this month.
3 Because I've sold my old one.
4 It's been a really long day.
5 It's been very successful so far.
6 He's gone to Sydney for the week.
7 I don't know. I haven't seen it.

a	b	c	d	e	f	g	h

Practice 5

Complete the text with the verbs in the box, using either the Past Simple or the Present Perfect.

acquire	add	create	finish	increase
launch	open	reach	start	turn

The Inditex group consists of almost a hundred companies dealing with textile design, production and distribution. Its unique management techniques and its successes (a) .... Inditex into one of the world's largest fashion groups.
The first Zara shop (b) .... in 1975 in La Coruña in northern Spain. Over the years, the group (c) .... other chains to the original Zara, each covering a different market sector. In 1991, the group (d) .... Pull & Bear, and in 1995, (e) .... 100% of Massimo Dutti. Bershka (f) .... its activity in 1998, followed by the acquisition of Stradivarius in 1999. Two years later, Inditex (g) .... Oysho, a chain specialising in fashionable lingerie and underwear.
In the last four years, the number of shops in the group (h) .... a figure of over three thousand, and the group now has operations in 64 countries worldwide. In the same period, sales (i) .... by 22% and net profits by 25%.
Despite its size, the group still controls its activities from a logistical centre in Arteixo, a village in the north-west of Spain, but in 2003 it (j) .... work on 'Plataforma Europa', a new distribution centre in Zaragoza.

Answers on page 141.

TOPICS

10 STRESSED TO THE LIMIT

Pressure is part and parcel of all work and helps to keep us motivated. But excessive pressure can lead to stress, which undermines performance, is costly to employers and can make people ill.

UK HEALTH & SAFETY EXECUTIVE - HTTP://WWW.HSE.GOV.UK/STRESS/

Discussion

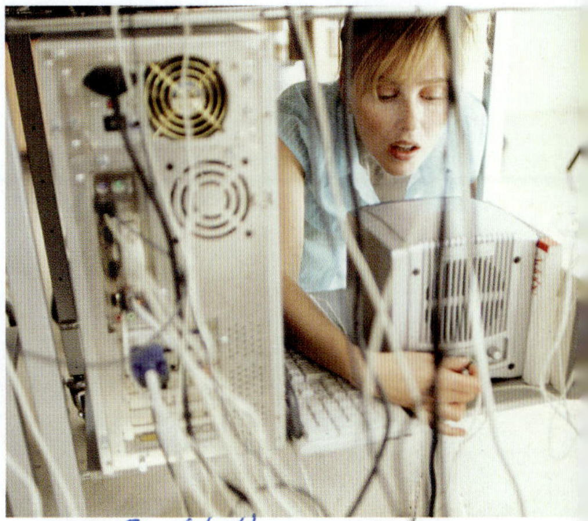

1 Work with a partner. Which of these factors produce the most stress? Add your own ideas.

being promoted   being responsible for people's lives
dealing with big sums of money   dealing with the public
doing boring, repetitive tasks   learning to use new technology
looking after children   making phone calls
meeting deadlines   travelling
waiting for other people to do things   working long hours

2 1.37–1.40 An interviewer for the radio programme *Work Today* spoke to four people in the street about stress. Listen to the interviews and answer the questions.

		interview 1	interview 2	interview 3	interview 4
a	What does the speaker do?				
b	Does the speaker suffer from stress?				
c	What causes the stress, according to the speaker?				
d	Does the speaker mention any of the reasons in 1? Which?				

3 The last speaker says that stress is more a problem of mental attitude than what you do. Do you agree?

4 In your opinion, what are the three most stressful jobs? Use the list below to help you.

accountant   air traffic controller   architect   chief executive   computer programmer   doctor
factory worker   firefighter   journalist   lawyer   middle manager   miner   pilot
police officer   shop assistant   secretary   stockbroker   taxi driver   teacher   telephonist   waiter

Now compare your ideas with the list on page 135. Are you surprised? What do you think are the least stressful jobs?

have to

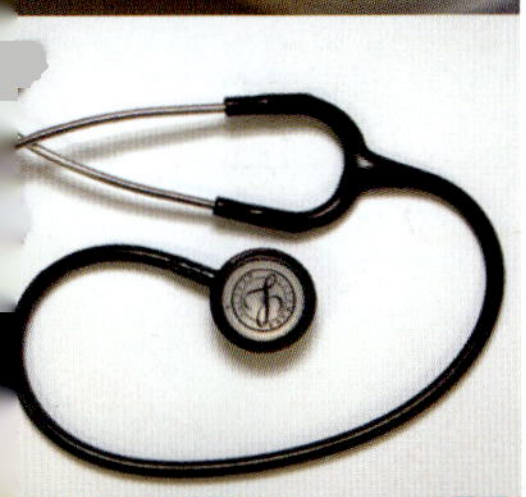

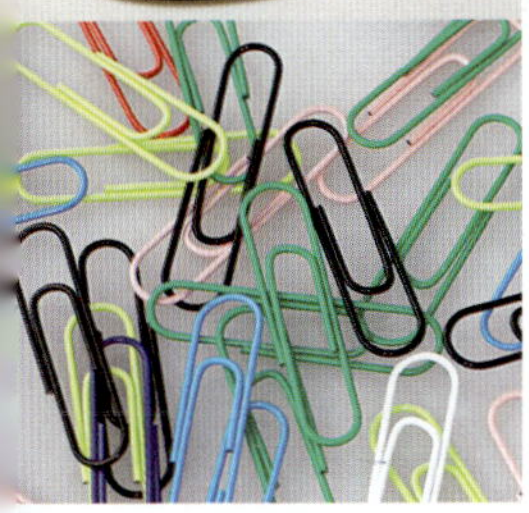

5 For each set of prompts a–g, make at least two sentences with *has to/have to/doesn't have to/don't have to.*

air traffic controller   factory worker   take decisions   be creative
An air traffic controller has to take decisions very quickly. (It's necessary)
A factory worker doesn't have to be creative. (It's not necessary)

a lawyer   secretary   wear a suit   type letters
b middle managers   chief executives   solve day-to-day problems   take strategic decisions
c shop assistant   computer programmer   deal with the public   know computer languages
d lorry driver   taxi driver   drive long distances   memorise street maps
e nurse   factory worker   wear special clothes   work at night
f accountant   telephonist   use a computer   be honest
g teacher   engineer   tell people what to do   wear a tie

Make sentences about the other jobs in 4.

6 Now interview someone about their job like this:
In your job do you have to …? No, but I have to … / Yes, and I also have to …

7 You are going to read an article about stress. All the words and phrases on the left are from the article. Match them to the definitions on the right.

a linked to	1 doing too much work
b root cause of	2 is good for the company
c overwork	3 principal reason for
d staff turnover	4 connected to
e makes business sense	5 money for getting better results
f performance-related pay	6 people joining and leaving a company
g morale	7 positive or negative attitude

a ☐ b ☐ c ☐ d ☐ e ☐ f ☐ g ☐

8 In your opinion, are the sentences below true or false?

a	Stress is always a bad thing.	true ☐	false ☐
b	Work-related stress can cause health problems.	true ☐	false ☐
c	Bad management is the main cause of stress.	true ☐	false ☐
d	Reducing stress costs companies money.	true ☐	false ☐
e	It's easy for companies to reduce stress.	true ☐	false ☐

9 Read the article below. Does the writer agree with your opinions in 8?

Stressed to the limit

Deborah Houlding of BMG online magazine explores the problem of work-related stress and examines ways in which it can be avoided.

Stress is not an illness or a negative condition. A certain amount of pressure brings out the best in our work. In the initial stages of stress there is a sensation of excitement and increased mental concentration.

However, too much stress is negative. It is bad for the individual. It is also bad for the employing organisation. In the UK, for example, stress-related illness is the cause of half of lost working days.

The negative impact of stress is linked to heart disease, alcoholism, nervous breakdowns, job dissatisfaction, certain forms of cancer, migraines, asthma, hay fever, insomnia, depression, eczema and many other medical and social problems.

Many surveys confirm the root cause of work-related stress to be bad management and overwork. Too much pressure, long hours and poor communication are the main factors. Reports and studies have identified the principal cause of stress as 'new management techniques' designed to 'improve performance'. Policies such as 'performance-related pay' increase stress and demotivate a work force.

Many legal and medical experts are advising companies to consider the costs and legal implications of stress-related illness. They emphasise the benefits of reducing stress as:

- better health
- reduced sickness absence
- increased performance and output
- better relationships with clients and colleagues
- lower staff turnover

Taking the decision to reduce stress makes sound business sense. It's better for profits and better for staff morale.

Managers should learn to motivate but not exhaust employees. There is a balance between obtaining maximum efficiency, and a worker's need to rest and recuperate their creative energies.

10 Complete the chart with the correct form of the word.

noun	verb	adjective
stress	stress	.... /stressed
motivation	....	motivating/ ....
creativity	create	....
....	excite	.... /excited

11 Complete the sentences using the words from 10.

a Working with the public can be very ....
b When the new boss arrived, staff morale was very low and nobody was very ....
c I'm a graphic designer so my job requires a lot of ....
d I don't find the new project very ....

12 Make similar sentences about your own company.

should/shouldn't

13 Look at these sentences.

Managers ***should*** *recognise their mistakes.* (It's a good idea.)
Employees ***shouldn't*** *work under unnecessary pressure.* (It's not a good idea.)

Make sentences that are true for you using *should/shouldn't* and the prompts below.

work well / have a certain amount of pressure
To work well, you should have a certain amount of pressure.

a companies / try / reduce the level of stress
b workers / work very long hours
c managers / communicate / ideas
d companies / invest money / improve conditions
e managers / learn / motivate workers
f workers / have time / rest

14 Make sentences about your company like this:

In my company ... should / shouldn't ... but often / in fact they/he/she/we ...

Include the ideas below and add your own.

- distribution of work
- communications
- performance-related pay
- sufficient training
- new technology

THE CONSULTANT'S REPORT

You are going to write a report on a company with problems. Follow steps 1–4 below.

Work with a partner. Create your own company.

▶▶ Step 1

a What line of business is the company in?
b What's the name of the company?
c Where is it located?
d Is it an old-fashioned or a modern company?
e How long has it existed?

▶▶ Step 2

You are going to perform a roleplay with a new partner. First, with your original partner, decide who is the employee and who is the consultant. Then find a new partner who is playing a different role to you.

Employee: You work for the company you invented. You are completely negative about every aspect of your job and company. Criticise everything and everybody.

Consultant: You are a management consultant hired to interview the staff of the employee's company to assess the levels of stress and morale. Interview the employee and note down the answers. Ask questions about

- working hours
- company organisation
- internal communication
- pay
- training provided
- holidays
- (your own ideas)

▶▶ Step 3

Work with your original partner from Step 1. Write a report of the management consultant's interview.
Use the framework below or adapt it to suit the interview.

- According to … the main cause/s of stress in his/her work is/are …
- Communications in the company are …
- The system of payment is …
- With regard to training, the situation is …
- Other causes of problems are …
- To reduce the level of stress the company should …
- In conclusion, …

▶▶ Step 4

Work with your partner from Step 2 again. Check that the report of your interview is accurate.

MQSC
CONSULTING

Interview report

Company: ....

Name of Interviewee: ....

Interviewer: ....

Date: ....

10 STRESSED TO THE LIMIT

LANGUAGE LINKS

Phrase Bank: Talking about your health

What symptoms do you notice?
I get a lot of headaches.
I sleep badly.
I get a bit on edge at times.
I have a horrible rash on my neck.
I suffer from stress.
Stress is linked to heart disease.

Vocabulary

Stress at work

1 Complete the sentences with the correct form of the word in brackets.

a An air traffic controller has a very .... job. (stress)
b A .... has to answer the phone all day. (telephone)
c His work involves a lot of different .... (responsible)
d Our boss is always shouting at us. I don't find it very .... (motivate)
e Too much stress is bad for the workers, and it's also bad for the .... (employ)
f Stress-related .... is the cause of half of lost working days. (ill)
g It's a problem of .... – we never know what's happening in the company. (communicate)
h Nobody knows how to use the new machine – we need urgent .... (train)
i Employees shouldn't work under .... pressure. (necessary)
j You should .... your mistakes and correct them. (recognition)
k One of the benefits of reducing stress is better .... with clients and colleagues. (relate)
l Workers need to rest and recuperate their .... energies. (create)
m The experts say that bad .... is the main cause of stress. (manage)
n Policies such as ....-related pay demotivate a work force. (perform)

2 Complete the second sentence so that it means the same as the first.

a Does your work cause you stress?
Do you find *your work stressful?*
b My boss makes life difficult.
My boss doesn't make life ....
c My husband isn't very helpful.
My husband doesn't ....
d At times I get nervous.
At times I get a bit on ....
e 75% of visits to the doctor are because of stress.
75% of visits to the doctor are the .... of stress.
f People don't think that teaching is a difficult job.
Everyone thinks that teaching is an ....
g I hope things improve for you.
I hope things get .... for you.
h Worrying about things doesn't help you.
There's .... in worrying about things.
i I don't work for anyone. I'm self-employed.
I work for ....

Grammar

have to and *should*

have to		
I You We They	**have to** **don't have to**	work at night.
He She	**has to** **doesn't have to**	work at night.
Do **Does**	I/you/we/they he/she	**have to** work at night?

should		
I You He/She We They	**should** **shouldn't**	do that job for free.

You use *has to/have to* to show that it is necessary to do something.

- *Everyone **has to pay** taxes.*
- *We all **have to use** the same computer programs.*

When you want to show that it isn't necessary to do something, you can use *doesn't have to/don't have to*.

- *He **doesn't have to travel** much in his job.*
- *We **don't have to dress** formally for work.*

You use *should* or *shouldn't* to show that it is a good or bad idea to do something.

- *You **should use** the Internet for getting new ideas.*
- *You **shouldn't work** so hard if you want to live to an old age.*

Practice 1

Complete the sentences in an appropriate way. Use *has to, have to, doesn't have to* or *don't have to* and the verbs in the box.

come	do	finish	get	get up	go
make	show	sign	wear	work	

a All visitors to the factory .... a register.

b Our company has a 'casual Friday' policy, which means you .... formal clothes in the office on Fridays.

c 'Why are you working so late?' 'Because I .... this report for tomorrow.'

d To get to work on time, he .... at 5.30 a.m.

e Every Monday morning, we .... to a departmental meeting.

f I like holidays because you .... anything.

g If you want to see Mr Smith, you .... an appointment. He's a very busy man.

h You .... if you don't want to. We can do it without you.

i You .... a visa if you travel to certain countries.

j When you cross an international border, you usually .... your passport.

k He's so rich he ...., but he still does. He's a workaholic.

Practice 2

Reorganise the words to make questions.

a finish this do have I today to

....

b dress do have work for to you formally

....

c year abroad how to go many you times a do have

....

d complete when have order we the to do

....

e do English go this have year classes we to to

....

f your have drive do in you job to much

....

Practice 3

Give appropriate advice using *should* or *shouldn't* and the verbs in the box.

go (x 2)	have	leave	set up	spend	work

a I can't get a job because I don't speak any foreign languages.
You should go to English classes.

b I don't know how to use this new accountancy program.
.... on a course.

c I keep getting these headaches.
.... so much time staring at figures.

d My plane is at 2.30.
.... now or you'll miss it.

e I have this constant pain in my chest.
.... a check-up.

f My family is complaining they never see me.
.... so late.

g I don't like working for someone else.
.... your own business.

Practice 4

Complete the sentences using a form of *have to* or *should* (affirmative or negative). Sometimes there are two possible answers.

a The doctor says I .... take things easy.

b You .... spend so much time in front of a computer – it's bad for your eyes.

c Managers .... be good communicators.

d You .... just give people orders, you .... motivate them to do a good job.

e I .... do this job even if it is stressful – I need the money.

f I'm going home now because I .... get up early tomorrow to catch my plane.

g If you need travel information, you .... look it up on the Internet.

h You .... speak to the boss like that.

i If you want to know more about the company, you .... visit them.

j You .... come with me. I can do the presentation on my own.

A study by the Consumer Federation of America confirms that 25% of us think that the lottery is the best bet for becoming a millionaire.

HTTP://WWW.TEACH-NOLOGY.COM/FINANCE/NO_MILLIONS/

Present Perfect for unfinished past

1 Read the information about Nokia. Complete it using the words in the box.

acquires | announce | appears | becomes | begins | founds | launches | merge | puts | sets

Nokia - Company History

Nokia is a leading international communications company and a pioneer in digital technology and wireless data communications which has continuously brought innovations to the highly competitive and growing telecommunications markets.

1865: The Nokia story (a) ......begins...... in south-western Finland with the establishment of a paper mill at the Tammerkoski Rapids.
1912: Eduard Polón (b) .... Finnish Cable Works, the foundation of Nokia's cable and electronics business.
1898: Arvid Wickström (c) .... up the Finnish Rubber Works.
1967: Nokia Ab, Finnish Rubber Works and Finnish Cable Works (d) .... to create Nokia Corporation.
1982: Nokia (e) .... Mobira, which later becomes the Nokia Mobile Phones division.
1986: The company (f) .... the first Nokia mobile telephone on the international market.
1993: The first Nokia digital cellular phone (g) .... on the market.
1998: Nokia (h) .... the world leader in mobile phones.
1999: The Internet goes mobile when Nokia (i) .... the world's first WAP handset, the Nokia 7110.
2006: Olli-Pekka Kallasvuo becomes Nokia's President and CEO. Nokia and Siemens (j) .... plans for Nokia Siemens Networks.

2 Complete the sentences about Nokia using the verbs in the boxes.

has produced | started to produce | still produces

a Nokia .... mobile phones in 1986.
b It .... mobile phones today.
c It .... mobile phones since 1986.

became | has been | still is

d Nokia .... the world leader in mobile phones in 1998.
e It .... the world leader in mobile phones today.
f It .... the world leader in mobile phones for over ten years.

3 Match the sentences in 2 to the tenses below.

Past Simple ☐ ☐
Present Simple ☐ ☐
Present Perfect ☐ ☐

4 Make similar sentences about Nokia with these prompts using the Present Perfect, *since* and *for*.

a A company with the Nokia name / exist
b The company / be / involved in the cable and electronics business
c The company / have / mobile phone division
d Nokia / sell / digital cell phones
e Nokia / produce / mobile phones with access to the Internet
f Olli-Pekka Kallasvuo / be / president
g Nokia and Siemens / work / on a joint venture

since & for

5 Put the following time expressions in the correct column.

1945 20 years 5 o'clock a couple of days a few years a long time five minutes
he arrived I was born last year months this morning yesterday

SINCE	FOR

6 Write sentences which are true for you. Use the Present Perfect, *since* and *for*.

I've been in my present job for two years. I've had a PDA since Christmas.

TELL ME MORE

How long

1 Make questions with *you* using the prompts. Use the Present Simple, Past Simple and Present Perfect, as appropriate.

a	What kind of car / have? How long / have / it? Why / choose it?
b	have / a mobile phone? How long / have / it? use it / a lot?
c	Where / live? How long / live / there?
d	Who / work? How long / work / there? What / job?
e	How long / have / present job? Like / it?
f	know
g	be interested in

2 Work with a partner. Ask and answer the questions in 1. Try to get more information about each subject, if you can.

3 Change partners. Tell each other about your previous partner. For example:

Lucien lives just outside Toulouse. He has lived there for three years. He works as a research scientist at the university. He's worked there since last June.

YOUTUBE

1 1.41 The words and phrases below are from a radio programme about a business personality. Listen to the extract and number the words in the order you hear them.

co-founders ☐	employees ☐	entrepreneur ☐	management roles ☐	West Germany ☐
millionaire ☐	smaller stake ☐	university professor ☐	video-sharing ☐	

2 Read the script of the radio programme on page 148 and correct ten mistakes in the article below. Then listen again and check your answers.

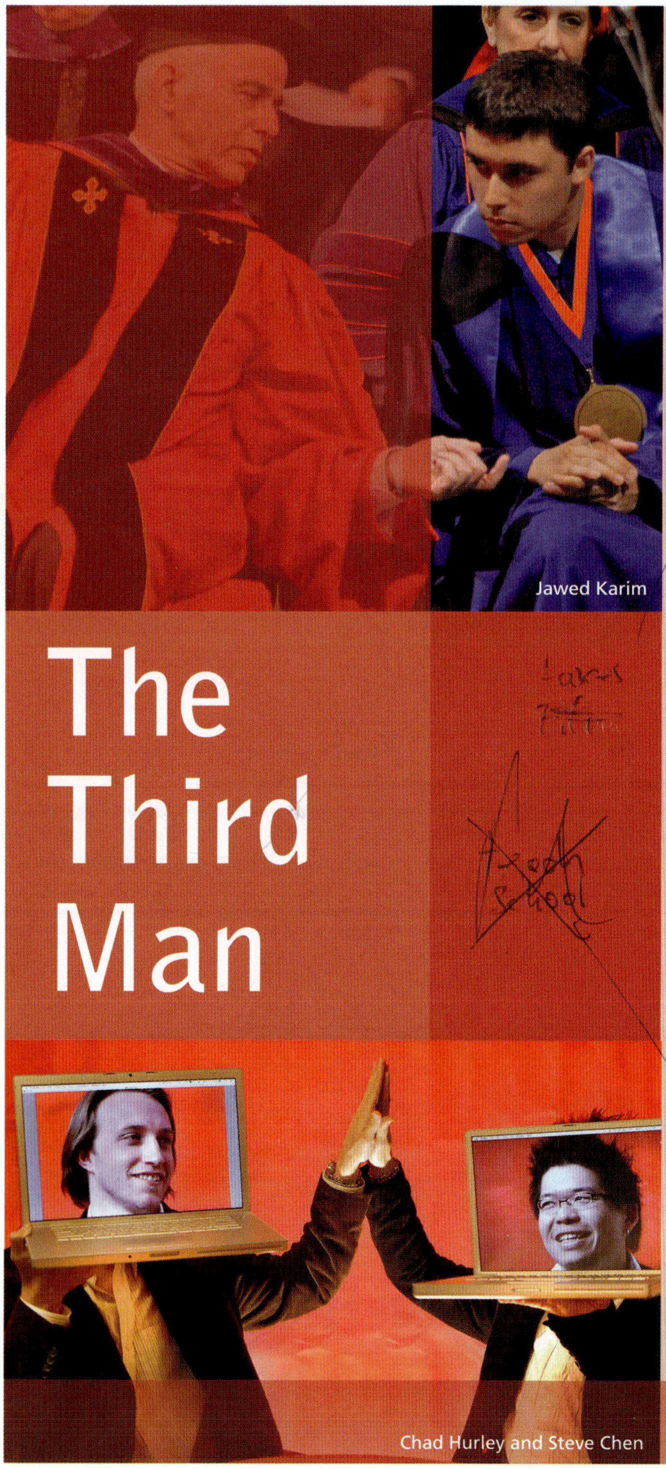

Jawed Karim

Chad Hurley and Steve Chen

The Third Man

JAWED KARIM is a college student with a difference. For a start, he is not worried about the $100,000 cost of his Ferrari because he is already a millionaire. He first hit the Internet jackpot in 2002 when eBay bought the online payment company he was working for. Then, in November 2006, he got lucky again when Microsoft agreed to buy YouTube for $1.65 billion.

When the deal was signed, everybody was talking about two of YouTube's co-founders – Chad Hurley and Steve Chen. After all, they were the public face of YouTube. Most people didn't know that there was also a third co-founder of YouTube, Jawed Karim. In fact, he was the person who actually uploaded the first video.

Karim grew up in West Germany, but has lived in Canada since his family emigrated there when Karim started high school. His Bangladeshi father is a chemist at 3M, and his German mother is a professor at the University of Minnesota. Karim obtained his degree in economics and engineering in 2004 at the University of Illinois.

Hurley, Chen and Karim have known each other since they met as employees at PayPal, the payment service. When eBay bought PayPal for $1.5 billion in 2002, they all received substantial payments. Now rich, the three men often met late at night for brainstorming sessions at Max's Opera Café near Stanford, and discussed possible film plots. Karim says he originally pitched the concept of a video-sharing website to his friends because at the time it was difficult to watch them on TV.

The three agreed to divide up the work based on their different skills. Hurley designed the site's interface and logo, while Chen and Karim shared responsibility for technical aspects. At a later stage, when it was necessary to take on management roles, Hurley became CEO and Chen the Chief Technology Officer. However, Karim really wanted to relax, so he chose not to be part of the management team. As a result, he agreed to take a smaller stake than the other two founders, and not to take a salary or even a formal title because, in his own words, he was 'focused on school'. Although since then he has continued in an informal advisory role, he denies it was the other two who actually turned the basic idea into reality.

Jawed Karim is not the first entrepreneur to lose his place in history. Popular wisdom, for example, says that Bill Gates started Microsoft and Sam Walton founded Wal-Mart on their own, but they too had co-founders. In any case, it is not likely that Karim has too many regrets. While his former colleagues continue to run YouTube, his dream is to teach and run a school. Whatever he does, money is not likely to be a problem.

3 Underline three examples of the Present Perfect in the script which tells us when a present situation started.

4 How much of the story can you remember without looking? Use the words in 1 to summarise the story with a partner.

5 Find words and phrases in the text which mean the same as the following.

a win a lot of money ……………………………………

b had good luck ……………………………………

c agreement ……………………………………

d got his university qualification ……………………………………

e meeting to swap ideas ……………………………………

f presented an idea ……………………………………

g graphic layout ……………………………………

h stockholding ……………………………………

i large sums of money ……………………………………

6 Use the words and phrases in 5 in the correct form to complete the following sentences.

a I know people who ……………………… and are now very rich.

b The company is a co-operative, so all the employees have a ……………………… in it.

c In my country, it takes most people three years to ……………………… .

d Many people in the financial world get ……………………… as bonuses for their work.

e We had a ……………………… to find a solution to the delays in production.

f If you ………………………, it is always possible you will win the lottery.

g Our company website has a very nice ……………………… which is simple for customers to use.

h I have to ……………………… to some important clients this afternoon, so I'm a bit nervous.

i If you manage to negotiate a good ………………………, we'll go out to celebrate this evening.

7 Write sentences which are true for you using the words and phrases in 5.

headhunter /ˈhedˌhʌntə/ *noun* a person or company who searches for good staff and tries to persuade them to leave their jobs and go to work for another company

Definition from Macmillan Essential Dictionary

HEADHUNTERS

1 1.42 Peter Davis is in the office when he receives an unexpected call from John Lindsay. Listen to the conversation and answer the questions.

a Why does John Lindsay call Peter Davis?

b When did Peter Davis start work for Blueprint International?

c What did he do before?

d How long has he been in charge of the international division?

e When did he get married?

f Has he got any children?

g Is he interested in what the caller has to say?

Discussion

2 Discuss the following questions with other people in the class.

a What type of management consultants does John Lindsay work for?
b Do you think what he does is ethical?
c How would you react in this situation?

Writing

3 Read the report for *People Search* below. Write a similar report about your partner or teacher. First ask questions about his/her career history to be able to write the report.

How long have you ...? When / Where did you ... before? When did you start / leave / finish ...?

PEOPLESEARCH ▶▶▶▶▶

Report

Peter Davis has worked for Blueprint International since 2003 where he has been head of their International Division for one year. Before Blueprint International he was at Navigate for three years. This was his first job after university where he studied engineering. He graduated from Nottingham University in 1999. He has been married for two years and has one child.

LANGUAGE LINKS

Phrase Bank: Money and the company background
He's now a millionaire.
He hit the jackpot.
They bought the company.
She became the CEO of the company.
He joined the management team.
He had a small stake in the company.
She was the co-founder of the company.
We don't get a bonus at the end of the year.

Vocabulary

Company news

Match the parts of the sentences.

a Dan Colman graduated from York University in 1980 with …
b He and some student friends founded …
c In 1998 they moved …
d At the beginning it was a small firm which produced components …
e The company quickly expanded and set …
f Recently, it has launched …
g The engineers responsible …
h It has also entered the …
i Dan Colman has held …
j The company has recently celebrated …

1 … for other manufacturers.
2 … mobile phone market.
3 … the top position since it was founded.
4 … a degree in electronic engineering.
5 … a range of computer accessories, which is doing very well.
6 … its thirtieth anniversary.
7 … up new divisions.
8 … its headquarters to Milton Keynes.
9 … for this success have become directors of the company.
10 … the company ALTS in 1982.

a	b	c	d	e	f	g	h	i	j

Grammar

Present Perfect – the unfinished past

You use the Present Perfect to say when present situations began. For example:
Past Simple: *I started working here 25 years ago.*
Present Simple: *I work here now.*
Present Perfect: *I've **worked** here for 25 years.*
NOT ~~*I am working here for 25 years.*~~ *
Past Simple: *I met John for the first time in 1985.*
Present Simple: *I still know him.*
Present Perfect: *I've **known** John since 1985.*
NOT ~~*I know John since 1985.*~~ *

* In many languages, you use a present tense to express this idea so these are very common mistakes. In English you can only use the Present Perfect.

To say when the action began you use *since* or *for*. You use *since* with a point in time and *for* with a period of time.

since	for
8 o'clock	2 years
2001	a month
August	a few minutes
last week	half an hour
I was born	ages
he arrived	hundreds of years

*Things have been better **since** we changed offices.*
*He has lived here **for** ten years.*
NOT ~~*… since ten years ago.*~~

You can also use *for* with the Past Simple. Compare these sentences:
Present Perfect: *I've **lived** in Manchester **for** three years / **since** 1998.* (I still live in Manchester.)
Past Simple: *I **lived** in Manchester **for** three years / **from** 1995 **to** 1998.* (Now I live somewhere else.)

Practice 1

Complete the sentences with *since* or *for*.

a Mr Bianchi has been out of the office .... last Thursday.
b We haven't had a holiday .... the summer.
c They have been friends .... they were at university together.
d He's had his own business .... a few years now.
e I haven't seen you .... a while. How are things going?
f I've known Pete .... we met at a trade fair nearly ten years ago.
g They've had that old car .... years.
h Mr Gonzalez has been here .... 9.30. He's waiting for you in reception.
i .... his wife had a baby, he's spent more time at home.
j He's waited for this promotion .... months.

Practice 2

Write questions with *How long …?* and the Present Perfect.

a you / work / here
How long have you worked here?

b he / know / about this problem

c she / be / a director of the company

d you / want / change jobs

e they / have / their website

f he / be / interested / in working for us

g he / have / a company car

h she / be / responsible for that account

Practice 3

Rewrite the following sentences using the Present Perfect.

a He works here – he started work in January.
He's worked here since January.

b He lives in Paris – he was born there.

c He's a computer programmer – he became a programmer when he left university.

d They make furniture – they started making furniture over a hundred years ago.

e She owns a business – she set it up five years ago.

f They lead the market – they became market leaders in 1998.

Practice 4

Rewrite the following sentences using the Present Perfect.

a I met him at university.
I've known him since university.

b Mr Jones arrived here hours ago.

c When did you buy your car?

d I got this job in January.

e They told me about the problem yesterday.

f They got divorced two years ago.

Practice 5

Read the biographical details of James Rodgers. Then use the prompts to write sentences using either the Present Perfect or the Past Simple and *for*, *since*, or *from … to*.

James Rodgers

1984 started smoking
1986 went to university to study engineering
1989 graduated with a degree in engineering
1990 got a job with Rolls Royce as an aeronautical engineer
1991 became interested in boats
1992 got married
1993 bought his first yacht
1995 got a job with P & W in Canada and moved to Montreal
2001 moved back to the UK and went to work at the P & W factory in Manchester
2003 gave up smoking
2006 moved to a new job in the P & W offices in Portsmouth

a be / an aeronautical engineer
He's been an aeronautical engineer since 1990.

b smoke

c study engineering / university

d be / interested / boats

e be / married

f work / Rolls Royce

g have / yacht

h live / Canada

i live / the UK

j have / job / Portsmouth

k work / for P & W

l not smoke

12 CONVERSATION GAMBITS

gambit /ˈgæmbɪt/ *noun* something that you say or do in an attempt to gain an advantage

Definition from Macmillan Essential Dictionary

The things most people want to know about are usually none of their business.

GEORGE BERNARD SHAW

1 Read the article below and think about the following questions. Then discuss them with your teacher or a partner.

a Do you have any strategies like the ones in the article for starting conversations with people you don't know?

b Do you think it's possible to learn the skills the article describes?

c Which of the strategies do you think are valid?

How to start a conversation

The ability to establish contacts and network is critical in business. Good communication skills project an image of confidence and intelligence. Although these are natural to some extent, they can be acquired by practice and preparation. Sometimes it is useful to develop a strategy for when you want to start a conversation with someone you don't know.

1 Start with 'hello' and then simply tell the other person your name and ask them theirs. Then offer your hand to shake.

2 Look around and see if there is anything unusual to point out. (Talking about the weather is probably not a good idea unless there is something very unusual about it - a storm, snow, tornado, etc.) 'Have you seen that picture over there?' 'This is an interesting building – I wonder how old it is?'

3 If you can, offer a compliment about something, but only if it is sincere and not too personal. For example, 'That's a great tie, where did you get it?' Or 'I saw you using a Palm Treo Pro earlier – looks very nice. Are you happy with it?'

4 Ask questions which will make the other person feel that they are interesting. People like talking about themselves but don't make the questions too personal. Ask for their opinions about things and their possible experience of current issues and situations. 'What did you think of the presentation?' 'Have you been affected by this postal strike?' It's not a bad idea to mentally prepare a list of possible topics before you begin the conversation. Avoid politics and religion because they are sensitive subjects for some people.

5 Instead of worrying about what you are going to say next, listen carefully to what the other person is saying and take up any conversation opportunities they offer you. Agree, disagree, ask follow-up questions and offer opinions to show that you are interested.

6 Look the other person in the eye, but don't stare or get too close. Occasionally smile, but avoid using a fixed grin like a lunatic.

All the strategies above are really just tricks to get going. Once you have broken the ice, hopefully the ongoing conversation will be relaxed and enjoyable. If things don't go well and the rapport really isn't there, it's better to give up and back off gracefully.

Introducing yourself

2 2.01–2.04 You are at a conference and you don't know anybody. What can you say to start a conversation with someone? Listen and complete the four conversations below.

1 **A** Excuse me, ... the ITM conference?
B Yes, that's right.
A Me too. ....
B I think it's over there.
A Oh, yes. Right, I'm Paulo, ...
B Hello, Paulo, I'm Kate. ....

2 **A** Phew! ....
B Yes, they always seem to have the heating on full.
A So, it's not ....
B No, it's my fourth time here.
A Oh, right, so .... I'm Boris.
B David. ....

3 **A** Is it ...., or is there some problem with coverage here?
B Oh, ... No, mine seems .... okay.
A Typical, flat batteries and nowhere to charge up.
B .... ?
A Oh, ..., but I was expecting a call on this number.
B I see.
A .... Nadine, by the way. From Xanadu Electronics.
B Pleased to meet you. I'm Miko.

4 **A** Excuse me, ... ?
B No, I'm sorry, I don't.
A ....
B Oh, here. ....
A Thanks. By the way, I'm Bill Smart from Silicon Technologies.
B Right, ... ? I'm Kazuo Yamada from Lexico.

Starting a conversation

3 Allan Vilkas is having a quiet drink in a hotel in Dublin after dinner. The other customer in the bar has a newspaper, but he's not reading it. What do you think Allan says to begin a conversation?

4 2.05 Complete the conversation using the phrases in the box. Then listen and check your answers.

finished with it	go ahead	here on	if I had a quick look at	the way	to check out	your time

Allan Excuse me, would you mind a) .... your newspaper?
Stranger Er, no, b) .... I've c) ....
Allan There's just something I want d) ....
Stranger No problem. Take e) ....
Allan Thanks. By f) ...., my name's Allan. I'm g) .... a business trip.
Stranger Oh, right.

5 2.06 Now Allan has the newspaper. Giving it back is another excuse to begin a conversation. Which of the following do you think he does?

a mention the political situation
b comment on the weather forecast
c say something about sport
d invite the other person for a drink

Listen to find out.

6 In first meetings, people often ask each other some of the following questions. Reorganise the words to make questions. Then match them to the answers 1–10. There are two possible answers for each question.

a you where are from *Where are you from?*	1 I'm from Turkey. 2 Until Friday.
b been have long you how here	3 Another four or five days. 4 It seems very nice.
c long staying how are you	5 I've been here for a couple of days now. 6 Yes. I'm visiting some customers.
d think what you Dublin do of	7 I come from South Africa. 8 It's a bit cold for me.
e business here you on are	9 Since Saturday. 10 Yes. I'm here to buy some machinery.

a ☐☐ b ☐☐ c ☐☐ d ☐☐ e ☐☐

7 2.07 Listen to the conversation. Which of the questions and answers in 6 do the speakers use? Circle them.

Conversation topics

8 The two men in the conversation in 7 talk about football and golf. Sport is a 'safe' topic. What other topics are safe? Which should you avoid? Circle the safe topics.

art business cars local attractions money and personal finance music personal life politics and the state of the world religion the opposite sex the stock exchange the weather

Saying goodbye

9 2.08 Complete the conversation. Then listen and compare your answers.

Sean Oh, well, Allan, it's getting late. I have to a) .... Thanks for the b) .... , and good luck with your c) ....

Allan Right, it was nice d) ....

Sean It was nice to e) .... Cheerio, then.

Allan Bye.

10 When Sean wants to end the conversation, he says *It's getting late. I have to be off.* Match the parts of the sentences below to make other ways to end a conversation.

a Excuse me, but I've just …	1 … a call on my mobile. I'll catch you later.
b I think they're going …	2 … someone is trying to catch my attention.
c Excuse me, but I think …	3 … seen someone I have to talk to.
d Hang on a minute, but I think I have …	4 … to start. I'll see you later.
e Sorry to cut you off, but I arranged …	5 … to meet someone at the bar five minutes ago.

Fluency

11 Work with a partner. Look at the headlines below. Imagine you borrowed your partner's newspaper and you are now giving it back. Start a conversation about one of the headlines. Maintain the conversation as long as possible. Begin: *Thank you for the newspaper. Have you seen this article about …?*

Prime Minister says economic situation 'hopeless'

Dog wins lottery

SCIENTISTS DISCOVER LINK BETWEEN GOLF AND IQ

First genetically modified human being

Mobiles banned on public transport

Princess Diana alive and living in New Jersey

UK TO DRIVE ON RIGHT

US PRESIDENT CONSULTS PRIVATE ASTROLOGER

CASE STUDY

STAFF APPRAISAL

appraisal /ə'preiz(ə)l/ *noun* an interview between a manager and an employee, which allows the manager to judge how well the employee is doing their job

Definition from Macmillan English Dictionary

1 Discuss these questions in groups. Do you have any experience of a staff appraisal system? If you do, was the experience positive or negative? What are the advantages of such a system from a) the employee's point of view and b) the company's perspective? What are the disadvantages?

2 2.09 Listen to the Director of a company describing their staff appraisal scheme. Has it been a success? Number the words below in the order you hear them. You will hear some of the words more than once.

anonymous ☐ chat ☐ expectations ☐ feedback ☐ form ☐ formal ☐ goals ☐
issues ☐ measure ☐ motivation ☐ objectives ☐ report ☐ scale ☐ timescales ☐

3 Is the appraisal scheme successful? Work with a partner. Use the words in 2 to summarise what Alison Lea-Wilson says.

4 Staff appraisal is very much 'in fashion' but recently some experts have begun to question how useful it is. Read these quotes from different blogs and match the extracts to the problems.

a It is inaccurate and subjective Extract B
b It is unpopular with both managers and employees. ....
c It is uneconomic and not good for company performance. ....
d It creates a bad atmosphere between members of staff. ....
e Does not work because managers don't have enough time to do it well. ....

logout

Blogs

A It's coming to that time of year again. And everyone hates it. Employees detest performance appraisals because they are totally useless and achieve nothing. Managers hate giving them because they're usually badly prepared and they have too many other things to do. Employees worry about them because they are often measured on things over which they have no control.

internalblog

B Research conducted by Personnel Decisions International (PDI), a global consultancy firm, finds the majority of employees who report to more than one boss get inconsistent marks. In a study of 5,970 employees reporting to two bosses, employees who were rated 'outstanding - one of the best' by the first boss, were rated lower by the other boss 62% of the time and only 'somewhat above average' or less 29% of the time.

BLOGS AND NEWS

C If you're looking for ways to improve performance, or cut costs, you should think about getting rid of your company's performance appraisal system. It uses a tremendous amount of time and energy, depresses and de-motivates people, as well as destroying any trust and teamwork. The whole system simply reinforces the values and prejudices of those in power at great cost to your company.

5 You work for a medium-sized engineering company which manufactures specialist machine parts. Your company introduced a staff appraisal scheme five years ago. Recently it seems that everyone (in private at least) is complaining about the system. Work in groups of four. You are going to take part in a meeting to decide what to do. Each take a role: A, B, C or D.

A

The Financial Director

You think staff appraisal is a waste of time unless it is linked to pay. You want to decide annual salary increases based on performance. You don't agree that staff in the same post should get the same pay-rise when some people are better than others. You want managers to come up with an objective system which rewards hard work and results.

B

The Production Manager

One of the things that most irritates you about your job is having to do staff assessments. In your opinion they are time consuming, costly and provide no clear benefits. A good, efficient working atmosphere depends on a manager being a good leader and knowing how to motivate his or her team without all this Human Resources nonsense. If you treat people like children, they will behave like children.

C

The Human Resources Manager

This is really your area and a major part of your job. You can't understand the attitude of other managers in your company who don't see how important staff appraisal is for making the company more efficient. You think it is their fault that the system does not work at the moment. If they change their attitudes you think it is possible to change the atmosphere in your company and that people will feel positive about evaluation.

D

The Union Delegate

Your position is clear. Staff appraisal is just another technique for management to exploit employees more. Usually it is an excuse for not promoting members of staff. Nobody trusts the system and the way people are currently evaluated and rated is clearly unfair because it depends on the opinion of each individual manager. The only people who like the system are those who get positive results and promotion by 'sucking up' to their line-managers.

6 The article below describes an alternative to traditional staff appraisal called '360-degree feedback'. Do you think that this sounds like a good solution to the problems you discussed in 5?

360-Degree Feedback

'360-DEGREE FEEDBACK' is an alternative performance appraisal system, where feedback comes from different people, all of whom work with the employee. Feedback can be obtained from colleagues, subordinates, managers and even customers to have a clear understanding of the employee's contribution and needs. '360' refers to the 360 degrees in a circle. It happens on a regular basis and the individual performance objectives are things which can be objectively measured. The focus of this kind of feedback is on developing relevant plans and training opportunities for each staff member. Both the employee and the manager have an equal opportunity to make contributions. The organisation has an open and public commitment to help each person expand his or her knowledge and skills. This is the foundation upon which a continuously improving organisation can build.

TOPICS

13 AIR TRAVEL

It might be cheap, but it's going to cost the earth. The cut-price air ticket is fuelling a boom that will make controlling global warming impossible.

THE INDEPENDENT (LONDON) FRONT PAGE ON SUNDAY 28 MAY 2005.

Discussion

1 Discuss the following questions with other people in the class.

a How often do you fly?
b What things can go wrong when you travel by air?
c Have you had any bad flying experiences?

2 2.10–2.11 Listen to the conversations. Someone is checking in. What goes wrong in each case?

3 Complete the conversations using the words in the box. Listen again and check your answers, if necessary.

check in	excess baggage	long queue	look it up	main desk	suitcase
passport	queue up	reference number	straight to the front	ten pounds	

Conversation 1

A Good morning. Is this where I a) .... for flight RA 264?
B Yes. Can you give me your b) ...., please?
A I'm afraid I've lost the paper I had it on, but here's my c) ....
B I'm sorry, but if you haven't got the reference number, I can't check you in. You'll have to go to the d) .... over there. They'll give it to you.
A But can't you e) ....? You've got my name.
B I'm not allowed to.
A Do I have to f) .... again?
B No. Just come to the front.
A OK.
B Next, please.

Conversation 2

A Can I have your reference number and passport please?
B Here you are.
A You've just got one g) .... to check in.
B Yes, this one.
A I'm afraid it's over fifteen kilos. You'll have to pay h) ....
B It's only just over.
A Actually it's seventeen kilos.
B Are you sure? How much will it cost me?
A It will be i) ...., but you have to pay over there at the main desk.
B What, over there? There's a really j) .... Can't I pay here?
A No, I'm sorry. But come k) .... when you come back.
B OK. Thanks.

BATTLE OF THE ARMRESTS

1 Read the introduction to an article on avoiding a travel problem. What do you think the 'strategies' are?

It's happened to everyone – even the most experienced business traveller and frequent flier. A last-minute trip, no seat assignment on the aeroplane and the only seat left on a packed flight? You've guessed it – the middle seat. It can make your trip miserable. Here are some strategies to help you avoid the worst seat.

Source: www.about.com

Conditionals with *will*

2 Look at this First Conditional sentence.

Condition	**Consequences**
If + present	*will* + infinitive

If you check-in early, you'll be able to choose your seat.
or *You'll be able to choose your seat if you check in early.*

Match the conditions to the consequences. Make as many logical combinations as possible.

a	if you book months in advance	1	you'll get on and off the plane faster
b	if you sit at the front	2	you'll be too early for a seat assignment
c	if you check in late	3	you'll have to go to the toilet a lot
d	if you're polite to the check-in attendant	4	you'll be able to stretch your legs
e	if you pretend to be ill or pregnant	5	you'll sometimes be able to change your seat
f	if you trust your instincts	6	you'll get more personal space
g	if you dominate the armrests	7	you'll pay for it with an uncomfortable seat
h	if you use your laptop	8	you'll choose better seatmates
i	if you drink too much	9	you'll feel claustrophobic
j	if you get up during the flight	10	you'll feel guilty the entire flight

a ...(2) 5, 6... b .... c .... d .... e ....
f .... g .... h .... i .... j ....

3 2.12 Listen to someone giving advice about getting a good seat. Circle the combinations in 2 which correspond to what the speaker says. Do you agree with the advice?

Discussion

4 Work in groups. Make a list of five *dos* and five *don'ts* for business air travellers.

BUYING AN AIRLINE TICKET

1 Read the article and answer the questions.

a Why won't you have anyone to blame if you get a bad deal on your airline ticket?
b If more than nine seats are empty, why will EasyJet not be happy?
c If you ask RyanAir about their prices, what will they say?

CUT-PRICE TRAVEL

HOW is it possible that two passengers sitting shoulder to shoulder in the same plane can pay such different prices for their tickets? Buying an air ticket has become a test of skill and timing where the customer is responsible for getting the best deal possible. With the online reservation systems of cut-price airlines it is your fault if you get a bad deal because there is no travel agent to blame.

Nowadays all airlines have a 'pricing' department which is responsible for 'yield management'. In other words, their job is to adjust the price of tickets in order to get the maximum possible profit for each seat on the flight. Ticket prices vary according to supply and demand and depend on how full the flight is, and when you make your reservation. The result is a tremendous difference in prices. In one investigation, Le Monde newspaper made enquiries at different times about Air France tickets on the same flight from Paris to New York in economy class. They were quoted 17 different prices, ranging from €467 to €3228.

Airlines justify these variable pricing policies on the extremely narrow profit margins of the business. To illustrate this, EasyJet use a graphic which shows the seating plan of a plane with 155 seats. They need to sell 39 of these seats to cover airport costs. 37 seats go in fuel costs and 15 to pay the pilots and crew. That leaves just 9 seats for profit.

Another airline, RyanAir, blames special extra fees for pushing up the prices. For example, each passenger pays 50 cents for the wheelchair that the plane is obliged to carry and since the attack on the twin towers in 2002, €5.29 for insurance against the risk of terrorism. However, it is also true that if your luggage is just over the allowed weight, or you have an extra piece of luggage, they will charge you a fortune for 'excess baggage'. At the same time you can't claim a refund if a flight is delayed, but if you're five minutes late for check-in, they won't let you through and you'll miss your flight.

2 Complete the following sentences based on the information in the article.

a If you book your ticket at a different time to another passenger, the price of your tickets ....
b If there isn't much demand for seats on a flight, the price ....
c You will only have yourself to blame if you .... deal.
d If they only sell 91 seats, ... profit.
e EasyJet don't make a profit on a flight if .... seats left.
f If you have an extra bag, ...
g They won't let you get on your flight if ....

3 What is your experience of cut-price travel? Tell your teacher or the other students in the class.

4 The verbs in each of the four lists below often accompany the nouns on the right. One verb in each list is wrong. Delete the verbs which are wrong.

get buy offer see negotiate	**.. a good deal**	cover estimate reduce increase delete	**.. costs**	cost do pay make charge	**.. a fortune**	adjust increase reserve lower reduce	**.. the price**

5 Use the verb + noun combinations in 4 to complete the sentences below.

a It is difficult to .... without customers changing to suppliers who are cheaper.

b Nowadays if you need to fly somewhere you can always .... on the Internet.

c Companies use computers to .... , but in fact they often create more work and are expensive.

d It is not possible to .... without hard work and good luck.

e Low-cost airlines .... if you book just before you travel, so you should make your reservation well in advance.

f Some cut-price airlines .... on their web pages, but often there are a lot of hidden charges, so they are not really as cheap as they seem.

g Airlines say that extra costs which they can't control .... of an air ticket.

THE NEGOTIATION GAME

1 2.13 You are going to play a game in which you have to negotiate the price, quantity, delivery time, payment terms and guarantee period of a product to gain points. Before you play, listen to two people playing the game as an example.

Fluency

2 Work with a partner. First of all, decide what the product is.

Speaker A: You are the buyer. Look at the instructions and chart on page 136.
Speaker B: You are the seller. Look at the instructions and chart on page 141.

13 AIR TRAVEL

LANGUAGE LINKS

Phrase Bank: Air travel

Is this where I check in for flight BA 264?

Is it okay if I take this bag on as hand luggage?

Did you pack your bag yourself?

Could you show me where the available seats are?

The flight will be boarding at gate number 23 in 20 minutes.

Have a good flight.

Vocabulary

Negotiating

1 Complete the dialogue with the words in the box.

10% accept business deal deliver discount do more order payment price up

A Okay, we want to do (a) .... with you, but we need to talk about the (b) ....

B Well, the catalogue price is $30.25.

A I know, but we're talking about a big (c) .... here. If we order 100 units, for example, what (d) .... will you give me?

B If you order (e) .... than 100 units, I'll give you a discount of (f) ....

A 10%. And for 150 units?

B For 150 units, I'll go (g) .... to 12%.

A 12%. That sounds good. What about (h) .... ?

B Payment is within 60 days.

A Er, if you let us pay within 90 days, I'll (i) .... a lower discount … say 10% on 150 units.

B So, you're saying that if I offer a discount of 10% on the catalogue price for an order of 150 units, with payment within 90 days, we'll have a (j) .... ?

A Yes, we'll have a deal … if you can (k) .... in two weeks.

B All right, then. I think we can (l) .... that. It's a deal!

2 Complete the dialogue with the phrases below.

I'll ask you to take me | I'll just take a taxi then | if I can get a room | I'll ask him to take me What will you do | I'll take the new metro | If there's nothing on Tuesday | if I can finish this report

A Have you got your trip next week organised ?

B More or less. I haven't actually booked anything yet.

A You know it's a long weekend. There'll be a lot or people travelling on Tuesday. (a) .... if you can't get a flight?

B (b) .... , I'll go on Wednesday and re-schedule a couple of meetings.

A What about getting to the airport?

B If Derek is free, (c) ....

A And if he isn't?

B Well if you're available,(d) ....

A Sorry, I can't.

B (e) ....

A How are you getting into town?

B Unless I'm pushed for time, (f) .... It's very convenient because there's a stop near the hotel.

A Oh, will you stay at The Majestic again?

B I will (g) .... It might be difficult with the conference on.

A You'd better get on and make some reservations.

B Yes, (h) .... , I'll get on the Internet or give them a ring before I go to lunch.

Air travel

1 Imagine you are flying from Europe to the USA. Number the following events in a logical order.

- ☐ a Book your flight over the Internet or by phoning the airline.
- ☐ b Check in at least 45 minutes before your flight.
- ☐ c Go through the metal detector and wait for your flight to be announced.
- ☐ d Fasten your seat belt and take off.
- ☐ e Show your boarding pass at the boarding gate and get on the plane.
- ☐ f Check the details of your reservation and seat assignment.
- ☐ g Dominate the armrests!
- ☐ h Go through customs.
- ☐ i Take a taxi to your hotel.
- ☐ j Land at JFK airport and get off the plane.
- ☐ k Go through passport control and pick up luggage in baggage reclaim.

2 Match the parts of the sentences.

a You should ask for the seat you want when you book …

b It's important to be polite

c There was a traffic jam and I missed …

d The flight was overbooked, so they offered me …

e If you don't get a good deal on your ticket, …

f If your flight is delayed, you …

1 … your flight

2 … my flight.

3 … to the check-in attendant.

4 … you can only blame yourself.

5 … can't claim a refund.

6 … a refund or a later flight.

a	b	c	d	e	f

Grammar

Conditionals with *will*

If + Present, *will/won't* + infinitive

- *If I **have** time, I'**ll finish** the figures this afternoon.*
- *If they **don't offer** me more money, I **won't accept** the job.*

will/won't + infinitive + *if* + Present

- *He **won't wait** if you **arrive** late.*
- *I'**ll phone** you if my mobile **works** there.*

You can use conditionals with *will* to talk about future events which depend on other things happening.

Practice 1

Match the parts of the sentences.

a If you don't leave now, …
b You'll be late …
c If I get a promotion, …
d I'll buy a better car …
e If people are rude to the ground staff, …
f If we make a good offer, …
g I'll take longer to get to the airport …
h I'll put on weight …
i If you don't have any plans for tonight, …
j They'll get more work done …

1 … they won't be able to get on the plane.
2 … if I go to so many business lunches.
3 … you'll miss your flight.
4 … if you don't keep interrupting them.
5 … if you don't call a taxi now.
6 … if we coincide with the rush hour.
7 … I'll earn more money.
8 … if they increase my salary.
9 … will you have dinner with me?
10 … we'll get the contract.

a	b	c	d	e	f	g	h	i	j

Practice 2

Complete the sentences using one of the verbs below in the correct tense.

adopt be find have improve
lose need pay phone tell

a If I see John, I ………………… him what you said.
b If anyone ………………… to contact me, tell them I'll be back at four.
c We ………………… able to get the 10.14 train if we hurry.
d If you ………………… my keys, will you let me know?
e Your English ………………… if you spend some time in the USA.
f I ………………… you if there's any news.
g If we ………………… within 30 days, will you drop the price?
h If BA's policy on rude passengers is a success, other airlines ………………… it.
i If he checks in late, he ………………… his seat assignment.
j You ………………… to hurry if you want to catch your flight.

Practice 3

Write a sentence using the conditional with *will* based on each piece of advice.

a You should confirm your booking or you won't get a good seat.
If you confirm your booking, you'll get a good seat.

b You should pretend you're not interested in buying from them or they won't drop the price.
…………………………………………

c You should apologise to the boss or you will have problems.
…………………………………………

d You shouldn't drink too much on the flight or you'll have to keep going to the toilet.
…………………………………………

e You should leave for the airport now or you'll miss your flight.
…………………………………………

f You shouldn't be rude to airport ground staff or they won't let you on the plane.
…………………………………………

g You should study something practical or you won't get a job.
…………………………………………

h You shouldn't work too hard or you'll get ill.
…………………………………………

i You should take the client out to lunch or you won't get his business.
…………………………………………

14 HIRING AND FIRING

Hiring or firing an employee is a challenging, emotional experience and a pathway to possible lawsuits. The decision to employ or terminate someone will influence you, that individual, his or her family, your team, your customers, and your stakeholders.

THE INDUSTRIAL PHYSICIST

1 Look at the headline below. What do you think the article is about?

2 Read the article to see if you are correct. Then answer the questions.

a Do you think the sacking was justified?
b Would this be possible in your company or in your country?
c What advice would you give to Nicola?

Ibiza phone-in prize winner fired

Nicola Williams, a 31-year-old single mother from Newbridge in South Wales, couldn't believe her luck when she was told she was the winner of a Mediterranean holiday for herself and her six-year-old daughter.

The week's break on the sunshine island of Ibiza was the prize in a radio phone-in competition. She told reporter Hefina Rendle on BBC Wales television that she was 'totally over the moon, really excited'. However, only minutes later she was laid off. Nicola, an electronic parts worker, who phoned the radio station from work using her own mobile phone, was unaware that her boss was standing nearby. He asked her to hang up, took her into his office, and told her she was sacked. She was ordered to leave the factory immediately.

This was her first job since the birth of her daughter, and she was fired by the same manager who originally hired her.

But the story may have a happy ending. The commercial radio station which ran the competition is now trying to find her another job. A spokesman for the station said that people should be allowed to take part in competitions from work, as they are in general life. He said it was sad that the manager couldn't see the good side and just congratulate Nicola on her good luck.

Skytronics, Nicola's former employer, refused to be interviewed by the BBC, and later issued a statement supporting the action of their manager.

3 Find two more verbs in the article that are similar in meaning to 'sack'. Which verb is more formal?

The passive

4 Find sentences in the article that are similar in meaning to the following:

a They laid her off. ....
b They ordered her to leave the factory immediately. ....

5 Compare the two pairs of sentences in 4.

a Which are active and which are passive?
b Who is mentioned first in the active sentences?
c Who is mentioned first in the passive sentences?
d Who is the story about?
e What is the advantage of using the passive sentences?
f The agent in the active sentences is *they*. What happens to it in the passive sentences? Why?

6 Read the manager's report of the incident in 2. He uses the passive to sound more objective and formal in style. Complete the report using the verbs below in the passive.

ask give (x 2) inform (x 2) note warn

RE: NICOLA WILLIAMS

On two occasions in November Ms Nicola Williams, an employee in the assembly plant, (a) .... that using a mobile phone in work hours was against the company rules. Both these warnings (b) .... by another supervisor, and (c) .... in her file. Then, in December, on a further occasion, she (d) .... a written warning. Finally, on Friday, 12 January at 10.30 I (e) .... of a problem on the factory floor. When I arrived there, I found a lot of noise and shouting going on. Ms Williams was using her mobile phone to participate in a radio phone-in programme. Apparently she had won a prize. I asked her to put the phone down immediately, and to come in to my office. I decided to terminate her employment, and in the presence of Ms Jones, my deputy, Ms Williams was told that she was being sacked. She became hysterical and abusive, and (f) .... to leave the factory immediately. She (g) .... that her possessions would be forwarded to her by post.

7 In what way are the details about the incident different?

8 Improve these short texts by changing one verb to the passive in each text.

a They have laid off over 35,000 people in the last five years, unemployment is rising, and there are social problems in the region.
35,000 people have been laid off in the last five years, unemployment is rising, and there are social problems in the region.

b The business is a great success. They are hiring new staff and it is expanding fast.

c As there was a recession and the number of orders decreased, they closed one of the factories.

d To improve margins, it is making the new model in Hungary, where labour costs are lower.

e Ford has several plants in Europe. One of them is in Valencia and it produces the Escort there.

f They have announced plans for the new industrial estate. It will cover ten hectares and create space for over 15 business ventures.

Discussion

9 Work in groups. In what situations do you think sacking is justified? Think about the following:

dishonesty disrespect to superiors
inappropriate dress
industrial action (going on strike)
not meeting objectives or achieving results
punctuality revealing company secrets
violence

Add your own ideas, if you like.

APPLYING FOR A JOB

1 2.14–2.17 Listen to four people talking about their approach to applying for a job. Take notes and match the people on the left to the summaries below.

a I'm looking for a chance to develop and demonstrate my true potential. ☐
b My qualifications and experience speak for themselves. ☐
c I'm so brilliant at whatever I do, they would be lucky to have me working in their company. ☐
d There may be people with better qualifications and experience, but no one is more enthusiastic or hard working than me. ☐

2 Which speaker(s) do you agree with? What approach did you use to get your present job? Does the approach you use depend on the job?

3 Read the following extracts from letters of application. Match them to the summaries in 1.

☐ i I am very keen to work for your company because of its excellent reputation. I do not have the specific qualifications or experience referred to in your advertisement. However, I am applying because I feel I am able to make up for this through hard work and willingness to learn.

☐ ii If you believe in the pursuit of excellence, then I am interested in joining your company. I set high standards for myself and expect them from others, especially the organisations that I work for. I look forward to an opportunity to add to the list of already outstanding achievements, which are outlined in my CV.

☐ iii From my CV, you will see that five years at a chemicals multinational have given me a solid business background. I am responsible for my department's logistical planning, which has developed my organisational skills. However, I am now looking for opportunities for further development and responsibility, which my present employer cannot offer.

☐ iv As a commercially aware and linguistically trained university graduate, I have a broad range of employment experience at blue-chip companies in both the USA and Europe. I am dynamic and creative, with a strong team spirit and leadership qualities. I have a proven record of working with individuals at all levels through highly developed interpersonal and communication skills.

Reading between the lines

4 Read the extracts in 3 again. There are certain formal phrases people use in letters of application to talk about their qualities and achievements. Underline phrases which mean the following:

a I'd really like to work for you because you're such a great company.
b If you think doing things well is important, I'd like to work for you.
c I don't really have the profile of the ideal candidate.
d I've worked with many different, important companies.
e I've shown I can work with all kinds of people and get on with everyone.
f I look after the practical day-to-day aspects of department organisation.
g I want a new job because my company probably won't be able to promote me.
h I have five years of international business experience working for a chemicals company.

5 Use some of the phrases in 3 to write a paragraph introducing your own CV.

A JOB INTERVIEW

1 Read the job advert and CV below. Why do you think Sara applied for the job?

MULTINATIONAL FOOD PACKAGING EQUIPMENT MANUFACTURER

seeks International Sales Manager to call on Europe and Latin America.

Base $80K and commission, full benefits and expenses.
Prefers: fluency in one or more foreign languages.

Send resumé with cover letter indicating citizenship and salary requirements.

CURRICULUM VITAE

NAME	Sara Verkade
ADDRESS	58, Stoppard Drive, London SW16
TELEPHONE	Tel: 353 865 344872
E-MAIL	sara.verkade@gmz.net
DATE & PLACE OF BIRTH	23.7.78, Maassluis, The Netherlands
MARITAL STATUS	Single
NATIONALITY	Dutch
QUALIFICATIONS	September 1996 - July 1999 BComm, Marketing Management, Haagse Hogeschool, The Hague
EMPLOYMENT HISTORY	June 2000 - present Management Team Co-ordinator, Helena Rubinstein, L'Oreal Organising meetings, events and conferences. Analysing sales figures and producing relevant reports and charts. Customer relations and responding to complaints and queries.
	June 1999 - June 2000 SPC Professional, Sales Productivity Centre, IBM Sales team support. Research, pricing and proposal-writing on million-dollar bids.
LANGUAGES	Dutch, English, German, Spanish
IT SKILLS	Proficient user of Microsoft Office suite

2 2.18 Sara was interviewed for the job. Listen to the interview. Questions a–i below are typical in an interview for a job. Which of the questions does the interviewer ask? (He does not use the same words.)

a Why did you apply for this job?
b Why should we employ you?
c When are you free to start?
d Does your present employer know that you want to leave?
e Have you ever done anything like this before?
f How do feel about travelling?
g How good are your computer skills?
h What are your language skills like?
i Do you have any questions?

3 Do you think the interviewer was fair in the interview? Do you think Sara got the job?

Asking for clarification

4 Listen again and complete the phrases below.

a How much managerial experience do you have ? It's .... your CV.
b Yes. .... you're the leader of a team?
c Oh, I see. .... of personal assistant?
d But .... a manager?
e .... in your previous position, you were 'an SPC professional'. What .... ?
f .... you were directly involved in sales?
g So, ... involve?
h Can .... specific, please?

Fluency

5 Write a brief CV for yourself and give it to your partner. Then take it in turns to interview each other for the job Sara wanted or another job. Ask for clarification of the details of the CV.

WHAT ABOUT THE WORKERS?

1 What is happening in the photograph on this page? How do you think this situation relates to employment and staffing?

2 Work with a partner. You will each read an article relating to the employment situation in a country and do three exercises. When you have finished, turn back to this page.

Student A: Look at page 136. **Student B**: Look at page 137.

3 The noun / verb combinations in the box were in the articles in 2. The verbs were in the passive. Can you remember the sentences? Tell your partner.

A

conditions / agree   firms / contact   salaries / negotiate   staff / pay   survey / carry out

B

anyone / sack   country / bring   offers / put   reforms / defend   strike / call

Discussion

4 Discuss the following questions in relation to your country.

a What are the laws about unemployment benefits? Do you think they are fair?
b What rights do workers have? How do they affect employment?
c Why do you think there is a shortage of skilled workers? Do you think the use of temporary labour is a good solution to the problem?
d 'It is increasingly difficult to provide people with jobs for life.' Do you think this is true?

LANGUAGE LINKS

Phrase Bank: Asking for clarification

Now, can we just check out some details?

Does that mean ... ?

But do you/are you ... ?

It says on your CV/in your e-mail that ... What exactly does that mean?

What does ... involve?

Could you be a bit more specific about ... , please?

Vocabulary

Procedures

1 Match the parts of the sentences.

a She was employed ...
b The incident was reported ...
c John was consulted ...
d The staff have been informed ...
e She was sacked ...
f The conditions were agreed ...
g He didn't accept the offers which were put ...
h The worker was injured ...
i The flight was delayed ...
j The passive is used ...

1 ... on a temporary basis.
2 ... about the decision.
3 ... for writing reports.
4 ... for stealing office stationery.
5 ... to him by the employment office.
6 ... by the bad weather.
7 ... to the supervisor.
8 ... at a company wide level.
9 ... of the new working hours.
10 ... by an explosion in the chemical plant.

a	b	c	d	e	f	g	h	i	j

2 Combine one word from column A with one word from column B to complete each sentence below.

A	B
electronics	application
written	secrets
job	position
company	rights
workers'	needs
job	security
previous	workers
skilled	warning
temporary	staff
unemployment	benefits
staffing	industry

a For young people .... is not usually as important as a good salary.
b We gave the employee a .... for arriving late to work two days running.
c In the summer there is more work so we have to take on more people to meet our ....
d He was accused of revealing .... to a competitor.
e A hundred years ago .... didn't exist because there were no unions.
f You always have to include a CV in your ....
g Education is important because industry needs a supply of ....
h Was your .... a full-time post?
i In many countries there are no .... for people who have no work.
j At Christmas, shops take on .... because it's a busy time of year.
k The .... is an important sector of the local economy.

3 Reorganise the letters to form words to complete the sentences.

kasc veritwine kemart girinf
dali fof revbal nowd

a Two hundred workers at the factory have been .... because of the bad financial situation.
b This mobile phone is the smallest on the ....
c I asked her to put the phone .... and come into my office.
d They can't .... you without giving you at least two warnings in writing.
e .... someone is one of the most difficult things a manager has to do.
f The first thing you have to do is give the employee a .... warning.
g How did your .... go, then? Do you think you got the job?

Grammar

The passive

The object in active sentences becomes the subject in passive sentences.

Active	**Passive (*to be* + past participle)**
Someone ***services*** *the machine every year.*	*The machine* ***is serviced*** *every year.*
They ***have closed*** *down five factories.*	*Five factories* ***have been closed*** *down.*
They ***decorated*** *the offices last year.*	*The offices* ***were decorated*** *last year.*
They ***are encouraging*** *her to apply for the job.*	*She* ***is being encouraged*** *to apply for the job.*
They ***don't clean*** *the office on Friday.*	*The office* ***isn't cleaned*** *on Friday.*

You often use the passive to put the important information at the beginning of a sentence. The passive can be more impersonal than the active. For this reason, you can use it in formal documents such as reports.

You can use *by* to emphasise *who* or *what* performed an action.

- *The book was written* **by** *Peter Hudson.*
- *The equipment is damaged* **by** *prolonged exposure to sunlight.*

Practice 1

Reorganise the words to make correct sentences.

a June was at the contract the signed end of

....

b sacked slowly Sheila was working too for

....

c damaged fire the the in was office

....

d workers accident injured were the in some

....

e measures announced the have new been

....

f staff employed new no year this be will

....

g redesigned corporate is image being our

....

h salaries increased year have this been our

....

Practice 2

Rewrite the sentences in the passive.

a They have cancelled the order.
The order has been cancelled.

b They haven't finished the new building.

....

c Someone told him about the meeting.

....

d Someone stole the plans for the new engine.

....

e Someone will pick you up at the airport.

....

f They didn't ask him if he wanted the job.

....

g Did anyone tell you about what happened at the meeting?

....

h They hold a sales conference every year.

....

Practice 3

Answer the questions using a sentence in the passive and *by*.

a Who was the inventor of the light bulb?
The light bulb was invented by Thomas Edison.

b What currency was the replacement for the peseta, franc and lira in 2002?

....

c How many countries form the United Kingdom?

....

d Who is the author of this book?

....

e Who is the owner of this book?

....

f What type of heating have you got in your office – oil, gas or electric?

....

g Who was the director of the film *Some Like it Hot?*

....

h Which company was the original manufacturer of the PC?

....

Answers at foot of page.

Answers (Practice 3)
b euro c four d Simon Clarke
g Billy Wilder h IBM

TOPICS

15 TIME

Here are some basic rules on time management:
Tell people how you want them to work with you, or how to use your time.
Return the favor, treat their time as you want your time treated.
No meetings without agenda.
No long documents without a short summary.
Make sure you know what is expected of you.

STEFAN TÖPFER, CEO & CHAIRMAN OF WINWEB (HTTP://WWW.SME-BLOG.COM/CATEGORY/HOW-TO/MANAGE-YOUR-TIME)

Collocations

1 Put vowels in the spaces to complete the verbs below.

sp_nd |
s_v_ | money
w_st_ |
h_v_ | time
_nv_st |

2 Complete the sentences using words from 1. Are they true for you?

a At work, I .... a lot of time on the phone to people and answering e-mails.
b I plan my day carefully. If you prepare things well, you can .... a lot of time.
c I don't .... much time for myself, but when I do, I like to get some exercise.
d Computers should make you more efficient, but they can also make you .... time.

Discussion

3 Discuss the following questions with a partner.

a Some people say 'Time is money'. Do you agree?
b In what ways do you think you waste or save time and money?
c What are your working hours? If you could choose, how would you organise your working hours?
d What do you think of Stefan Töpfer's basic rules of time management?

THE NEW DATABASE

1 Match the words and phrases on the left with the definitions on the right.

a	deadline	**1**	a hold-up
b	a delay	**2**	point in time by which something must be done
c	behind schedule	**3**	late
d	timeframe	**4**	period in which something is expected to happen

2 2.19 Listen to the conversation and answer the questions.

a What problem is the conversation about?
b When was the system supposed to be online?
c When is it going to be ready now?
d What do you think of the IT technician's attitude?

3 Listen again and complete the phrases with one word for each gap. Contractions count as one word.

a We're worried because it's ....
b Well yes, I'm sorry about .... , but there have been some problems …
c … the system was supposed to be online last October. You .... , and it's now February.
d … not compatible with the new design. That means we have a ....
e What do you mean? How .... ?
f Are you saying that .... for all this is now next October?
g Can you guarantee that you're giving us priority on this? Will .... ?

4 Complete the phrases so they are true for you. Then compare your ideas with your teacher or a partner.

a It takes me .... to get to work in the morning.
b I .... meet my deadlines.
c In my company we .... timeframes for getting things done.
d When people are not on time for meetings ....
e IT projects .... behind schedule.
f At work the schedules for projects are ....
g When things are delayed I ....
h In my country, ... on time.

THE MYTH OF TIME MANAGEMENT

1 2.20 Listen to a talk on the topic of time management. The speaker deals with the topics below. Put them in order.

- [1] Introduction – Does time management work?
- [ ] Dealing with interruptions
- [ ] Defined tasks v. problem-solving
- [ ] Factors beyond our control
- [ ] Making useful investments in time

2 Complete each of the gaps in the text with a word from the box. Then listen again to check your answers.

box	efficient	expectations	intelligence	internet	operators	problem	tasks

Good afternoon. The subject of my presentation today is 'The Myth of Time Management'. Why is it a myth? Well, there are thousands of books and (a) internet courses on the market which are designed to help people be better managers of their time. They all suggest techniques for using our time more efficiently. They recommend making 'to do' lists, prioritising, and not answering the phone as ways to make us more time (b) .... But do these techniques really work?

Well, they say that time is money. That may be true, but time is certainly not like other resources which we manage, such as materials and machines. It is much more complex than that because use of time depends to a big extent on personality and attitude. Sometimes we can change our own behaviour, but time management really depends on changing the behaviour of other people around us and the demands they make on our time. At best, this is difficult, but more often than not it is beyond your control. As a result, you can be a very efficient user of your time – disciplined, organised and choosing the right moment to do vital (c) .... – yet still feel stressed and overworked. To be honest, in many cases, this is simply because you are being asked to do more than is possible in the time available.

This leads me on to the next point, because in fact, time management is frequently about making choices that in reality we don't have. One of the recommended techniques is to close your door at certain times, or leave your voice (d) .... to deal with calls. That's fine, but if interruptions and dealing with unpredictable human problems are part of your work, then those techniques don't help very much.

Another time-management technique is to analyse what you are doing and decide if it is important or not. Well, I think most people of average (e) .... can normally distinguish between activity which is useful and activity which is a waste of time. Unless they dislike their job or their employer, they will do useful things in their work time. In fact, often the problem is feeling guilty about using time to think or acquire skills and ideas which are not immediately productive. What apparently is a waste of time, is actually extremely useful because in the long run, it will make you more efficient.

Time management may work with jobs with very defined tasks, where procedures and processes are very clear. Machine (f) ...., for example, don't have to worry much about managing their time because the pace of work is imposed from outside. On the other hand, if you are faced with a task which involves creativity or (g) ....-solving, how to go about performing the task may not be clear. It could also be that you are in a job where you lack either the necessary skills or appropriate training to carry out your duties.

I will go on to look at these different aspects of time-use in more detail, but we have to remember that there will always be more work than time. This is what keeps us employed. How effectively you use your time is to some extent a question of ability, training and proper planning. But above all, it is about having a positive attitude towards your work, combined with reasonable (h) .... about how much you can do.

OK, that's a brief summary of the points I'd like to cover. Now let's go back to look at the question of how we can change .....

Discussion

3 Is the speaker for or against time management techniques? Do you agree? Why/why not?

4 Underline four phrases in the script which can be useful in a presentation.

5 How well do you manage your time? Complete the 'You' column with approximate percentages for the time you spend on the different activities. Add other activities, if necessary. Then complete the 'Your partner' column by asking *How much time do you spend on …?* Then change round.

Activity	You	Your partner
planning & delegating		
meetings		
correspondence		
telephoning		
reading		
dealing with problems		
....		
....		
	100%	100%

What differences are there between the way you and your partner manage your time? Why do you think this is?

JUST IN TIME

1 Read the article and answer these questions.

a How did AOL try life without time?
b What was the aim of the experiment?
c Why do companies use time as a measure of productivity?
d Why is the normal working timetable (nine to five) inefficient?
e What was the result of the experiment?

LIFE WITHOUT TIME

How dependent are we on time? Is life without clocks less stressful? One company decided to find out. At AOL, they removed all the clocks from their UK headquarters. Then everybody carried on working as usual.

They wanted to investigate how pressure of time can lead to stress, and to see how an environment without clocks would affect productivity. They say that time is money, and most companies use time to control their activities because it is easy to measure. On the other hand, humans have a biological clock which doesn't necessarily correspond to the standard eight-hour working day. We are more productive in the morning, and then our efficiency tends to drop off after lunch. So, if you're feeling hungry, why not have something to eat instead of waiting for the lunch break? Or, if you've finished your work, don't hang on until it's time to clock off, just go home.

So, what happens when you rely on your own body clock instead of artificial deadlines? According to one worker, 'Most people carried on as normal, although some took advantage of the opportunity to have an early lunch.' Another said 'This is great. It makes sense to be able to work when you need to and leave the office when you don't.' On the other hand, one secretary found the experience 'disorientating'. However, one office manager was in no doubt: 'Thank goodness we are going to bring the clocks back tomorrow. Make no mistake, a clockless office leads to chaos. Some people may be less stressed without clocks, but you need to know where people are and when, and meetings, for example, can last forever if you don't have a time limit.'

2 Discuss the following questions.

a What do you think of this experiment? Is it useful, interesting, or a waste of time?
b How aware do you need to be of time in your job?
c Could you work without a watch or clocks?
d Do you have lunch etc. at the same time every day?

Vocabulary

3 Find words and phrases in the article which mean the same as the following:

a continue ....
b fall quickly ....
c result in ....
d wait ....
e quantify ....

4 Use the words and phrases in 3 to complete the following sentences.

a Time management methods .... to unnecessary stress.
b In some businesses, it is difficult to .... efficiency.
c When you have to make a decision, it's best to .... until the last minute.
d If you .... in the same job for a long time, you lose interest.
e The amount of activity in an office .... on a Friday afternoon.

5 Which of the sentences in 4 do you agree with?

6 Look at this sentence from the article on page 97 and answer the questions. *Thank goodness we are going to bring the clocks back tomorrow.*

a Does the sentence refer to the past, present or future?
b Which of the following is closest in meaning to *we are going to bring the clocks back?*

We would like to bring the clocks back …
We are intending to bring the clocks back …
We have to bring the clocks back …

7 Plan how you are going to spend your next working day. Then explain your plans to your partner like this.

At 9.00, when I arrive at work, I'm going to check my e-mail. Then …

8 2.21–2.23 Complete the following conversations using the verb in brackets with either *going to* or *will*. Then listen and check your answers.

Conversation 1

A Where are you going?
B Well, I've finished everything I had to do, so I (a) .... (leave) early.
A What about the sales predictions for next month?
B Oh, I'd forgotten about that. I (b) .... (start) on them tomorrow first thing. I've arranged to meet someone at five.

Conversation 2

C Have you planned Mr Logan's visit? What about lunch tomorrow?
D I (c) .... (take) him to The Redwing.
C I seem to remember he's a vegetarian.
D Is he? In that case, I (d) .... (phone) to check they have a vegetarian menu.

Conversation 3

E Is everything confirmed for your trip to San Sebastian?
F Yes, the plane goes to Bilbao. I (e) .... (take) the train from there.
E No, don't do that – it takes forever. The bus is much faster.
F Is it? Well, I (f) .... (take) the bus, then.

9 Read the conversations again and look at how *will* and *going to* are used. Underline the correct option in the following sentences.

You can use *will* or *going to* to talk about decisions and plans:

a ***Will / Going to*** shows that you are making a decision now.
b ***Will / Going to*** shows that you made the decision earlier.

10 Work with a partner. Have similar conversations as in 8 using the prompts below and following this pattern:

A Say what you are going to do. *I'm going to walk to the station.*
B Mention a problem with the plan. *But it's raining.*
A React with an alternative plan using *will*. *Oh, in that case, I'll take a taxi.*

Plan	Problem	Alternative
walk to the station	it's raining	?
attend Japanese classes	you're too busy – you'll miss classes	?
buy a bargain computer	it's an old model – it'll be obsolete very soon	?
give up smoking	you'll get fat	?
get an easier job	you'll earn less money	?
take a taxi to the airport	the taxi drivers are on strike	?
take up roller skating	it's dangerous – there are lots of accidents	?

WASTING TIME

Collocations

1 Match the words to make four common collocations.

a bottom — 1 balance
b delicate — 2 caught
c get — 3 time
d waste — 4 line

a ☐ b ☐ c ☐ d ☐

2 Use the collocations in 1 to complete the article.

wasting time at WORK

Lots of people are so afraid of getting caught, they never (a) .... at work. They work the entire eight hours. They are right to be afraid. There is a (b) .... between not doing any work and doing too much. The (c) .... is you must get your work done. If you start wasting hours at a time, you'll (d) .... To be an effective time waster, you have to find small ways to eat up time. Remember, you can't waste the company's time if you don't work for the company. However, with a little effort, no one will ever know how little you do.

Source: www.vgg.com

3 Here are the headings from the rest of the article. What tips do you think the author gives under each heading?

- Be sloppy
- The computer
- The Internet
- Office conversations
- Meetings

4 Look at page 138 to see what the author recommends.

5 Complete the sentences below with words or phrases from the text on page 138 that mean the same as the words in brackets.

a 'Your papers are ....' 'Yes, but I know where everything is, so don't touch anything.' (untidy)
b Before making an important call, you should .... time to prepare it. (reserve)
c I only use the Internet to get specific information. I don't have time to .... the Web. (move around from link to link with no particular aim)
d My job requires a lot of .... , so I need a good Internet connection. (information searching)
e People who always .... and agree with everything are no use at all. (move head up and down)

6 Work with a partner. What other ways of wasting time can you think of?

15 TIME

LANGUAGE LINKS

> **Phrase Bank: Presentations**
> Good afternoon. The subject of my presentation today is …
> This leads me on to the next point …
> I will go on to look at these different aspects of time-use in more detail, but …
> Okay, that's a brief summary of the points I'd like to cover. Now let's go back to look at …

> **Phrase Bank: Talking about time**
> It's behind schedule. What is the situation?
> I'm sorry about the delay but there have been some problems.
> How long is it going to take?
> I think we should be ready by …
> It shouldn't take longer than that.
> Will it be on time?

Vocabulary

Working conditions

1 Combine one word from box A with one word from box B to complete each sentence below.

A	B
realistic	planning
eight-hour	deadline
long	forecasts
sales	line
forward	hours
bottom	day

a Monday is too soon for us: next Friday is a more ....

b The traditional .... does not suit our natural daily rhythm.

c According to our .... we are going to sell over 20% more next year.

d In any business the .... is that you have to make enough money to survive.

e You should give priority to important tasks such as .... and problem analysis.

f In the UK, people work .... but their productivity is not as high as in France or Germany.

2 Complete the sentences using the correct form of the words in brackets.

a Most people .... better in the morning. (performance)

b A psychologist is going to .... the staff to see how they work. (observation)

c Time management .... will not be impressed by the results of the experiment. (specialise)

d We are not so .... after a good lunch. (production)

e They .... to reduce the working week to 35 hours in some countries. (intention)

f Have you .... what to do about the situation? (decision)

g The .... went on for hours and the meeting ended very late. (discuss)

Grammar

be + *going to* + infinitive

Affirmative & Negative		
I	**am** **'m not**	**going to apply** for the job.
You We They	**are** **aren't**	
He She	**is** **isn't**	

Interrogative		
Are(n't)	you they we	**going to phone** later?
Is(n't)	he she	

You can use *going to* to talk about intentions and decisions you have made about the future before the moment of speaking.

- *We're **going to** open a new office in Berlin.*
- *I'm **going to** ask for an application form for the new post.*

going to or *will*?

You use *will* to show you are making a decision at the moment of speaking.

A *Could I speak to Mr Gomez, please?*
B *I'm afraid he's out at the moment. Can I take a message?*
A *No thanks, **I'll phone** later.*

Practice 1

Write sentences using *going to* and the word prompts.

a this evening / meet / friends / a drink.
This evening, I'm going to meet some friends for a drink.

b they / employ / more staff / deal with the new order

c you / meet / me / airport?

d what / you / say / at / meeting?

e next year / I / study / German

f he / look for / new job

g she / not / accept / our offer

h we / take / train / bus?

Practice 2

Read the sentences and make responses with *will* and an idea from the box.

call the office and apologise
take the team out for lunch
take a taxi back to the office to collect them
take an aspirin and go home
switch it off
call the IT department
ask her for her business card

a Your sales team has met its targets for this month.
I'll take the team out for lunch.

b You're at a meeting and your phone rings.

c Your computer has just crashed.

d You've forgotten some important documents for a meeting.

e You suddenly have a terrible headache and feel sick.

f You see an important client at a conference and you can't remember her name.

g You've overslept and you're going to be late.

Practice 3

Complete the responses with the verb in brackets using either *going to* or *will*.

a We've run out of toner for the photocopier.
Have we? I .... (order) some more.

b What are your plans for the weekend?
We .... (visit) some friends in the country. Do you want to come?

c Did you remember to book the hotel?
No, I forgot! I .... (phone) them now. I hope they still have some room.

d You should consult George about the production problems.
I've already mentioned it to him. We .... (discuss) it this afternoon.

e Have you seen their offices? They're miles from anywhere in this really old building.
Yes, I know. But they .... (move) to a new place next year.

f I'm dying for a cup of coffee.
All right, I .... (make) you one now. Do you take sugar?

g Why are you working so hard?
Because I .... (leave) on time today, for a change, and I want to finish this before I go.

h I have to go to the airport and my car won't start.
Don't worry. I .... (lend) you mine.

Practice 4

Complete the conversation using the words in the box.

do easier information learn someone start strategy time urgent

A What are you doing?
B I'm putting this customer (a) .... into the database.
A Why don't you get (b) .... else in your team to do it?
B Well, it's (c) .... if I just do it myself.
A Yes, but if you do it yourself, they'll never (d) ....
B Yes, you're probably right. I'll (e) .... that next time.
A Anyway, have you finished the marketing (f) .... for the new product launch?
B No, I'm going to (g) .... that this afternoon.
A Oh, come on! It's really (h) .... We're all waiting for it.
B I know, but I haven't had (i) ....

16 GETTING THINGS DONE

Often, a telephone call is required to get things done, possibly to someone you haven't spoken to before. You imagine that person doesn't take calls, is very frightening and hates you and your ridiculous plan. But most people are glad to hear from new people, as it adds to the richness of life.

GUY BROWNING THE GUARDIAN SATURDAY JUNE 4, 2005 - HTTP://WWW.GUARDIAN.CO.UK/WEEKEND/STORY/0,,1497435,00.HTML

ASKING FAVOURS

1 2.24–2.25 Complete the extracts from two conversations below which take place in an office. Then listen and compare your answers.

Extract 1

A I .... go to the Post Office to pick something up and it's .... lend me your umbrella?

B Of course. As long as ....

Extract 2

A The thing is that I need .... where we won't be interrupted. .... use your office?

B All right, as long as .... I've got a meeting myself.

What's the difference between *Could I …?* and *Could you …?*

2 Work with a partner. Act out conversations using the prompts below. Use the conversations in 1 as a model.

Problem	Request	As long as …
phone home / mobile batteries flat	use / your mobile	just a short call
send an e-mail / computer not working	use / computer	not take too long
be at airport at five / taxi services not answering	give / lift	get back before six
post a letter / can't leave the office	post it on your way home	have it ready by five o'clock
translate this letter / no dictionary	borrow yours	get it back by this afternoon
take notes / no pen	lend me one	give it back later
make copies / photocopier not working	take / photocopy shop	answer the phone while I'm out

Saying *no*

3 2.26 It is important to say *no* to a request tactfully. Otherwise you can create problems for the future. Listen to the conversation and answer the questions.

a What favour does the speaker ask Richard?
b How does Richard react?

4 Use the phrases in the box to rewrite the conversation so that it sounds more polite.

I'd take my own, of course, but it's being repaired. Nothing serious, I hope.
What's the problem? Well, actually, I'm not very keen on the idea.
It's just that I don't feel happy about other people driving my car. Oh, all right. Not to worry.

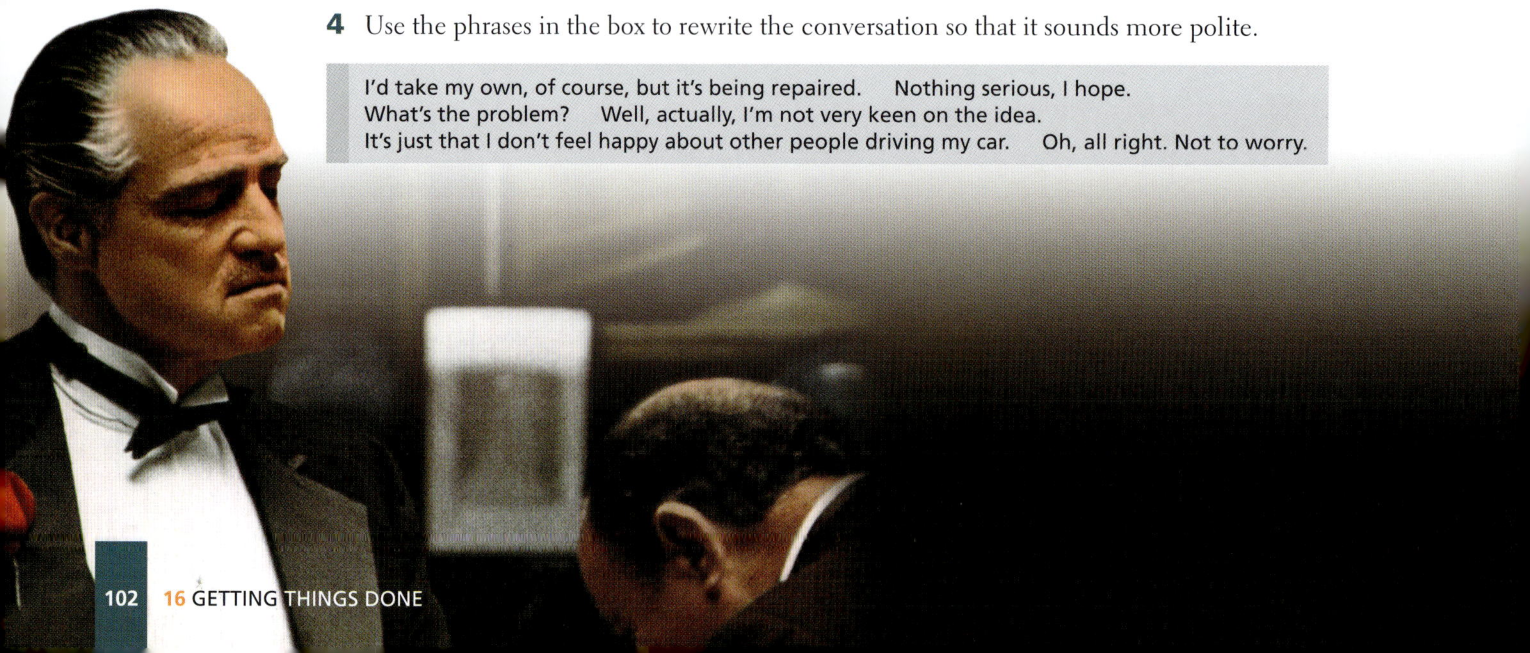

Requests, persuasion and threats

5 2.27 Put the conversation in the correct order. Then listen and check your answer.

Jeff

☐ a … but on the other hand, if you do it, I'll see it as a personal favour.
☐ b I know, but you can take the time later on.
☐ c No, there isn't. Look, I know it's inconvenient, but I can't think of any other solution.
☐ d Sandra, we need someone to answer the phone from 2.00 til 4.00 while Julia is off sick. Could you do it?
☐ e Yes, in principle, yes. But you never know. Your contract is up for renewal next month. Enough said?
☐ f No, it isn't, and obviously I can't force you to do it, but …
☐ g Not really. It creates such a bad impression. Listen, I'd do it myself, but I've got to be somewhere else.

Sandra

☐ h From 2.00 to 4.00? It's not my hours.
☐ i Well, can't we just put the answerphone on for a couple of hours?
☐ j Yeah, enough said.
☐ k It's not the time. I'll have to get someone to pick the kids up from school. Isn't there anyone else?
☐ l I see. I don't really have much choice, do I? I hope it's just this time …
☐ m But?
☐ n I'm sure you would, but it's not my problem, is it?

6 Identify phrases in 5 for the following:

a a request ....
b a suggestion ....
c emotional blackmail ....
d a threat ....

UPGRADE

1 2.28 A passenger is checking in for a flight. Listen to conversation 1 and answer the questions.

A Good afternoon, sir.
B Hello. I'm on flight IB 603. I was wondering if there's any chance of an upgrade to business class.
A Well, I don't know. It depends how crowded the flight is.
B Yes, I quite understand, but I'd really appreciate it if you could have a look. I don't mind paying the extra. It's just that I've had a really hard day, and it'd be really nice to have a bit more space and comfort.
A Just a minute, sir.
B I'm sorry to put you to any trouble.
A No, that's okay. Oh, yes, there's lots of space in business class. I think we can do it.
B Oh, fantastic. How much is that?
A That's all right, sir. Don't worry.
B Oh, thank you ever so much.
A You're welcome. Have a good flight.

a Do you think the passenger really expects to pay for the upgrade?
b Is the passenger polite?
c Does he get what he wants?
d Underline the phrases in the conversation which the passenger uses to sound polite.

2 2.29 A guest is checking in to a hotel. Listen to conversation 2 and answer the questions.

a Do you think the guest's request is reasonable?
b Is the guest polite?
c Does he get what he wants?

3 Work with a partner. Find conversation 2 on page 152 and act it out. This time the guest is polite. Use the phrases you underlined in conversation 1. If you are the receptionist, decide what to do.

COMPANY STRUCTURE

1 Read the information about different types of company structure and answer the questions which follow.

Company Structure

Businesses can be organised by:

- function
- geographical area
- product or customer
- project

FUNCTION

Larger businesses are traditionally organised into departments according to their role. Employees with similar jobs (functions) are grouped together. E.g. production, financing, marketing and human resources.

AREA

Some businesses organise their activity according to geographical area. This is common in large multinational companies but it might also be appropriate for medium-sized businesses. E.g. a small retail chain or a fast-food chain with branches.

PRODUCT/CUSTOMER

This involves organising the business into departments which focus on different products. Employees with different skills work in departments according to the product they are developing. Departments can also be organised to serve groups of customers with specific needs. E.g. a bank may have separate departments for personal accounts and business accounts.

PROJECT MANAGEMENT

Project-based management is becoming increasingly popular. Employees are grouped in two different ways, for example by function and by project. In many cases, this is a temporary arrangement due to a special project. Project teams have specialised employees working for them from other departments. These employees therefore report to two managers – departmental and project.

a What kind of structure does your organisation have? (Or one you know about.) Why is it organised like this?

b What are the advantages and disadvantages of the different types of company structure? Compare your ideas with the ideas on page 142.

2 You are going to take part in the meeting to decide what the best organisation for a company is. Read the background information below and then each take a role: Consultant A, B, C or D.

WILLIAM TUCKER LTD is a British transport and logistics company which was founded 20 years ago. During this time it has grown from a small lorry transport company with 10 employees to become a leader in the sector with a fleet of over 300 trucks.

The company has a structure based on geographical areas with branch offices/depots distributed over the UK. Each branch has a team run by a manager who is responsible for a profit and loss account. This structure was efficient in the early days when the company just had one main activity. However, the company has diversified and provides many different services. In transport, there are large loads, packet delivery and liquid and gas transport lines. It has also developed logistics support (movement and control of stock) for the automobile and steel industries. These activities have very different operational needs and the company needs to re-think its structure. The Managing Director has contracted four consultants to advise on how to organise the company. ■

Consultant A
You think the company should centralise its administration in a headquarters. Departments should then be organised according to the main functions in the company - operations, finance, HR and R&D. This will make it easier to establish policies which will make the company more efficient. Costs can be reduced by providing central services such as HR and finance from a centralised headquarters. You believe the modern technology makes it possible to do this from a distance.

Consultant B
You believe that every part of the company structure must be responsible and accountable for its results. You are also against having a large central administration and recommend that the company continue operating from a small headquarters - any change would cost a lot of money. Your solution is to maintain the present structure of branch offices. However, certain branch managers with specialist knowledge and a concentration of a particular activity in their area will have a double role. On one hand they will continue to run a branch office/depot, but on the other hand they will have overall responsibility for a line or activity over the whole company. This means they will have two 'profit and loss' accounts under their control. This means that some middle managers may report to more than one boss.

Consultant C
You argue in favour of a 'matrix' organisation where employees report to a 'product line' boss in the headquarters, as well as to a local branch boss. This means that product line bosses will have to co-ordinate with branch bosses to make the most efficient use of each specialist in the organisation. This will require improved communication in the company but will help distribute the available talent and skills in the companies to meet the needs of each branch office.

Consultant D
Your solution is radical. Your advice is to break the present company up into separate companies within a group. Each separate company will operate independently and concentrate on one particular activity. This will encourage competition, clear accountability and profit responsibility. In some cases this will mean creating new offices. You believe future growth will be faster as a result because each company will have the organisation that fits its needs. For example, the logistics support to car factories is more concerned with stock control in warehouses than transport.

3 Now look at page 139 to read about a similar company in Spain. Is its organisation similar to what you discussed in 2?

TOPICS

17 OFFICE GOSSIP

gossip /ˈgɒsɪp/ *noun* a talk or conversation about things that are not important or about other people's private lives

Definition from Macmillan Essential Dictionary

Gossip is the cement which holds organisations together. Providing communal space such as coffee areas or lunchroom, allows employees to share information, knowledge and build relations that benefits both company and the employee.

JUDITH DOYLE HTTP://WWW.PERSONNELTODAY.COM/ARTICLES/2000/11/22/3125/WORK-LIFE-BALANCE-DEBATES-OVER-SIMPLISTIC.HTML

1 2.30 Listen to the conversation and answer the questions.

a Why has Trixy been out of the office?
b What is the news which she hasn't heard?
c Is Prescott their boss or a colleague?
d Why are they worried?
e Why don't they think that Maureen will be worried?
f The expression 'There's no smoke without fire' means that when people gossip about something, there's usually some truth in what they say. Do you have an equivalent saying in your language? Do you think it's true?

Reported speech

2 Look at this sentence from the conversation in 1.

… *he said that we were overstaffed.*

The original statement was *You are overstaffed.*

Listen to the conversation again and complete the reported statements.

a 'You will have to let some people go.'
This consultant chap .... have to let some people go.
b 'How many people does it involve?'
Prescott .... it involved.
c 'It depends on individual performance and attitude.'
He .... on individual performance and attitude.
d 'I often see them coming out of *The Green Man* together.'
I'm not saying who, but someone .... them in *The Green Man* together.
e 'Will you stay behind to work on something with me?'
The other day he .... stay behind to work on something together.

say and *tell*

3 Which of the sentences below needs *said* and which one needs *told*?

a He .... we were overstaffed.
b He .... me we were overstaffed.

What is the main difference between *say* and *tell*?

Question words

4 What words are missing from the following sentences?

a 'Where are you going?' He asked me .... I was going.
b 'When are you going?' He asked me .... I was going.
c 'Are you going?' He asked me .... I was going.

When reporting questions, when do you use the word *if*?

Tenses

5 Complete the sentences below.

a 'I'm busy.' He said he .... busy.
b 'I'll start straight away.' He said he .... straight away.

What changes do you make to the Present Simple in reported speech? What changes do you make to *will* in reported speech?

6 2.31–2.34 Look at the conversations below. Complete them with words and phrases which make sense. Then listen and compare your answers.

Conversation 1

A Jeff, a) .... last month's production figures?
B No, Jane, I'm b) .... Can I give them to you this afternoon?
A It's no good being sorry. There's always some c) .... If they're not on my desk by four o'clock, I'll have to d) .... Mr Bradley.
B Yes, Jane. I'll start e) ....

Conversation 2

C David, have you got f) .... ? There's something I want to g) .... with you … in my office.
D What's it about?
C Oh, well, we're missing a laptop h) .... from the store.
D What has that got to do with me?
C Well, you are the only other person with a i) .... to the store and …

Conversation 3

E Marie, the figures you need are j) ....
F Thanks, Pedro. Is everything k) .... ?
E Yes, no problems. Would you like to l) .... them with me?
F Yes, but I'm a bit m) .... this afternoon.
E Me too. Er, do n) .... that new café they've just opened? It's nice and o) .... We can go through them there after p) ....
F Oh, I q) .... so, but I won't be able to stay for long.
E Great. r) .... there at about six, then?
F Yes, all right. See you there.

Conversation 4

G Hi, Monica.
H Oh, hello, Jim. s) .... things going?
G Great. In fact, you can be the first to congratulate me.
H Yes, you look very t) .... with yourself. What's up?
G I'm the new u) .... of the eastern sales team.
H Oh, really? What salary are you on now, then?
G v) .... a year.
H I can't believe it. Sixty thousand!
G And they're giving me a new w) ....
H Oh, really? Congratulations, then. The x) .... are on you. See you later.
G Yes. Bye.

7 You are at the coffee machine having a gossip with a colleague. You have overheard the conversations in 6. Use the frameworks in the box to tell your partner what you heard. It is not necessary to report everything.

I heard ... talking to ...	... said that ...	... told ... that ...	... asked ...

GOSSIP

1 Read the following news article.

a What is the new law?
b Do you think it's a good idea? Why/why not?

City Council gags workers

Municipal employees in the Brazilian city of Cascavel have been banned from gossiping during working hours. Under a new law approved by the city council, public employees who spread rumours or gossip about their colleagues face the sack. The city says civil servants have the right to work in a professional environment and claim the new law will promote integrity in public offices.

2 Underline words and phrases in the text which mean the following:

a ordered not to do something
b pass on information which is not official and may not be true
c be in a position where you can be dismissed

Discussion

3 Discuss the following with other people in the class.

a How do you define gossip?
b Is it always a bad thing?
c Is it possible to ban it?
d Does your company have a policy on gossip? Have you ever heard of a company that does?

4 The comments below were made on a website for office workers. Read them and classify them in the table. Then compare your answers with a partner.

Gossip is good	Mixed feelings	Gossip is bad

OFFICE WORKERS FORUM

A Posted by James Pittman, England	A friendly and chatty work environment makes employees happy. This results in a better level of work from employees, which means the company makes more money. Any employer who bans office gossip will lose money by making the workforce less productive.
B Posted by Janet Jones, Wales	In my place of work gossip is the only way of finding anything out about the company strategy. The management refuse to talk to most of the staff.
C Posted by Luke McCarthy, Australia	There's nothing worse than gossip – and it's mostly propagated by women who have nothing better to do than YAP YAP YAP.
D Posted by Nicole Martin, France	Gossip isn't a bad thing. Is there another way to learn about office politics? I see it as a healthy activity and part of working in an office.
E Posted by Pieter Groot, Netherlands	Gossip is what someone, somewhere, doesn't want you to know. A delicious pastime – unless you are the one being gossiped about. And certainly not a sackable offence.
F Posted by Sanjay Patel, India	Having started a new job a year ago, I made an effort never to engage in gossip. If I'm in a group where gossip starts, I find a reason to leave the area. It can be very damaging to your career and general workplace relations.
G Posted by Claudia Weber, Germany	Isn't freedom of speech a basic human right? However, there's a fine line between harmless and hurtful remarks. I think it's best left to individuals to decide which is which.
H Posted by John Mason, Scotland	Some of my biggest insights into problems at work have occurred while chatting by the coffee machine. Having a (brief) chat about totally unrelated matters, although not directly productive, can actually improve productivity by breaking up the day a little.

5 The phrases below are from the comments above. Complete the sentences with your own words and ideas.

a In my place of work, ...
b Any employer who .... will ....
c There's nothing worse than ....
d .... isn't a bad thing.
e I make an effort never to ....
f A .... work environment makes employees ....

6 You are going to listen to an interview about office gossip from a radio programme. The words and phrases on the left are from the interview. Match them to the definitions on the right.

a	drive for efficiency	1	talking informally
b	scrapped	2	mobile refreshments service
c	human resources	3	effort to get more work done
d	encouraged	4	seen as positive
e	chatting	5	not continued with
f	tea trolley	6	organisation and management of company staff

a ☐ b ☐ c ☐ d ☐ e ☐ f ☐

7 Before you listen, decide if you agree with the following statements.

a Companies who provide an opportunity for their workers to socialise are making a mistake.
b People have less time to talk to each other and socialise than before.
c The differences between a good job and a bad job are the social aspects.
d Employees are more productive when they are happy.
e When employees share information and knowledge, the company benefits.
f Companies should take measures to encourage gossip.

8 2.35 Listen to the interview to see if the speaker agrees with you.

Roleplay

9 Work with a partner and perform the following roleplay about office policy on coffee breaks and gossiping.

Speaker B: Look at the instructions on page 139.
Speaker A: You are one of the management consultants who prepared the study mentioned in the interview in 8. In a client's company you see the notice below next to the coffee machine. Try to persuade the client to change the policy.

COMPANY NOTICE

- Employees may take up to three coffee breaks per day.
- Maximum time at coffee machine: four minutes.
- All 'gossip' or discussion of non-work related matters is prohibited.

Writing

10 Complete the form below.

FROM: Personnel Manager
TO: Managing Director

With regard to the company policy on coffee breaks, ...

....

In my opinion, ...
According to a report by the Industrial Society, ...

....

In the report the author says that ....
It is a question of balance, but ....
In conclusion, ...

17 OFFICE GOSSIP

LANGUAGE LINKS

Phrase Bank: Social chat

How's it going?

Where have you been?

Have you heard the news? What news?

I can't believe it!

Really! Is it official?

Apparently they are going to ...

That's awful/terrible/ wonderful/incredible.

Catch you later.

See you there at about six.

Congratulations!

Vocabulary

Relationships at work

1 Combine one word from box A with one word from box B to complete the sentences below.

A	B
coffee	consultant
company	room
human	policy
meeting	resources
management	machine

a People have the best ideas in conversations around the ....

b The company has hired a .... to give advice on improving internal communications.

c What do you think about this idea of removing the chairs from the .... so we don't spend so long talking about things?

d What is the .... on taking coffee or tea breaks?

e Nowadays people say .... instead of 'personnel'.

2 Complete the puzzle using the clues below. Sometimes the first letter has been given.

1 Having communal areas benefits relations in the w.................. .
2 We are having a .... for efficiency. (You also .... a car.)
3 What this unit is about.
4 Let's make an .... not to waste time.
5 It's not a good idea to .... rumours.
6 Have you heard the .... ?
7 There's no .... without fire.
8 We have banned smoking in the o.................. .
9 They don't a.................. of people taking long tea breaks.
10 Let's go to the pub for a .... on Friday night.
11 We should encourage employees to .... their ideas.
12 What has happened to the tea .... ?

Grammar

Reported speech

say & tell

You can use *say* or *tell* to report what someone said.

say + something

- *He **says** (that) he is happy in his new job.*

tell + somebody + something

- *He **tells** everyone (that) he is the company boss.*

Tense

If you use the past forms *said* or *told*, you have to change the verbs in the original.

Present → Past

- *'I **like** working on my own.' → He said he **liked** working on his own.*

***will → would*:**

- *'I'll help you.' → He **said** he **would** help me.*

Pronouns

I ➔ *he/she*
me ➔ *him/her*
my ➔ *his/her*
your ➔ *my*

- *'I speak to* ***your*** *secretary every day.'* ➔
  He told me ***he*** *spoke to* ***my*** *secretary every day.*

Adverbs of time & place

now ➔ *then/at that moment*
today ➔ *that day*
here ➔ *there*
tomorrow ➔ *the next day/the following day*
yesterday ➔ *the day before/the previous day*

- *I'll see you* ***here tomorrow****.* ➔
  He said he would see me ***there the next day****.*

Most of these changes are logical and natural and often similar in other languages. They depend on the differences in time, place and people between the original conversation and the reported conversation.

asked

For reported questions you can use *asked* + *what/when*/etc.

- *What do you want?* ➔ *He* ***asked*** *me* ***what*** *I wanted.*

or *asked* + *if* for reporting yes/no questions.

- *Is it official?* ➔ *He* ***asked*** *me* ***if*** *it was official.*

Practice 1

Complete the second sentence to report the first one.

a I'm really enjoying my job at the moment.
She says she's really enjoying her job at the moment.
b It's too late to cancel the meeting.
I said ……………………
c We are having a lot of problems with the production department today.
He told me ……………………
d What time is Mr Keegan going to arrive?
He asked ……………………
e We should buy a new computer system.
He keeps telling me ……………………
f Is Mr Merchant available?
She asked ……………………
g The fixed costs include the office rent and equipment hire.
She said ……………………
h Where do you work now?
They asked me ……………………
i I'll meet you at the airport at eight o'clock.
She said ……………………
j I want to see you about the arrangements for tomorrow.
He told me ……………………
k Does the office open on Saturdays?
He asked me ……………………
l When will the documents be ready?
She asked ……………………
m I'm the best salesman in the company.
He keeps saying ……………………
n Can I make a phone call?
He asked if ……………………
o What do you think of the new website?
He asked me ……………………

Practice 2

Complete the sentences with *say/says/said*, *tell/told*, or *ask/asked*.

a Why didn't you …………… me you weren't happy with your job?
b What will people …………… if we try to ban office gossip?
c Did he …………… what time you had to be there?
d The boss always …………… that I should keep my desk more organised.
e He …………… me he was having second thoughts about applying for the job.
f Will you …………… him if he's going to come?
g I can't read the small print on this. What does it ……………?
h Every time I visit them they …………… me how you are.
i I'll …………… you if you promise not to …………… anything to anybody else.

TOPICS

18 E-COMMERCE

A report, to be released by leading insurer AXA next week, has found Britain's pensioners have become a generation of silver surfers.

HTTP://WWW.AXA.CO.UK/MEDIA/PRESSRELEASES/2007/PR20070202_1100.HTML

1 Complete the sentences using the phrases in the box. Then compare them with those on page 139. Do you agree?

you're interested in quality · who cares? · you're interested in price · you're interested in quality and price

a When you buy something for yourself with your own money, ...
b When you buy something for someone else with your own money, ...
c When you buy something for yourself with someone else's money, ...
d When you buy something for someone else with someone else's money, ...

Discussion

2 Work with a partner. Ask each other the following questions.

a When was the last time you bought something for:
- yourself?
- somebody else?
- a customer or client?
- your company?

b What did you buy?
c What factors influenced your decisions?
d What kind of shopping do you like/dislike?
e How often do you buy things on the Internet?

E-commerce – advantages and disadvantages

3 E-commerce has advantages and disadvantages. Work with a partner. Decide if the features on the left are plus factors or negative factors for the seller (S) or the customer (C). Add your own ideas.

	+	-
open for business 24x7x365		
competitive pricing		
no need for physical premises		
low selling costs		
updated stock information in real time		
credit card payment		
fast communication (e-mail/phone) with client		
cost and time of delivery		
collection of marketing data		
uncertainty about delivery		
difficulty of returning goods		
not good for perishable goods		
online information limited to text and photos		

snail mail /ˈsneɪl meɪl/ *noun* letters that are sent by post

Definition from Macmillan Essential Dictionary

4 2.36 Listen to a radio program where experts discuss e-commerce. Which of the ideas above do they mention? Are their ideas the same as yours in 3?

Discussing advantages and disadvantages

5 Listen again and complete the phrases. There is one word for each gap.

a Paul, how do you see the future? .... ?

b The .... : access to products that may not be available locally.

c Yes, for the customer .... – convenience and lower prices.

d That's absolutely right, but .... as well.

e After-sales service is ....

f On .... the seller can deal directly with the manufacturer …

g For me security is .... in people's minds.

h Yes, buying online will inevitably make groceries more expensive, so what's the point? Actually, ...

i Not .... when you go to a shop and pick something up, you choose what to look at and how to look at it.

j There's .... Because payment is by credit card, very small or very large transactions tend not to be conducted online.

6 2.37 Look at this phrase from the discussion.

Books and DVDs are one thing, but fruit and vegetables are another.

Make similar sentences using the following prompts.

a the right qualifications / have experience
The right qualifications for a job are one thing, but having experience is another.

b a high turnover / make good profits

c have a good idea / put into practice

d high productivity / improve staff motivation

e create a good product / sell it

Now listen and compare your answers.

7 Work with a partner. Brainstorm the advantages and disadvantages of the following:

a Working for a company and working for yourself.
b Living in the country and living in a town.
c Having children and not having children.
d Going to university and starting work straight after school.

Roleplay

8 Work in groups of three. You all work for a marketing company. Market studies have shown that retired people spend a significant amount of their free time surfing the Internet. You have formed a focus group to explore the possibility of marketing to the over-sixties using the Internet. Make notes about what you are going to say. Use some of the expressions in 5 and 6 in your discussion.

Speaker A: You think this is a fantastic idea. Think of arguments to support it.
Speaker B: You think this is a ridiculous idea. Think of arguments against it.
Speaker C: You are the focus group leader. You are not sure about this idea. Lead the discussion, listen to the others and ask questions.

THE FUTURE OF THE INTERNET

1 The words and phrases (a–h) are from a text on the future of the Internet. Match them to the explanations (1–8).

a devastating attack
b computing devices
c government and business surveillance
d virtual classes
e a wide public
f digital products
g healthcare problems
h social networks

1 lessons where the students are not physically in a classroom.
2 a large group of different people.
3 software, DVDs, mp3 music, etc.
4 electronic chips which can control things and communicate.
5 difficulties looking after people who are ill.
6 groups of people who have friendship, relationships or interests in common.
7 companies and the state watching what people do.
8 a violent action which completely destroys something.

a ☐ b ☐ c ☐ d ☐ e ☐ f ☐ g ☐ h ☐

2 A group of technology experts have answered a survey about the future of the Internet. They were asked their opinion on the following statements. Work with a partner and say if you agree (✓) or disagree (✗) with each prediction.

	agree or disagree?
At least one devastating attack will collapse the Internet in the next ten years.	
Manufacturers will use computing devices in appliances, cars, phones and even clothes. As a result, there will be more government and business surveillance. The authorities will arrest more people using this evidence.	
In ten years, most students will spend at least part of their 'school days' in virtual classes.	
Tele-work and home-schooling will grow, and the barriers between work and leisure will be less clear. Everyday family life will change as a result.	
The Internet will make people more creative. They will collaborate with others to make more music, art, and literature. Their work will circulate freely online and will command the attention of a wide public.	
All media, including audio, video, print, and voice, will stream in and out of the home or office via the Internet. Computers that control video games, audio, and video will become the centre of the living room. They will link to networked devices around the house, replacing the television's central place in the home.	
Internet users will continue to easily copy and distribute digital products freely through anonymous peer-to-peer networks. It won't be possible to stop this.	
The number of dangerous fanatics in politics, in religion and in groups which believe in using violence will increase as their networks grow online.	
Online medical resources will help solve healthcare problems such as rising costs, poor customer service and lack of access to medical care.	
The size of people's social networks will grow. People will have a much wider range of information about job opportunities, personal services, common interests, and products.	
People will vote in elections online without problems of security. More people will participate in elections as a result.	

3 Compare your answers to what the experts thought on page 140.

4 Complete the sentences below with the vocabulary items in 1. Each sentence expresses an opinion. Do you agree?

a People should be allowed to share .... like music and films.
b .... in cars will make them safer and more ecological.
c I like the idea of children being at home and studying in ....
d .... will increase as the average age of the population goes up.
e State-funded television should appeal to .... and not just people who want to watch documentaries.
f As people spend more time online they spend less time with their friends and their .... are getting smaller.
g One day terrorists will use a very harmful computer virus to make a .... on all our communication systems.
h You don't need to worry about .... if you haven't done anything wrong.

MAKING PREDICTIONS

1 Look at this sentence from the survey on page 116.

At least one devastating attack will collapse the Internet in the next ten years.

This is a prediction. You express predictions about the future using *will*. Underline other predictions in the article.

2 Do you agree with the predictions in the article? Discuss them like this:

A I think the security issues of the Internet will be solved.
B Do you? I don't. / Me too.
A I don't think terrorists will attack the Internet.
B Don't you? I do. / Me neither.

3 What other predictions can you make about the Internet?

In ten years, all banking will be online.

Discussion

4 Tick Y (yes) or N (no) against the predictions in the chart so that they are true for you. Then discuss them with a partner.

A *Do you think you'll change your job in the next five years?*
B *Yes, I do. I don't really like what I do now. How about you?*
A *No, I don't think I will. Things are going well and I like my job.*

	next year	**Y**	**N**	**in five years**	**Y**	**N**	**in the next ten years**	**Y**	**N**
my life	I'll change jobs.			I'll leave and start my own company.			I'll make a million and retire.		
my company	Our main competitor will go bankrupt.			Everybody will work at home most of the time.			Most employees will be replaced by computers.		
the world	There will be an economic boom.			The USA will have a female president.			There'll be a world government.		

LANGUAGE LINKS

Phrase Bank: Advantages and disadvantages
What are the pros and cons?
The advantages / benefits / disadvantages / drawbacks are …
That's a negative/positive factor.
Security is an issue.
Another point is …
Having a good job is one thing, but earning a lot of money is another.

Vocabulary

Shopping & the Internet

1 Match each verb on the left to the item on the right that it collocates with. Then use the phrases to complete the sentences.

a	compare	1	a bill
b	influence	2	the conversation
c	listen to	3	a network
d	run up	4	prices
e	try on	5	the decision
f	access	6	a sweater

a I like to .... before I buy anything expensive.
b His children have .... of over $300 by surfing on the Internet all day long.
c When she asked to .... they told her they didn't have one in her size.
d To .... you have to obtain a user name and a password from the administrator.
e Did you .... in the canteen yesterday?
f What factors do you think will most .... on salaries?

2 Complete the anecdote using the words in the box.

button came charge clicked complain crashed download
e-mail message online pay reply security website

Why I will never buy anything on the Internet again
Ask most people how shopping will be in the future and inevitably they will mention the Internet. Well, the other day I had a bad enough experience shopping (a) .... to put me off for life. I heard about a book you could download from a (b) .... before it was published and sold in bookshops. As it was by an author I adore, I decided to investigate.

I found the page and read the information. They charged thirty euros for the (c) .... Not a massive amount but you had to use a credit card. I completed the form with the endless details requested, including my (d) .... address. Finally I entered my credit card number, because they solemnly promised that there was no (e) .... risk. When the payment was authorised – it took about a minute – a new screen appeared with a (f) .... which said 'download now'. I (g) .... on the button but nothing happened so I clicked again. Then a (h) .... came up saying 'Download suspended due to network overload. Please try again later.'

Finally the system (i) .... and I had to turn off the computer. When I reconnected, the same forms as before (j) .... up but I didn't want to risk paying again, so I wrote an e-mail to the company explaining the problem. I never got a (k) ....

I assumed that as I never got the book I wouldn't have to (l) .... , but when I got my credit card statement at the end of the month I saw the (m) .... for thirty euros was there. It was too late to do anything and there was no one to (n) .... to. Okay, so it was only thirty euros – no big deal – but the question I ask myself is this: why risk buying online when it amounts to what is basically an act of faith? In any case, it will be a long time before I try buying something over the Internet again.

Grammar

will for future predictions

Affirmative		
I You He She It We They	**will** **'ll**	work

Negative		
I You He She It We They	**will not** **won't**	work

Interrogative		
Will **Won't**	I you he she it we they	work?

You can use *will* + infinitive to express predictions or beliefs about the future.

- *This year the economy* ***will grow*** *by 3%.*
- *I'm sure we* ***will finish*** *the order on time.*

The negative of *will* is *won't*.

- *I'm sorry, but things* ***won't get*** *any better.*
- *No, there* ***won't be*** *a recession.*

Put *will* before the subject to make questions.

- ***Will*** *people use the Internet for most of their shopping in the future?*
- ***Will*** *the economy recover by next year?*

You often introduce predictions with *I think* …

- ***I think*** *the DVD* ***will replace*** *the CD.*
- ***I think*** *the meeting* ***will end*** *on time.*

Avoid saying *I think … won't …*
Use *I don't think … will …*

- ***I don't think*** *the keyboard* ***will become*** *obsolete.*
  (NOT ~~*I think the keyboard won't become obsolete*~~.)
- ***I don't think*** *the meeting* ***will end*** *on time.*
  (NOT ~~*I think the meeting won't end on time*~~.)

Practice 1

Join the sentence beginnings with the endings using *will* + the verbs in the box.

affect	arrive	be	continue	get	go	have	retire	take

a Prices … will continue … public by next year.
b There … … with a massive golden handshake soon.
c The managing director … … better.
d The government … … a boom in the economy.
e Young George … … late as usual.
f The company … … measures against inflation.
g Life here … … a very successful career, I'm sure.
h The plane … … to rise.
i The political situation … … the economy.

Practice 2

Reorganise the words to make correct sentences.

a any new you system won't with have problems the
You won't have any problems with the new system.

b information think the Internet I you'll on find the

c Berlin you'll good have time think I a in

d Juan Montes think see you'll there don't I

e think do write report time you'll the you to have?

f time you what arrive will?

g long how us it will get there take to?

h we'll shopping I to think go time any don't have

i make think money I he'll lot a of

j want people see buy will always to products they before them most

Practice 3

Make questions with *do you think … will …?* and then write answers that are true for you.

a What time / get home tonight?
What time do you think you'll get home tonight? About 7.30.

b What / have / dinner?

c Where / go / next holiday?

d change / jobs / next five years?

e lose / weight / this month?

f How long / take / do this exercise?

g ever have / own business?

h ever drive / Ferrari?

i work as hard / five years from now?

19 E-WORK

We are a society overwhelmed by pollution, traffic jams, and seemingly endless commutes to work. Time with our families is often minimal. And we look to teleworking as one solution to these formidable problems.

UNITED STATES OFFICE OF PERSONNEL MANAGEMENT

1 Discuss these questions with a partner or your teacher. What is e-work? Choose the best description from a–d below.

a Working for a company from an office in your home.
b Working at home a couple of days a week and going into the office on other days.
c Using a laptop and electronic equipment to work when you are travelling.
d Setting up your own Internet-based business at home.

Do you have any experience of working like this?

2 Read the article below and answer the questions.

a Which of the types of e-work in 1 does the article mention?
b Why is it difficult to say how many people are doing e-work?
c What is the typical idea that people have of e-work?
d What is the most common form of e-work?
e What form of e-work does the article say is not likely to grow very quickly?

e-work in the EU

How many teleworkers are there in Europe and how fast are their numbers growing? The answers to these questions are important for policy-makers in employment, transport, environment and social development. They are difficult to answer because many countries have no statistics and definitions of telework vary from country to country. However, a major survey of employers in 18 European countries has made some estimates. The survey found that there are big differences between countries both in the quantity and type of e-work done. The definition of e-work used included all work done away from a company office using a computer and a telecommunications link, by either direct employees or self-employed workers. The study made estimates for four different types of 'individual' e-workers:

Type of e-worker	Use of ICTs (information and computer technologies)	Number in EU
Fully home-based employees.	Employed by a company to work from home all the time.	810,000
Multilocational employees.	Employed by a company to work either at home and in the office, or do mobile work from a home base.	3,700,000
Freelance workers.	As self-employed worker to supply information-based services to companies from home.	1,450,000
Self-employed with own business.	As self-employed worker to run their own business from home.	3,080,000

The study concluded that there were over 9 million e-workers in Europe. The largest single group were multilocational e-workers, estimated at 3.7 million. This group includes employees who work partly at home and partly in the office, as well as those who work while travelling or from clients' premises. Surprisingly, only 810,000 employees worked exclusively from their homes. The media often presents these people as the 'typical' e-worker.

There were, however, an estimated 1.45 million freelancers supplying business services to companies and a further 3 million-plus self-employed people with home-based businesses. This makes a combined total of some four and a half million self-employed teleworkers across Europe - approximately half of the total number of teleworkers.

The study also makes estimates for the future. It suggests that if technological and organisational change continues at current rates, the total number of e-workers will triple, to reach 27.12 million by 2010. The biggest area of growth will be in the 'multilocational' type of work and freelancers providing business services to companies. The number of independent home-based businesses is not expected to increase so fast.

3 Say if the following statements are true (T) or false (F) according to the article:

a People have different ideas about what telework is. ☐
b The survey only included people who worked for themselves. ☐
c The biggest group of teleworkers were those who only worked at home. ☐
d The survey looked at four different types of telework. ☐
e Approximately half the teleworkers have their own businesses. ☐
f In 2010 there will be three times the number of home-based businesses. ☐
g The number of people who do telework for companies will increase a lot. ☐

STAY AT HOME AND GET RICH?

1 There are a lot of adverts for e-work on the Internet. Look at the example below. Have you ever seen an advert like this? How do you think you can make money working from home?

Make money while you work at home

No skill required.

2 2.38 Listen to a conversation where two people discuss the advert in 1 and answer the questions.

a Do the speakers think that the advert is about a real job?
b What do they think are the advantages of working at home?
c What do they think are the disadvantages?

Conditionals

3 Complete the phrases from the dialogue with the missing words. There is a gap for each word - contractions count as one word. Then listen again to check your answers.

a If it .... so easy, everyone .... do it.
b That's a shame. I .... mind working at home if I .... the opportunity.
c I'm not so sure. I wouldn't miss travelling in to work every day, but if I .... at home, ... the contact with people here.
d That's true, but if you .... just come in a couple of days a week, it .... okay. On the other hand, unless you .... somewhere quiet to work, it .... be difficult to get anything done.
e 'Do you think .... be disciplined enough?' 'I don't know. I .... if it .... my own business, but otherwise who knows?'
f They do talk about telework a lot these days. Some people say that if people .... commuting, it .... be much more ecological.

4 The phrases in 3 are all examples of how we use *if* + past + *would/could* to talk about hypothetical or imagined situations. Complete the phrases with your own words.

a If I worked at home/if I didn't work at home, my life ....
b I'd be happier about my job if ....
c I wouldn't be happy about work if ....
d If my company introduced/stopped flexible working, ...
e If I spoke fluent English, ...
f I would say 'no' if ....
g My company would be more efficient if ....
h If people could predict the future, ...

5 A company manager is sitting in his office dreaming about how he could change his life. Put his ideas into a chain of conditionals to recreate his dream like this:

If I left my job, I'd spend more time at home. If I spent more time at home, …

be an enormous success   be completely stressed out again   be more relaxed
come up with a really great business idea   have a lot of responsibilities   have time to think
have to work harder than I want to   set up a company

6 In what circumstances would you …

- start your own business?
- stop working altogether?
- change jobs?
- refuse a promotion?
- ask for a pay rise?
- accept a cut in pay?

I'd start my own business if I had a good idea.

TELEWORKING

1 2.39–2.40 Listen to two interviews with people who telework.
Which speaker:

a has children? ....
b lives in the country? ....
c doesn't have fixed hours? ....
d gets up later than before? ....
e wears her slippers to work? ....
f is self-employed? ....
g works for a company? ....

2 Listen again and complete the chart.

	Speaker 1	Speaker 2
Country		
What did she do before?		
What does she do now?		
What are the advantages of her new work?		
What are the advantages for her employers/clients?		

Discussion

3 Which of the speakers is making a better use of technology, in your opinion? What would the main advantages and disadvantages of working from home be for you?

4 Read the advantages and disadvantages of working from home in the magazine article below. Put each in the correct category in the chart below. The first one has been done for you.

Does working at home really work?		
	Advantages	**Disadvantages**
The workplace		
The working day		
Commuting		
Technology		
Efficiency		
Costs		
Motivation		
Family		1

WORKING AT HOME

The advantages and disadvantages

What do people really think about working from home? We interviewed a cross section of people from different industries about their experiences of teleworking.
As you will see, there was quite a wide variety of opinions.

1 'There is no getting away from the family. When you work in an office you get a chance to escape and meet new people.'
2 'I think us home workers get more done in a shorter time. There are no phone calls or colleagues to slow you down.'
3 'Without the journeys to and from the office you don't get a chance to relax and prepare your mind before you work, or to wind down before you get home. I miss the separation between home and leisure time.'
4 'You do get to see more of your children. The problem is, though, that you're supposed to be WORKING.'
5 'You don't have to sit in traffic jams or walk to work in the rain. Or listen to people talking loudly on their mobiles on the train.'
6 'I think financially you miss out on perks like subsidised refreshments or travel.'
7 'Life is definitely cheaper for the employee. You save on things like transport and smart clothes. It's also cheaper to have lunch at home.'
8 'It's a bit dangerous for workaholics. You can easily find your working time creeping into your leisure time.'
9 'Sharing ideas and problems with your colleagues can make you more productive in some jobs. And the gossip can be really inspiring!'
10 'Space can be a problem. Rooms can become an unpleasant mix of home and office.'
11 'You don't have to work with those obsolete office computers and the company intranet which always seems to be down.'
12 'The flexibility is great. You can work at five in the morning or on a Sunday afternoon.'
13 'I like the freedom. You can open the window, play music and generally make yourself comfortable.'
14 'It can be difficult to get down to work. You have to be very self-disciplined.'
15 'If you have a technical problem, you're on your own. There's no IT expert to call on.'
16 'No boss cracking the whip!'

5 Look at the chart on page 140 and check your answers.

Vocabulary

6 Find words and phrases in the text which mean the same as:

a relax ....
b queues of cars and lorries unable to move forward ....
c benefits not included in your salary ....
d people who can't stop working ....
e out of date and no longer useful ....
f informal exchange of news and information ....
g start ....
h trying to make people work harder ....

7 Complete the sentences with the words and phrases from 6.

a As I have to travel so much I don't hear any of the office ....
b When I get home, I like to .... by listening to some classical music with a glass of wine.
c My boss is a complete .... She just doesn't know how to relax and turn off.
d It's better to have a higher salary than .... like a company car or free meals.
e The problem with buying a computer is that in a couple of years it's ....
f I find it difficult to .... the accounts and usually leave them until the last minute.
g I leave home very early to avoid getting caught in .... on the way to work.
h .... is part of any manager's work.

8 Are the sentences in 7 true for you? If not, change them so that they are.

9 Work with a partner and perform the following roleplay about the advantages of working at home or in the office. Use the phrases in the box to help you.

Speaker A: You are a manager in your company. You are negotiating with the unions to introduce e-work in your company. Convince your partner of the advantages of working at home.
Speaker B: You are a union representative in speaker A's company. The management wants to introduce working from home but you are against it. Convince your partner of the advantages of office work.

If people worked from home, … Most people find / would find that …
From the worker's / company's point of view, it would mean … At the moment, people have to …
There'll be all sorts of problems if … I agree with that, but … That's not necessarily true, because if …

19 E-WORK

LANGUAGE LINKS

Phrase Bank: Explaining things

It's **not really about** working at home.

Then **you are supposed to** persuade your friends.

The **idea is to** …

I **doubt it really works.**

It **sounds more** attractive **than it really is.**

You **can do as little or as much** as you want.

The **basic tools** are …

Vocabulary

Teleworking

The text below is an extract from an article about teleworking. Complete it using the words in the box.

commute desk flexibility home local office

The key word for the future is (a) .... We're not suddenly going to see massive numbers of people working from (b) .... instead of going into the (c) .... We'll see a much more hybrid existence where some of the time people are in the office, maybe at a shared (d) ...., and some of the time at home. And there are of course 'telecentres' – serviced offices which provide an intermediate stage where people can find a (e) .... office instead of having to (f) .... into a town or city centre.

Grammar

Conditionals (future reference)

You can use *if* + past + *would/could* to talk about hypothetical or imagined situations in the future. This is often called the 'second conditional'. Look at these examples:

Condition	Consequence
*If I **knew** the answer,*	*I'd **tell** you.*
*If we **got** the order,*	*we'd **have** years of work.*

Compare these two sentences:

- *If the factory **shuts**, over 200 people **will lose** their jobs.* (The speaker thinks the situation is likely to happen in the future.)
- *If the factory **shut**, over 200 people **would lose** their jobs.* (The speaker thinks the situation is unlikely or improbable in the future.)

Practice 1

Match the parts of the following conditional sentences.

a If we worked from home, …
b If I spent less time travelling, …
c The company would save money …
d People would need good computers …
e Our quality of life would improve …
f If I never saw my colleagues, …
g There'd be problems with this plan …

1 … I'd have more time with my family.
2 … if the staff didn't agree with it.
3 … if they had to work from home.
4 … if we didn't have to commute.
5 … I'd miss the personal contact.
6 … we'd spend less time travelling.
7 … if it invested in home working.

a	b	c	d	e	f	g

Practice 2

David and Sarah are a couple who live in London with their two young children. Read their conversation and complete it using the verb in brackets in the appropriate tense.

Sarah Why don't we move out of the city into the country? I'm fed up with living here. It's so stressful.

David If we (a) .... (live) in the country, it (b) .... (take) about ten minutes for you to get bored with it.

Sarah No it wouldn't. We (c) .... (get) a nice big house – somewhere with a garden. The kids (d) .... (go) to a little village school, and we (e) .... (forget) about all the street violence, traffic and pollution.

David But they (f) .... (like) living in the city, and they (g) .... (miss) their friends. Also, if we (h) .... (move) into the country, we (i) .... (spend) all our time in the car travelling in and out to work.

Sarah Not necessarily. If you (j) .... (ask) your company, they (k) .... (let) you work from home some of the time, and mine would, too.

David I don't think so. I (l) .... (have) to be in contact with people in my job. Anyway, if I (m) .... (be) in the house all day, I (n) .... (go) crazy.

Sarah Don't be so negative. If you (o) .... (spend) more time at home, we (p) .... (see) more of you, and we could do more things like going for walks and playing tennis. You (q) .... (have) a better quality of life.

David I'm sorry. I just don't think you're being realistic. It (r) .... (be) a dream.

Sarah If you (s) .... (be) less selfish, you'd at least think about it.

David Okay, I promise I (t) .... (give) it some thought if that's what you want.

Practice 3

Write conditional sentences using the prompts.

a He doesn't work hard so he isn't very successful.
If he worked harder, he'd be more successful.

b You don't have enough experience so we can't give you the job.

c He can't drive so he has to take taxis all the time.

d I don't have the information so I can't help you.

e I don't like sport so I don't go to the gym.

f He works long hours because he enjoys his job.

g She only does the job because she hasn't got any choice.

h My car is in the garage so I can't take you to the airport.

i Things take him a long time because he isn't very organised.

j He drives an expensive car because he can afford it.

Practice 4

Give advice by completing the sentences.

a If you got up earlier, you wouldn't be late to work so often.

b If you did a computer course,
.

c You would make a better impression
.

d If you had a mobile phone,
.

e You wouldn't be so stressed
.

f If you used the Internet,
.

g You'd do better at the interview
.

h If you didn't complain all the time,
.

Practice 5

Reorganise the words to form questions.

a job do what would you if choose you could
What job would you do if you could choose?

b live you abroad you where if would to had go

c treat people boss how you would were if you the

d didn't language study would what you English you if learn

e would earn how a you the wasn't living salary if important

Practice 6

Respond to the sentences using the prompts. Decide if the situation is real or imaginary.

a Are you going to tell the boss about it? (If / tell / she / sack me)
No way. If I told her about it, she'd sack me.

b Do you think he is going to get the job? (Unless / get nervous / interview / not have / problems)
Yes, I think so.

c Are you going to invite Sarah to the party? (If / invite / Dave / have to invite Sarah too)
I don't have any choice.

d Are you going to invite Su to the party? (If / invite / Su / have to invite Dave too)
No, I can't.
and Jane would be upset.

e I've got an awful headache but we haven't got any aspirin. (If / take / aspirin / you / feel better.)
Oh dear.

f In this job you haven't got enough time to take up a hobby. (If / have / time / do some gardening)
Yes, it's a shame.

g He almost had a accident again on Friday. (Unless / stop / driving like a maniac / kill himself)
What, again?

h Can you give me his mobile number? (If / know / give / it / you)
No, I can't I'm afraid.

20 WORKING LUNCH

According to a poll conducted by the Creative Group, being rude to a restaurant employee is the No. 1 reason a business lunch goes bad.

CHRISTOPHER ELLIOT - HTTP://WWW.ELLIOTT.ORG/POWER-TRIP/FIVE-BUSINESS-LUNCH-FAUX-PAS

Discussion

1 Look at the quote above and discuss the questions with a partner or your teacher.

a Does the result of the Creative Group survey surprise you?
b What do you think the other reasons are? Compare your ideas with the article on page 141.

2 2.41 Neil Klein and Satoshi Tanaka are having a working lunch at a restaurant in Japan. Listen to their conversation and answer the questions.

a Why does Neil like the restaurant?
b Who orders the food?
c What does Neil want to eat?
d What does Neil decide to eat?

3 Put the lines of the conversation in 2 in order. Then listen again and check.

Neil Klein

[1] This looks like a very nice place, Satoshi.
[ ] I'll try the *unagi*, then.
[ ] Okay. Sounds good.
[ ] What's that?
[ ] Yes, I really like the decor. Er, could you order for both of us, Satoshi?
[ ] Hm, I'm sure it is. Actually, do you think I could have a steak?
[ ] No, no, let's have some sake.

Satoshi Tanaka

[ ] And then I think you should try some *unagi*.
[ ] It's eel – grilled and served on a bed of rice. It's delicious.
[ ] Yes, I thought you would like it.
[ ] Well, I'm afraid they don't serve steak here.
[ ] Fine. Would you like some sake, or would you prefer some beer?
[ ] Of course. I think we could have some miso soup to start with. They do it very well here.
[14] Right. Sake it is, then.

4 a Make a list of some of the typical dishes which restaurants serve in your area, using the local name.

Starters
Onion bhaji
Samosa

Main courses
Chicken Madras
Vegetable Biryani

It's	a type of	fish meat vegetable pie
	a	rice dish pasta dish
	made with made from	eggs fruit
	served with	vegetables a salad potatoes a sauce
	cooked	with garlic with spices with herbs in olive oil

b Imagine you are entertaining a visitor. Sometimes you can translate the names of dishes, but you may also have to explain how they are cooked. Act out a conversation with a partner and explain what each dish consists of. Use the phrases on the right to help you.

WHO DOES WHAT?

1 2.42 Complete the second part of Neil and Satoshi's conversation with the phrases in the box. Then listen and check your answers.

job title report to responsible for

Satoshi Neil, I met Jeff Segram earlier this year. What exactly is his a) .... ?
Neil He's the Managing Director.
Satoshi Do you mean the CEO?
Neil Yes, that's what the Americans say. He's the person on the board who is b) .... the day-to-day running of the company.
Satoshi And what about you?
Neil I'm the Product Development Director. I'm on the board as well, but I c) .... Jeff.
Satoshi Right, I see.

2 Find phrases in the conversation in 1 which are similar in meaning to the following:

a is in charge of ....
b Jeff is my boss. ....
c What does he do? ....

3 Act out conversations like the one in 1 using the prompts below. Use your own ideas, if you like.

Who you met	Job title	Responsibilities	Your job title	Who you report to
John Atherstone	Chairman/President	long-term strategy and planning	Managing Director	John Atherstone
Sisi Albright	Director of Marketing/ Vice-President Marketing	marketing policy and the worldwide sales force	Head of Asian Sales Department	Sisi Albright

4 Work with a partner.

a List five job titles in your company, or in other companies.
b Do you know the equivalent job titles in English?
c Explain what each person does.

DOWN TO BUSINESS

1 2.43 Listen to Neil Klein talking to Jeff Segram when he returned to head office, and answer the questions.

a Was the trip a success?
b What do you think happened when they got down to business?

2 2.44 Now listen to the conversation between Neil and Satoshi. What do you think Neil did wrong?

3 Read the information below about doing business in Japan. Does this confirm your ideas in 2?

The Hard Sell

A hard sell is often seen as offensive in Japan. Japanese businesspeople may think that you are trying to convince them because your product is no good. It is better to use a low-key sales pitch and give them objective information. The Japanese are not accustomed to aggressive American techniques that use a persuasive 'winning' argument. If you are not completely honest about your product, your credibility will be damaged and what you say will lose influence. Don't say that yours is 'the best on the market'. It is better to say, 'We sold two million units last year. As you know, our closest competitor sold less than a million.' At the same time, be careful not to criticise competing products. In fact, the Japanese will respect you if you mention the assets of the competition.

4 Act out the conversation between Neil and Satoshi, but this time Neil should follow the advice in the text.

5 Do you have any similar experience of doing business with different cultures? What other differences in the way of doing business do you know about?

LINUX

1 Discuss in groups. What operating system do you have on your work computer – Windows, Mac, Linux or some other? Do you find it easy to use? Have you any experience of other operating systems?

2 Read the article below. Why are some companies changing to Linux? What are the main IT issues that companies are concerned about?

SIEMENS BACK LINUX

One of the world's largest IT companies believes that Linux will take 20% of the market for desktop computers in large institutions within 5 years. Siemens Business Systems, the $6 billion global IT company, say that a desktop running Linux can be as effective as one using Windows, but at a significantly lower cost. Linux is an OS which in its most basic format is free. Users can also modify the program code and adapt it to their needs - this is not possible with commercial software.

Senior program manager Duncan McNutt says that Siemens has been encouraged to investigate the viability of Linux by customers who are annoyed by Microsoft's pricing and licensing policies. However, the risks are high - while lower IT costs are important, maintaining productivity is even more critical. Just one day of productivity lost to a technology problem can be disastrous when it is multiplied by 10,000 or more workers.

For this reason, they tested the software with secretaries and managers, and not IT people. Siemens believe two days of training are all that is needed for the change to Linux. This is the same as the standard time budget for upgrading to a new version of Windows/MS Office. McNutt says that Linux will save 20% to 30% in administration costs, 50% in hardware costs, and 80% in licensing fees. Linux also saves money on hardware because it needs fewer resources and can run on less powerful computers.

And it's not just about saving money. While Linux will save 80% over Microsoft's licensing fees, many large customers are even more unhappy about being in a position where Microsoft can dictate terms to them. Many European institutions are angry that Microsoft's licensing means they cannot afford both upgrades and support on their current budgets. In any case, they would prefer to use their IT spending to help encourage a local tech industry, rather than support a U.S. monopoly. There are now several examples of this at city government level in Germany and France.

Source: www.linux.com

3 Underline the phrases in the article which mean the same as a–h.

a one fifth of company computers in the world will run on Linux
b study if Linux is a good idea
c it is possible to make or lose a lot of money
d the time companies set aside for
e operate on
f demand as much as they want from them
g the money they have reserved for this
h company which has no competition

4 The boss of MedicoTek, a company which trades in medical supplies, has seen the article in 2 and wants the management team to evaluate the possibility of changing to Linux. Work in groups of four. You are going to take part in a meeting to decide if you should change. Each take a role: A, B, C or D.

A

The IT Manager

You agree that changing to Linux would save a lot of money, but there are problems. All your training and experience has been in Windows-based systems, and the move to Linux would mean a great deal of effort and extra work for you. You are also worried about the support available. However, you are also concerned about something else. You know that some of the programs that the company uses at the moment are illegal pirate versions. If the company paid for them, it would be very expensive, but if it gets caught, the consequences would be a large fine for the company and bad publicity.

B

Head of Sales

You spend most of your time travelling. You love technology and depend on lots of different gadgets when you are on the move. You don't think your toys will be compatible with Linux. Apart from that, you believe that there will be problems with your customers because they all use Windows. You also think it will be difficult for staff to adapt to something new and will require a lot of training. For these reasons, you are against any change.

C

The Company President

At present, your margins are not good, and any cost-cutting moves would help the situation. IT is a major part of your budget, and you are worried about the cost of software licences going up in the future. On the other hand, you suspect that the transfer to a new system will be difficult for the company and will possibly have a negative effect on efficiency. On a personal level, you are worried about having to adapt to new software. You also think that if you go ahead, it will be necessary to replace the present IT manager with an expert in Linux-based systems.

D

The Head of Research & Development

You are very keen on Linux and know a lot about it. In fact, many of the specialised scientific programs you use for your work are only available in Linux, and you are convinced that it is a more secure and stable system. You don't think that staff will find it difficult to change to the new software because the new versions are very similar to Windows. You are also part of a group on the Internet which is very critical of Microsoft. You don't like Bill Gates and as a question of principle you think people should use open-source software because it is better.

5 A company in Australia decided to use Linux. Read the article below. What happened? Why do you think the situation created by the new software was unacceptable 'from a business point of view'?

Linux misses Windows of opportunity

Crest Electronics adopted Linux as an operating system for their servers. Then, seven months later, the company made the drastic decision to switch to Windows. What happened?

Crest Electronics is a distributor of video and audio accessories in Australia. To standardise the company's business systems, Anthony Horton, IT manager, chose to move the operating system to Linux. However, the move didn't go as planned and several months later, Mr Horton abandoned Linux for Windows.

Mr Horton explains that stability issues and the complexities of keeping Linux up-to-date caused the problems. For some reason, with Linux the machines would unexpectedly crash, causing havoc for the company's production schedule. Each time the system stopped working, the company were unable to take orders from customers. From a business point of view, this was of course unacceptable. Apart from that, IT staff were spending a lot of time on routine maintenance and updates to the system.

Running out of patience and over budget, Mr Horton took the critical decision to drop Linux for Windows. It only took two days to install Windows on the servers and despite the cost of the licence, the total costs over time were actually lower than Linux because they spent less on IT support. The system proved reliable and easy to maintain and Mr Horton believes this justified the difficult decision to change the operating system again.

ADDITIONAL MATERIAL

01 INTRODUCTIONS

Answers: Language link (p11, crossword)

Across
2 website
3 list
5 e-mail
7 mouse
9 intranet
10 link
11 connection
14 virus
16 browse

Down
1 attachment
4 screen
6 download
8 online
12 click
13 site
15 surf

02 WOMAN AT WORK

Top earners (p13, ex3)

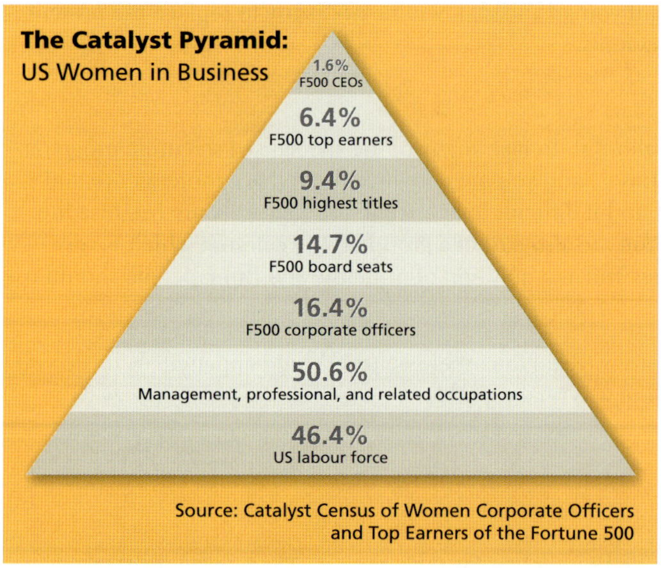

03 TELEPHONE TALK

Indirect questions (p20, ex 2)

A InterAir / help?
B Yes, please / like / information / flight / Munich
A Yes / know / flight number?
B The flight number? / sure / know / leaves Munich / 1730
A yes / IA 345
B Yes / tell / time / gets in?
A arrival / 1910
B 1910 / know / delay?
A No / flight / on time
B Right / thank / much
A welcome / goodbye

04 ASKING QUESTIONS

Answers (p26, ex4)

a Who do you work for?
b Where is your company based?
c Where are you staying?
d Do you speak (*German?*)
e Who is (*Alex*) talking to?
f What do you do? / What's your job?
g Have you got any children? / Do you have any children?
h Where are you from? / Where do you come from?
i Are you married?
j Do you play golf?
k Do you know (*Adriana Bellini*)?

05 COMPANY HISTORIES

Answers: Language link (Business verbs, p35)

a become
b launch/develop
c expand/grow
d produce
e found/start
f achieve
g negotiate
h buy
i provide
j increase

02 WOMAN AT WORK

Blogs (p14, ex4)

For

- People have an alternative source of information to TV, newspapers and radio.
- A more 'human' face for organisations.
- A good way of sharing information and ideas in an organisation.
- A good way to get feedback on ideas and developments - readers can make comments and suggestions.
- An opportunity for the writer - shows they have talent and helps career prospects.
- Sometimes writers can make a living through advertising.

03 TELEPHONE TALK

Sales contacts (p23, ex2)

Speaker B
Situation 1
You work for ADH Graphics. A potential client phones you. Listen to what the customer wants and complete the phone contact form below with the necessary information.

PHONE CONTACT FORM

ADH Graphics

DATE:

CALL INITIATED BY:

CALL HANDLER:

CLIENT:

ADDRESS:

CONTACT:

POSITION:

TEL:

E-MAIL:

NATURE OF BUSINESS:

PURPOSE OF CALL:

COMMENTS:

ACTION REQUIRED:

BY WHOM:

DATE AND TIME:

Situation 2
You work as the Marketing Manager in the marketing department of a clothes manufacturer, Lewis & Co. You are looking for someone to print some labels for your new range of jeans. The labels have to be printed on quality card in two colours. They also have to be cut to the shape of the company logo. You want 10,000 labels. Phone ADH Graphics for an estimate.

05 COMPANY HISTORIES

Answers: Language link (Practice 4, p36)

a Bill Gates didn't found Oracle, he founded Microsoft.
b The Wall Street Crash didn't start a worldwide economic boom, it started an economic depression.
c The six European states didn't sign the Treaty of Madrid, they signed the Treaty of Rome.
d The eleven member states of the European Union didn't adopt the pound as a common currency, they adopted the euro.
e Henry Ford didn't manufacture the first mass-produced electronic components, he manufactured cars.
f Napster didn't have problems over people downloading books, it had problems over music.

06 CORRESPONDENCE

Answers (p38, ex2)

Dear Mr Holmbrook,
Thank you for your order. I just wish to confirm that we have received your order details and we have started to process them. If your item is not in stock or if there are any dispatch problems we will contact you within the next 24/36 hrs. Please contact us if you have not received your order within 7 days at orders@ciclosciclone.com so that we can resolve the issue.
Thank you once again.
Best wishes,
CiclosCiclone (Dispatch Team)

Dear Mr Holmbrook,
We apologise for the delay, but we have worked out the shipping costs of your modified order. It will be an extra £6.99.
To activate this transaction we will need to re-take your card details by phone to process the payment manually. We will need the long number on the front of your card, the expiry date, and the security code on the back of the card.
Thank you for your patience and for shopping with CiclosCiclone.
I look forward to hearing from you.
Best wishes,
Diego Martin

Dear Mr Holmbrook,
Regarding the modification, it will not be a problem. The total amount for your order will be £84.85.
I look forward to hearing from you.
Best wishes,
Diego Martin

Dear Mr Holmbrook,
Please do not worry. We will sort the problem out for you, and your order will be with you shortly. Once again, please accept our apologies.
Best wishes,
Diego Martin

07 HOTELS

Room service (p48, ex3)

Speaker A: Phone room service to make requests for:

- a bottle of Glenfiddich whisky
- someone to fix the minibar
- someone to explain how the TV pay channels work
- someone to sew on a button
- an extra set of clean towels
- (*your own request*)

09 SPIRIT OF ENTERPRISE

Change (p60, ex4)

Speaker B: Look at the information in the table. Work with your partner to complete the missing information and find out how Inditex has changed over the last four years.

Inditex	**four years ago**	**now**
Shops worldwide	2,244	....
New stores in year	....	439
Employees	47,046	....
Countries where the group operates	....	64
% of international sales	55%	....
Chains in group	....	eight - Zara, Kiddy's Class, Pull & Bear, Massimo Dutti, Bershka Stradivarius, Oysho, Zara Home
Turnover	€5,569 million	....
Net profits	....	€1,002 million
Headquarters	Arteixo, La Coruña	

03 TELEPHONE TALK

Sales contacts (p23, ex2)

Speaker A

Situation 1

You work as the Publications Officer in the marketing department of Miki-chan Fashion Accessories. You are currently producing your new company brochure. This is a 32-page, full colour brochure on high quality paper. You need 30,000 copies. Phone ADH Graphics for an estimate. The only problem is that the brochure needs to be ready in ten days. Can they do it?

Situation 2

You work for ADH Graphics. A potential client phones you. Listen to what the customer wants and complete the phone contact form below with the necessary information.

DATE:

CALL INITIATED BY:

CALL HANDLER:

CLIENT:

ADDRESS:

CONTACT:

POSITION:

TEL:

E-MAIL:

NATURE OF BUSINESS:

PURPOSE OF CALL:

COMMENTS:

ACTION REQUIRED:

BY WHOM:

DATE AND TIME:

02 WOMAN AT WORK

What's in a job (p15, ex3)

Speaker A

Your partner has the missing information. Complete the chart by asking questions like the ones in exercise 2 on page 15.

Name	Janice	Delia
Job title		Director of Retail Sales
Type of company		chain of clothing stores
Working hours		45
Responsibilities		Leading a team of 25. Accounts and stock control. Maintaining inventory in stores.
Weekend/Late evening work		One evening and one weekend day a week. Sometimes 'on call' with a pager in case of emergencies.
Most enjoys		Satisfying internal clients. People she works with.
Travel		Not often. Trips to different stores. 3 trade fairs a year.
Holidays		2 weeks. 3 weeks after 5 years' service.
Ratio of women to men in position/field		60% male, 40% female.

10 STRESSED TO THE LIMIT

The ten most stressful jobs (p63 ,ex4)

Measured by level of 21 specific job demands, in the USA the ten most stressful jobs are:

1. Inner-city high school teacher
2. Police officer
3. Miner
4. Air traffic controller
5. Hospital doctor
6. Stockbroker
7. Journalist
8. Customer complaint worker
9. Waiter
10. Secretary

03 TELEPHONE TALK

Telephone frustration (p21, ex2)

The five main frustrations customers experience in dealing with telephone staff are:
- taking too long to answer
- being put on hold and forgotten
- being transferred and having to repeat their enquiry
- being answered by voicemail and other machines
- not having calls returned

13 AIR TRAVEL

The negotiation game (p85, ex2)

Speaker A: Buyer
Negotiate with your partner to get the best deal possible. You get points for each category of the deal – price, quantity, delivery time, and so on. For example, if you agree on a price of 6 euros, you get 2 points, or 3 points if the price is 5.5. Add your points for each category to get your score. To be a successful negotiator you have to get at least ten points.

Points	1	2	3	
Price	6.5	6	5.5	€
Quantity	200	150	100	units
Delivery	3	2	1	weeks
Payment	30	60	90	days
Guarantee	6	12	18	months

Useful language
Let's talk about (*price*)
That's my best offer.
Okay, I can go with that.
It's a deal!
I can't go any higher/lower.
I can't do that.
Can you help me on this?

06 CORRESPONDENCE

Answer: An important order (p41, ex7)

A: S-A-G, can I help you?
B: Yes, this is Elena Moretti from Stern Hydraulics. Could I speak to John Bird, please?
A: Oh, hello, Elena. I'm afraid John isn't here at the moment. Can I take a message?
B: Yes, he sent me an order confirmation – the reference is DH010601 – but the delivery date is wrong.
A: Oh, dear. Can you give me the details?
B: Yes, it says July 7th, but the agreed delivery date was June 22nd. It's really important.
A: I see. Well, I'll tell him as soon as he comes in.
B: Thank you. I'm not at all happy about this. A lot depends on this order.
A: Right, Elena, leave it with me. I'm terribly sorry about this.
B: No, it's not your fault. Just ask John to phone me.
A: All right, then. Bye for now.
B: Goodbye.

14 HIRING AND FIRING

What about the workers? (p92, ex2)

Student A
1 Read the article.
2 Find and underline in the article five examples of the passive.
3 Match the five words and phrases in bold in the article to five of the definitions below. Ask your partner which words match the other five definitions.
a compensate for ....
b percentage of working population without jobs ....
c employees with training and abilities to do technical tasks ....
d people who are unemployed for a long time ....
e what employees can legally expect from their employers ....
f motivating factors ....
g money paid to people who don't have jobs ....
h all the people who work in a country or for a company ....
i the number of employees a company requires to do its work ....
j workers who have contracts limited to a period of time ....
4 Which country do you think the article is about? Could it be your country? Why? Why not? Explain your reasons to your partner.

Skills shortage linked to job insecurity

According to a survey which was carried out by the Confederation of Industry, almost two thirds of the country's companies are experiencing a shortage of **skilled workers**. It is a problem which particularly affects the electronics industry.

The companies claimed that they provided training for their **workforce**, but that this on its own was not sufficient to cover their **staffing needs**.

In an attempt to **make up for** this lack of skilled workers, nearly half of the 670 firms which were contacted said that they had increased their use of **temporary staff**, and over a quarter intended to do the same in the next year.

According to a spokesman for the Confederation, a result of this skills shortage is an increase in feelings of job insecurity among a third of employees. 'It is increasingly difficult to provide people with jobs for life,' he said.

Although over 60% of firms said staff were paid based on their skills and level of competence, the Confederation noted that while salaries at management level were frequently negotiated individually, conditions for clerical and manual workers were usually agreed at a company-wide level.

06 CORRESPONDENCE

On-the-spot decisions (p39, ex 5)

Speaker B: Choose a problem from the table and tell Speaker A. Begin *I've got a problem …* Speaker A will offer a solution and then tell you about a problem. React using one of the solutions below. Say *Don't worry, I'll …*

B *I've got a problem, the battery in my mobile's flat.*

A *Don't worry, I'll lend you mine.*

Problems	Solutions
I can't understand these figures.	I'll look for information on the Internet.
My computer keeps crashing.	I'll send it to you again.
I can't get an answer from the taxi service.	I'll go through it and correct them.
I need to speak to you urgently.	I'll reserve the tickets for you this morning.
The printer is not working properly.	I'll look it up for you.
I don't know how to use this program.	I'll print them out for you.
Our e-mail system isn't working.	I'll get you an aspirin.

14 HIRING AND FIRING

What about the workers? (p92, ex2)

Student B

1 Read the article.

2 Find and underline in the article five examples of the passive.

3 Match the five words and phrases in bold in the article to five of the definitions below. Ask your partner which words match the other five definitions.

a compensate for ....

b percentage of working population without jobs ....

c employees with training and abilities to do technical tasks ....

d people who are unemployed for a long time ....

e what employees can legally expect from their employers ....

f motivating factors ....

g money paid to people who don't have jobs ....

h all the people who work in a country or for a company ....

i the number of employees a company requires to do its work ....

j workers who have contracts limited to a period of time ....

4 Which country do you think the article is about? Could it be your country? Why? Why not? Explain your reasons to your partner.

Unions general strike threat

The whole of the country will be brought to a halt if plans for a general strike go ahead. The threatened strike has been called by the unions in reaction to the government's attempts to cut **unemployment benefits.** With the proposed changes unemployed workers will have to take one of the first three 'acceptable' job offers which are put to them, if the place of work is within 30 km of their homes. If they refuse, they will lose their benefits. Also, anyone who is sacked from their job but appealing against the decision will lose their salary entitlement during the period of the appeal.

The two main unions, each with over a million members, say that the reforms are a direct attack on **workers' rights.** They say the changes will be especially negative for those who lose their jobs, and the **long-term unemployed.** They also claim that the new law will make it easier and cheaper for companies to lay off staff, and will lead to increased job insecurity.

With an 11.3% **unemployment rate,** the highest in the European Union, the reforms have been defended by the government, which says they are necessary in order to be competitive and provide an open and flexible labour market. It says the measures will help solve the problem of unemployment by increasing the **incentives** for people to find jobs. Although its relations with the labour movement have been generally good for the last six years, trade union officials say that this time the government has gone too far.

06 CORRESPONDENCE

An important order (p41, ex9)

Speaker B: You are John Bird. You understand why Elena Moretti is angry. Her company is one of your best customers. Your production department let you down. They promised to meet the delivery date but there was a transport strike and some components didn't arrive. Apologise as much as you can for what happened and invent excuses for everything. Offer to pay for a holiday weekend in London for Elena, but don't make any promises you can't keep.

15 TIME

Wasting time (p99, ex4)

BE SLOPPY

A good hour or two can be gained every few weeks if you keep your desk in a mess. Friday afternoons and Monday mornings are perfect times to set aside for cleaning up your work area. (28 minutes to an hour once a week)

THE COMPUTER

Load your computer with unnecessary programs that make your machine run more slowly. While you're waiting for the PC to process information, sit back and relax. If the boss questions you, just say, 'Damn computers.' He'll laugh and agree with you. (roughly 42 minutes a day)

THE INTERNET

Be very careful misusing the company PC to surf the Net for personal enjoyment. Your boss knows the Internet is a big waste of time and is watching for people who are doing web searches for MP3s and games. The best way is to use it for all research. If you need a phone number for a client across town, use the Internet to find it. Most people just reach for a phone book, which is faster than using the Internet. (roughly 9 to 33 minutes a day)

OFFICE CONVERSATIONS

Enter business conversations around the office that are taking place in the open. You don't have to be a part of the conversation very much. The important thing is to be there physically. Just listen and nod your head when appropriate. (23 minutes to 1.3 hours)

MEETINGS

Go to every meeting you can get into. You'd be surprised at how many people miss the opportunity to waste time by avoiding meetings. Once you're in a meeting, it's all about planning your weekend, or thinking about the football game you watched the night before. (According to Office Studies International the average meeting takes 42 minutes and meetings happen every 5 hours. Count on 2–3 meetings a week.)

Adapted from 'Wasting time at work' by Galen Black
Source: www.vgg.com

03 TELEPHONE TALK

Could you tell me ...? (p20, ex4)

Speaker B

You were just about to send this e-mail to a colleague, when they ring you. Answer their questions.

To:
From:
Subject: Annual sales meeting

You're on flight BA 44362 at 1955 on the 21st December from London Heathrow terminal 2. You'll be met by a taxi which will take you to the factory to meet Mr Fuentes. It's about 40 kilometres from the airport.

You've got one hour with Mr Fuentes. Then you leave to get to the hotel for the meeting. You'll need to go across country. Avis have either a Range Rover 3.6 or Jeep Grand Cherokee, whichever you prefer. An armed guide will accompany you. Don't forget that you'll need to carry your passport and international driving licence at all times.

The hotel is The Lodge. It's in the middle of the forest, twenty miles from the nearest town, and has 5 stars. All the rooms (including the meeting room) have been booked for the whole week.

All the best,

06 CORRESPONDENCE

Answers: On-the-spot decisions (p39, ex 5)

Problems	Solutions
I've got a headache.	I'll get you an aspirin.
I can't understand these figures.	I'll explain them to you.
My computer keeps crashing.	I'll call the IT technician.
We didn't get your fax.	I'll send it to you again.
This report has lots of errors in it.	I'll go through it and correct them.
I can't remember his phone number.	I'll look it up for you.
I need to speak to you urgently.	I'll phone you this afternoon.
I haven't booked my flight to Berlin.	I'll reserve the tickets for you this morning.
The printer is not working properly.	I'll change the ink cartridge.
I don't know how to use this program.	I'll show you how it works.
I need three copies of this proposal.	I'll print them out for you.
I don't know anything about this company.	I'll look for information on the Internet.
Our e-mail system isn't working.	I'll fax the details to you instead.
I can't get an answer from the taxi service.	I'll take you to the airport.

17 OFFICE GOSSIP

Gossip (p110, ex9)

Speaker B: You are the personnel manager of the company with the notice below about coffee breaks. You think a lot of time is wasted by people chatting and gossiping when they are supposed to be working. You are under pressure from the Managing Director to improve the efficiency of the company. Also, recently there have been a lot of rumours about staff cutbacks. Most of them are false but some are true, and this is creating a lot of problems.

COMPANY NOTICE

- Employees may take up to three coffee breaks per day.
- Maximum time at coffee machine: four minutes.
- All 'gossip' or discussion of non-work related matters is prohibited.

CASE STUDY 4 COMPANY STRUCTURE

Truck and wheel (p105, ex3)

Truck & Wheel

Truck & Wheel is a Spanish transport and logistics company which dates from 1975. It has a small headquarters in the north of Spain near the French border. It has 11 branch offices and depots distributed over Spain. It also has 3 offices in Portugal. It began life as a transport company and has grown over the years. It now has a fleet of over 350 trucks but the company has diversified. It supplies logistics support for the automobile, iron and steel industries. For example, in the Volkswagen factory in Pamplona it provides 'just in time' supply of parts for car production with only 90 minutes between the order for each individual car and delivery on the production line.

As the company has grown the structure has been adapted. Each branch has a manager with profit responsibility, but managers may have overall responsibility for particular customer groups or product lines on a national level. As such they are responsible for two profit and loss accounts. For example, the manager of the Madrid office is also responsible for Portugal as a geographical area which has a customer base with very different needs to Spanish clients. This means that middle managers often report to two managers as in a matrix type organisation. It also means that the company has continued to operate out of a small headquarters because top management is spread out over different branch offices. However, the company is now considering creating some separate companies in order to promote a more aggressive commercial approach for certain activities.

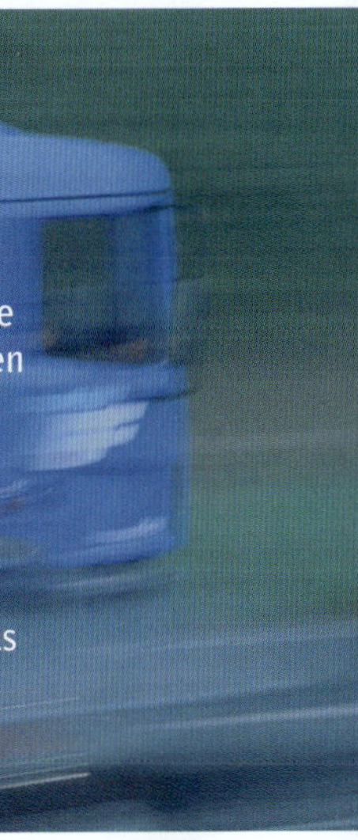

02 WOMAN AT WORK

Blogs (p14, ex4)

Against

- Most people don't have interesting things to say - most blogs are not very good.
- Most people are not very good at expressing their ideas clearly in writing.
- People with something to say don't usually have time to write and people with the time have nothing to say.
- A blog is easy to start but difficult and time-consuming to maintain. A blog which is not updated gives a very bad impression.
- It isn't always a good idea to let people to say what they think - it can create an image of confusion and conflicting messages. Companies are not democracies!

18 E-COMMERCE

Sentences for comparison (p113, ex1)

a When you buy something for yourself with your own money, you're interested in quality and price.

b When you buy something for someone else with your own money, you're interested in price.

c When you buy something for yourself with someone else's money, you're interested in quality.

d When you buy something for someone else with someone else's money, who cares!

18 E-COMMERCE

The future of the Internet (p116, ex3)

Some experts did not either agree or disagree. In some cases they did not answer and in others they gave a different answer.

	Agree	Disagree
At least one devastating attack will collapse the Internet in the next 10 years.	66%	11%
Manufacturers will use computing devices in appliances, cars, phones and even clothes. As a result, there will be more government and business surveillance. The authorities will arrest more people using this evidence.	59%	15%
In ten years, most students will spend at least part of their "school days" in virtual classes.	57%	18%
Tele-work and home-schooling will grow and the barriers between work and leisure will be less clear. Everyday family life will change as a result.	56%	17%
The Internet will make people more creative. They will collaborate with others to make more music, art, and literature. Their work will circulated freely online and will command the attention of a wide public.	54%	18%
All media, including audio, video, print, and voice, will stream in and out of the home or office via the Internet. Computers that control video games, audio, and video will become the centre of the living room. They will link to networked devices around the house, replacing the television's central place in the home.	53%	18%
Internet users will continue to easily copy and distribute digital products freely through anonymous peer-to-peer networks. It won't be possible to stop this.	52%	20%
The number of dangerous fanatics in politics, in religion and in groups which believe in using violence will increase as their networks grow online.	50%	23%
Online medical resources will help solve healthcare problems such as rising costs, poor customer service and lack of access to medical care.	48%	22%
The size of people's social networks will grow. People will have a much wider range of information about job opportunities, personal services, common interests, and products.	42%	29%
People will vote in elections online without problems of security. More people will participate in elections as a result.	39%	30%

07 HOTELS

World records (p49, ex2)

city	chain	price	city	chain	price
Amsterdam	Hilton International	272	London		476
	Accorhotels	238			408
	Crowne Plaza	195			329
	Best Western	178			188
Frankfurt		494	New York	Accorhotels	584
		330		Hilton International	457
		157		Crowne Plaza	268
		152		Best Western	260
Geneva	Crowne Plaza	394	Paris		420
	Hilton International	357			381
	Accorhotels	260			361
	Best Western	148			254

19 E-WORK

Teleworking (p123, ex5)

Does working at home really work?		
	Advantages	Disadvantages
The workplace	13	10
The working day	12	8
Commuting	5	3
Technology	11	15
Efficiency	2	9
Costs	7	6
Motivation	16	14
Family	4	1

06 CORRESPONDENCE

Answers: Language link (p42, crossword)

Across		Down	
1	delivery	2	immediately
6	prompt	3	expensive
8	informal	4	signature
9	handwriting	5	details
10	fax	7	courier
13	business	11	apologise
15	correspondence	12	reply
19	check	14	Internet
21	decision	16	worried
22	message	17	phoning
24	annoyed	18	mistake
28	welcome	20	that
29	down	23	skills
30	confirm	25	order
		26	send
		27	cost

09 SPIRIT OF ENTERPRISE

Answers: Language links (p62, Practice 5)

The Inditex group consists of almost a hundred companies dealing with textile design, production and distribution. Its unique management techniques and its successes (a) **have turned** Inditex into one of the world's largest fashion groups.

The first Zara shop (b) **opened** in 1975 in La Coruña in northern Spain. Over the years the group (c) **has added** other chains to the original Zara, each covering a different market sector. In 1991 the group (d) **created** Pull & Bear, and in 1995 (e) **acquired** 100% of Massimo Dutti. Bershka (f) **started** its activity in 1998, followed by the acquisition of Stradivarius in 1999. Two years later Inditex (g) **launched** Oysho, a chain specialising in fashionable lingerie and underwear.

In the last four years the number of shops in the group (h) **has reached** a figure of over a three thousand, and the group now has operations in 64 countries worldwide. In the same period, sales (i) **have increased** by 22% and net profits by 25%.

Despite its size, the group still controls its activities from a logistical centre in Arteixo, a village in the north-west of Spain, but in 2003 it (j) **finished** work on 'Plataforma Europa', a new distribution centre in Zaragoza.

13 AIR TRAVEL

The negotiation game (p85, ex2)

Speaker B: Seller

Negotiate with your partner to get the best deal possible. You get points for each category of the deal – price, quantity, delivery time, and so on. For example, if you agree on a price of 6 euros, you get 2 points, or 3 points if the price is 6.5. Add your points for each category to get your score. To be a successful negotiator you have to get at least ten points.

Points	1	2	3	
Price	5.5	6	6.5	€
Quantity	100	150	200	units
Delivery	1	2	3	weeks
Payment	90	60	30	days
Guarantee	18	12	6	months

Useful language

Let's talk about (*price*)
That's my best offer.
Okay, I can go with that.
It's a deal!
I can't go any higher/lower.
I can't do that.
Can you help me on this?

20 WORKING LUNCH

Discussion (p127, ex1)

A business lunch is part meal, part meeting. It's informal, but at the same time there's a long list of unwritten rules that can't be broken. According to a poll conducted by the Creative Group, an advertising and marketing firm in Menlo Park, Calif., being rude to a restaurant employee is the No. 1 reason a business lunch goes bad. What are other reasons?

- Arriving late.
- Bad table manners.
- Dressing too casually.

But what else can go wrong and how do you keep it from happening? Here's a look at some other common business-lunch 'faux pas' that are easily preventable:

- **Choosing the wrong restaurant.** For example: inviting a prospective client who is allergic to shellfish to a seafood restaurant.
- **Sitting at the wrong table.** What if you can't discuss the deal because of all the noise? Or the quiet restaurant where you have to whisper for fear of being overheard by the people at the next table? The ideal establishment is one where you don't have to shout but you have some privacy.
- **Saying the wrong thing.** At an American business lunch, it's considered inappropriate to get down to business before the waiter has handed you the menu. In other countries, you don't talk business until the first glass of wine has been poured and the host offers a toast. Elsewhere, ordering wine is considered inappropriate.
- **Ending it the wrong way.** A verbal "thank you" is always appropriate (even if it didn't go as you planned). If possible, send a thank-you note (which is also another opportunity to send your business card), noting what you specifically liked about the meal and, possibly, recapping the conversation.

Source: www.elliott.org

CASE STUDY 4
COMPANY STRUCTURE

Pros and Cons of Different Structures (p104, ex1)

	Advantages	Disadvantages
Functional	Specialisation – each department focuses on its own work. Accountability – someone is responsible for the section. Clarity – employees understand theirs and others' roles.	Closed communication could lead to lack of focus. Departments can become resistant to change. Coordination can be difficult and may take too long. Gap between top and bottom.
By Product/ Activity	Clear focus on market segment helps meet customers' needs. Positive competition between divisions. Better control as each division can act as separate profit centre.	Duplication of functions (e.g. different sales force for each division). Negative effects of competition. Lack of central control over each separate division.
By Geographical Area	Serve local needs better. Positive competition. More effective communication between firm and local customers.	Conflict between local and central management. Duplication of resources and functions e.g. a different sales force for each product.
By Project	Facilitates a multi-disciplinary or cross-functional way of working. Can flatten a business' hierarchy. Ensures a business is organised according to its core activities. Makes better use of employees' skills.	Can make organisational boundaries less clear. Confuses lines of accountability as employees may report to several different managers.

07 HOTELS

Answers: World records (p48, ex1)

Largest	MGM Grand	Las Vegas	6,276 rooms
Tallest	Rose Tower	Dubai	72 floors
Most expensive room	MGM Grand	Las Vegas	$5,000 room/night
Highest	Lhasa Hotel	Lhasa	12087 feet above sea level
Most northern	Ny-Ålesund	Svalbard, Norway	78°55'N 11°56'E
Most southern	Ushuaia	Ushuaia, Argentina	54°48'S 68°18'W
Oldest	Hoshi Ryokan	Awazu, Japan	It opened in 717

02 WOMAN AT WORK

What's in a job (p15, ex3)

Speaker B

Your partner has the missing information. Complete the chart by asking questions like the ones in exercise 2 on page 15.

Name	**Janice**	**Delia**
Job title	Production Manager	
Type of company	software company	
Working hours	Normally 40-50 hours but can be up to 75	
Responsibilities	Managing website. Liaising with international offices.	
Weekend/Late evening work	Not in her present position.	
Most enjoys	Doing something that makes a real difference to the company.	
Travel	Occasional trips to other offices.	
Holidays	3 weeks	
Ratio of women to men in position/field	Half the department are women but only two have technical skills.	

LISTENING SCRIPTS

01 INTRODUCTIONS

1.01

A: Okay everybody, can we make a start? First of all, allow me to welcome you all to Ashbourne Management College. My name is Mariah Wilson and I am the main tutor for our 'Performance Through People' course. It's always useful to know something about the background of the other participants so we normally begin by asking you to introduce yourself to the rest of the group. Perhaps we could start with you, Jan?

B: Yes, hello. My name is Jan Werner. **I work for Metronet Fibre**. Our main business is fibre optics. We install urban fibre-optic networks for telecommunication systems all over the world. I'm director of communications in the HR department. I'm Norwegian but I live and **work in the Czech Republic. Our head office is in Prague**. That's where I'm based. At the moment, though, I am spending a lot of time visiting our other offices in Europe. I organise and run different management training courses for our senior management.

A: Thank you Jan. Silvia?

C: Well, I'm Silvia Fortuni. I'm Catalan and I'm from Barcelona. **I work for a big retail chain** with franchises all over the world. We manufacture and sell clothes and fashion accessories but of course, my role is related to personnel. I work out of our headquarters in Barcelona and I am director of staff training responsible for recruitment and training in the European area. I have to say I love my job and I welcome the opportunity to learn something more about performance and motivation. I think that's it. If you want to know anything more, you can ask me.

D: My turn? Hi everybody. My name is Jean-Christophe Marchal but most people just call me JC. I'm here because I have a new job in the HR department of Aqualux. I'm mainly involved with staff training. As I say, it's a new job for me but I have five years' experience working in the HR field. You probably think from my accent that I'm French. Actually, I'm Belgian but I'm based in Paris where we have our main office. Aqualux is a utilities company and our main activity is the supply and treatment of water and waste.

A: Thank you JC. Now, Elena, I think it's your turn …

1.02

Hello and welcome to Business Talk. If you've ever had a meal in an Indian restaurant in the UK, you've probably sampled the subject of this week's programme. This month we are looking at the retail food trade and today we examine the amazing success of one of the fastest-growing beer brands in the UK. Cobra exports to more than 45 countries worldwide, and now with subsidiaries in India, South Africa and the US, it is becoming a mainstream, global beer brand. Later on we talk to the founder and managing director, Karan Bilimoria, but first, here's a quick profile of the company.

Back in 1989 an unknown Cambridge graduate with previous business experience set up Cobra Beer to fill a very specific gap in the market. Karan Bilimoria noticed how normal beers left eaters of curry feeling very full and bloated, so he had the idea of a lighter, less gassy beer. This is its USP or unique selling point but his aim was to brew the best Indian beer possible and to make it a global brand. He started by importing his beer from India, but nowadays Cobra is brewed in the UK, Poland, Belgium, the Netherlands and India. Cobra Beer uses only natural ingredients but retains a premium strength of 5%. As an indication of its quality, Cobra Beer won 6 Grand Gold Medals and 14 Gold Medals at the 2007 Monde Selection beer awards in Brussels.

Cobra Beer has a turnover of £75 million a year and supplies over 6,000 restaurants and most major supermarkets and retail drink chains in the UK. It is also available in nearly 6,000 pubs and clubs. The company is expanding rapidly with a growth rate of 42% in the last ten years.

The company headquarters are in Fulham, in southwest London but it now has subsidiaries in India, South Africa and the US. As a current development it is extending operations to meet the demand for Cobra in the European and worldwide market, but Karan says that innovation is still the key to the Cobra philosophy. His business principles from the outset are very straightforward. They are: the product comes first; be different and better; never ask for exclusivity; treat suppliers and customers with the same respect; maintain an informal yet professional office atmosphere.

02 WOMAN AT WORK

1.03

A: What's that?

B: Oh, it's a blog by a woman who's a top manager in a big telecom company.

A: What does she say?

B: It's about her daily routine. I wonder how she can survive on five hours' sleep.

A: It's probably not true. People can invent anything they like in blogs. **What do you think about** people blogging?

B: It depends what you mean by blog.

A: Well I'd say that most people who are normal don't have much to say that's of any interest to anyone else.

B: **Yes, you're probably right, but** it depends on the type of blog. Technical blogs can be quite useful.

A: **What do you mean?**

B: You have some problem with the computer, do a search on Google and find the solution in some techie's blog.

A: Okay, but that's an example of a blog which has useful information on a very specific subject. Most blogs are just people's opinions.

B: Well, that's democratic.

A: **I'm not sure about that.** The information might just be rubbish.

B: Aren't you being a bit negative? **For example, from a business point of view** they can be very useful.

A: Our company blog for example?

B: Yes, it's a good way for us to share information and ideas.

A: You mean complain about things and gossip. It's a good theory but in practice it doesn't work. In any case, you can't say what you really think because you might get into trouble.

B: Maybe, but look at Sally McDermott's blog. It makes her company look more human. It's good public relations.

A: **Do you really think** it makes any difference? Who's going to read it anyway?

B: Lots of people. Me, for a start.

1.04

A: Hi Eddie. How are you?

B: Oh hello Jennie. I'm fine. And you?

A: Fine thanks. How's Fiona?

B: Oh, she's okay. She's got a new job.

A: Really, that's good.

B: Well, yes, I suppose so but I'm worried she's working too hard.

A: Oh dear. Does it involve long hours?

B: Officially 40 hours but she often works late. We don't see her at home much.

A: What's she doing?

B: It's the same company - you know - educational software, but she's now regional marketing manager for Western Europe.

A: Sounds impressive. What does it involve?

B: Apart from being in charge of the sales reps she's also involved in new product development and the whole marketing strategy of the company.

A: Does it mean a lot of travelling?

B: It seems to. At least a couple of trips a month.

A: I see.

B: I don't mind that. It's the weekends that cause problems.

A: Does she have to work weekends?

B: Not every weekend but we can never make plans.

A: Oh dear. How much holiday does she get?

B: It's not bad. Three weeks a year. But that's a long way off.

A: You're being a bit negative. Does she enjoy it?

B: It's hard work but I think she enjoys the challenge.

A: But you're not very happy.

B: I'm happy for her. The money's good and it's great for her career but there is a downside.

A: Well, it's always difficult at the beginning. Anyway, give her my regards. Why don't we go for a drink sometime?

B: Okay, I will and yes, I'd like that.

Phrases in bold are from the Phrase Banks in the Language Links

03 TELEPHONE TALK

1.05

A A: Yes?
B: **Can I speak to** Derek LaMotte please?
A: Who?
B: Derek LaMotte. Is that ILM?
A: What number did you want?
B: 0837 621882.
A: No, I'm afraid **you've got the wrong number**.

1.06

B You have one message from 903586759 at 18.30 on April 1. … 'Hi, it's Dave here …

1.07

C C: **This is the** BetaGuide directory service. Donna speaking. Which city?
D: I'm in Portsmouth. **Can you give me the number of** Budget Car rental please?
C: Just one moment. I have three numbers.
D: Oh. I need to call them to report a breakdown.
C: Okay. It must be this one.
D: I think the number …
E: The number you require is 0453 678234. The number you require is 0453 678234.

1.08

D F: UKN Systems. Janet speaking.
G: Morning. My name's Peter Bland from Pressic SA. I arranged to meet Derek LaMotte at a factory out here on the Houghton Industrial Estate but I can't find it. Could you give me his mobile number so I can ask him where it is?
F: Err, yes. Just one moment.
G: It's probably just around the corner.
F: It's 07663493782.
G: I'm sorry. Could you say that again a bit slower?
F: 07663493782.
G: Right. Got it. Thanks.
F: Bye.
G: Yeah. Goodbye.

1.09

E Remember, you have the chance to win £1000. Ring now on 0902386980. I'll repeat that for you. If you know the answer, phone us now on 0902386980.

1.10

A: InterAir, can I help you?
B: Yes, please. I'd like some information about a flight arriving from Munich.
A: Yes. Do you know what the flight number is?
B: The flight number? I'm not sure. I know it leaves Munich at 1730.
A: Oh, yes, that's IA 345.
B: Yes, that's it. Could you tell me what time it gets in?
A: Yes, the arrival time is 1910.
B: 1910. Do you know if there's any delay?
A: No, the flight is on time.
B: Right, thank you very much.
A: You're welcome. Goodbye.

1.11

A A: **Can I have extension 305, please?**
B: I'm afraid **the line is engaged**. Will you hold?

1.12

B A: Could I just check that? You need 50 units by Friday, and Mr Johansson can contact you on 943 694726.
B: Yes, that's correct.
A: Right, Mr Smith. I'll give him the message as soon as he's free.

1.13

C A: … and it really isn't good enough.
B: Yes, Mr Wright. I understand what you're saying and I apologise for the error. As soon as Mr Downs is back I'll ask him to get in contact with you. I'm really sorry about this.
A: Right, thank you. I realise it's not your fault.

1.14

D A: Could I have the Sales Department, please?
B: One moment, please. Just putting you through now.

1.15

E A: Shonagh Clark speaking.
B: Hello, **I'm phoning about** your letter of 12th June.

1.16

F A: This is Jorgen Bode here. **Could I speak to** Jean Simmons, please?
B: Oh, I'm sorry, Mr Bode, but Ms Simmons isn't in the office right now. Can I ask her to call you back? Or I can contact her on her mobile if it's urgent.

1.17

A: Hello, **could I speak to** Mr White, please?
B: Speaking. How can I help you?
A: Hello, Mr White. My name is Clarkson, from Bellstone & Smith, the elevator manufacturers.
B: Yes, I think I've heard of you.
A: I'm in charge of the customer support department. I'm phoning to ask for an estimate. It's for a service manual we're preparing.
B: Oh, yes. I don't think we've done anything for you before.
A: No, that's right. We're in the process of updating all our manuals. If the price is right, it will mean quite a lot of work.
B: I see. Well, could you give me the details, then?
A: Yes, it's for a manual of just over 100 pages.
B: 100 pages. Could you tell me what size?
A: It's in A5. We want to print 20,000. But I'd like estimates for 10,000 and 30,000 as well.
B: I see. Is it in colour?
A: No, it's in black and white. Mainly text. The cover is in colour, though. I can put it all on a CD for you. Is that all right?
B: Yes, that would be perfect. Could I just read my notes back?
A: Yes, go ahead.
B: You want quotes for print runs of 10,000, 20,000 and 30,000 of an A5 100-page manual in black and white. The cover is in colour and you'll be presenting the material on CD.
A: That's right.
B: Would you like me to visit you with some samples?
A: Yes, okay.
B: Would tomorrow morning suit you?
A: No, I'm out of the office tomorrow. How about Friday? About ten o'clock?
B: Friday … the 16th … at ten. That's fine. I'll bring the estimates with me and we can discuss the details then.
A: Fine.
B: Oh, could you give me the address?
A: Yes, it's 14, Clapham Road, London SW14.
B: And your telephone number?
A: 0207 839 4216.
B: 0207 839 4216. Right. Oh, do you have e-mail?
A: Yes, it's clarkson.bellstone@lineone.com.
B: Can I just check that? clarkson, dot, bellstone at lineone, dot, com.
A: Okay, then, Mr White. See you on Friday.
B: Yes. Goodbye, then.
A: Goodbye.

04 ASKING QUESTIONS

1.18

Conversation 1

A: Hello, do you mind if I join you?
B: Er, no, not at all.
A: How do you do? My name's Rick Van Looy.
B: Hi. Pleased to meet you. I'm Florent Rondele.
A: Are you from around here, then?
B: No, but my company has a store in town. Actually, I live in France.
A: So, what do you do, Florent?
B: I'm in marketing. I work for a retail company. We deal mainly in leisure goods.
A: Do you mean sports equipment?
B: Well, both sports and casual wear. Clothes, shoes, accessories, stuff like that. We have stores in several countries.
A: Sounds like a big operation. How many stores have you got?
B: Nearly fifty in total. And what line of business are you in, Rick?
A: Well, quite similar really. I'm a sales manager for a large Dutch clothing firm, Verweij Fashion – do you know it?
B: Yes, of course. Are you opening a store here, then?
A: Yes, we're looking at possible sites at the moment.
B: Hm. That can be a slow process. Rick, do you fancy something to drink?
A: Erm, yeah, thanks.
B: Come on, then. There's a table free over there.

1.19

Conversation 2

A: Excuse me, does this belong to you?
B: Oh, thank you very much.
A: It was on the floor.
B: Yes, I was looking for it just now. I wanted to finish this crossword. I'm feeling a bit groggy, actually.
A: Yes, it's a long flight.
B: Isn't it? Have you got the time?
A: Yes, it's … erm … just after midnight.
B: So, do we land soon?
A: Yes, in about half an hour.
B: Oh, good. Do you know Bangkok?
A: Yes, I live there. Is this your first trip there?
B: Yes, it is actually.
A: On business, I suppose?
B: Yes, I'm visiting a supplier.
A: Oh, really? I wonder if I …

1.20

A: Do you know Jan Nowacki?
B: Yes, isn't he Director of Business Development at Guinness?
A: Not any longer. Now he's the Public Relations Manager at the National Bank of Poland.
B: The National Bank of Poland, that's interesting. Do you have any contact with him in your work?
A: Not really, but I occasionally play golf with him.
B: What's he like?
A: He's a nice chap. You'd like him.

CASE STUDY: INTERNET ACCESS

1.21

We introduced our policy in 1997, when we gave each employee access to e-mail and the Internet. It covered personal use, downloads, the use of e-mail between colleagues and what would happen if guidelines were ignored. We felt it was very important to have a policy - if your employees don't know the rules, you can't blame them for breaking them. The policy is two pages long and is part of our employee handbook. Each employee signs for a copy during their induction and it is then theirs to keep and refer to.

With the Internet, rather than ban personal use we allow our employees to do what they want, as long as they do it during a break. We do allow personal e-mails, but not during work time. The only thing completely banned is internal, non work-related e-mails. This is because if an employee gets an external message they could pass it around internally during their break to colleagues who are still working, and disrupt them.

We also won't tolerate anyone looking at adult websites and we ask employees to be careful with what they download. If you allow your employees to access the Internet freely, you have to protect your IT system against viruses.

We have only had a problem once – one of our key members of staff was sending personal e-mails back and forth to her boyfriend all day. When we did take action, it not only got her focused on her job once again, but also showed the rest of our staff that we would enforce our policy - even against a key employee.

05 COMPANY HISTORIES

1.22

Nintendo is one of the best-known brands in the world and the leader in interactive video entertainment - a multi-billion dollar industry. The company has a history which dates back to the nineteenth century. In 1889 Fusajiro Yamauchi founded a small company to manufacture playing cards. The company continued this activity over the years and in 1953 it manufactured the first mass-produced plastic playing cards in Japan.

In 1963 the company changed its name to Nintendo Co. Ltd. and started to manufacture games as well as playing cards. A couple of years later in 1965, company boss Hiroshi Yamauchi hired a young engineer, Gunpei Yokoi. Gunpei was later the engineer behind many of the company's most successful products.

In 1975 Nintendo formed a partnership with Mitsubishi Electric to take advantage of their micro-processor technology. Throughout the 70s Nintendo was the leader in video games for public arcades, but in 1983 it developed the NES, the first console for use at home. In another clever move, they negotiated deals with third-party companies to produce new games. This was easier and faster than producing the games themselves.

In 1989 Nintendo launched Game Boy – the first console you could carry around in your pocket. The package included Tetris - one of the most addictive games of all time. In 1990 Nintendo sales represented 10% of the trade deficit between Japan and the USA.

However, there were problems ahead and in 1994, Sony released the Playstation. The Playstation worked as a CD player as well as a console and was a huge success. Nintendo faced a major new competitor and as a result, its sales suffered badly.

In 2001 Nintendo launched a new console, the GameCube. Sales were poor but at the same time in the USA, their 'GameBoy Advanced' dominated the handheld market. With the disappointing sales of the GameCube and the success of GameBoy Advanced, Nintendo decided to concentrate on the portable market. In 2004 they released a new handheld console - the Nintendo DS (Dual Screen). The DS was popular but again had to compete against Sony and its new handheld, the PSP.

So, in 2006, things looked bad for Nintendo but once again, a brilliant innovation saved them from disaster - the 'Wii'. Its most brilliant feature is a 'wand' which allows players to physically move while they play a game on screen - a completely new concept because there are no complicated controls and anyone can play with it. With a clever advertising campaign in a very short time it achieved higher levels of sales than all its competitors.

1.23

How old is the Internet? It's difficult to fix a single date for the birth of any complex technology. In the case of the Internet, people suggest different dates. It depends on what they understand the Internet to be.

We know that in 1965, the Advanced Research Projects Agency (ARPA) under the US Department of Defence began work on a system to connect computers. They called the project ARPANET.

On September 2nd, 1969, in a laboratory at the University of California, Professor Leonard Kleinrock connected the first two machines. At its simplest level, the Internet connects computers so for many people that day the Internet was born. The next month they sent the first message to a computer at Stanford University. The message was 'lo'. They wanted to send the words 'log in' but when they typed 'g' the system crashed. So appropriately, this first word was a phonetic version of 'hello'.

By January 1970 ARPANET connected computers in four American universities, and by the following year there were 23 in the system, connecting different universities and research institutes. In 1973 Ray Tomlinson sent the first e-mail via ARPANET. In the same year the Net went international, connecting computers in England and Norway.

The ARPANET was a single network, but the next step was to connect different networks and to create an 'internetwork'. In 1974 Bob Kahn and Vincent Cerf invented a software that allowed networks using different operating systems to connect to each other. The software, called TCP/IP, became the universal language of the Internet on January 1st, 1983. Many experts argue that this event was the real birth of the Internet because it made it possible to link different networks in one web.

More and more networks joined the system and the number of connected computers increased dramatically: from 10,000 in 1984 to 100,000 in 1987. By the early 1990s the World Wide Web was the most popular way of browsing the web, and the network was accessible to anyone in the world with a computer. In 1992 the number of hosts reached 1,000,000.

In 1993 two programmers, Marc Andreessen and Eric Bina, launched the first version of Mosaic. This was the first graphics-based browser of the type we all use today and made possible what many people now understand as the Internet - an easy means to browse websites, get information and spread news.

06 CORRESPONDENCE

1.24

A: JFA Fabrics, can I help you?
B: Yes, I'm phoning from Natural Furnishings in Chelsea. Could I speak to Peter Simpson, please?
A: I'm afraid he's out of the office right now. Can I help you?
B: Well, I sent him a text message and he hasn't replied. It's really quite urgent.
A: Can you tell me what it's about?
B: It's a bit complicated to explain. I need a copy of a certificate for customs. Maybe he didn't get my message. Can I just check his mobile - 07636746384?
A: Hang on. Yes, that's the right number. Listen, why don't you send the details to me by e-mail and I'll send you a copy of the certificate as an attached PDF.
B: Yes, that's a good idea. What's your e-mail address?
A: Jim, dot. That's J-I-M, dot, J-F-A, at lineone, dot, net. Lineone is all one word.
B: Can I just check that? Jim, dot, JFA, at lineone, dot, net.
A: Yes, that's right.
B: Don't worry. **I'll deal with** the e-mail straight away. By the way, my name's Cathy, Cathy Slater. You must be Jim.
A: Yes, Jim Kutz. Don't worry about the certificate. You'll have it by this afternoon.
B: Okay, thanks for your help.
A: You're welcome. Bye.

1.25

A: Have we got a decision from Jim about the Mason contract?
B: No, don't worry, I'll ring him about it this afternoon.
A: I tried – there's no answer.
B: Well, I'll send him an e-mail, then.
A: You can't – our Intranet is down.
B: Never mind – I'll send him a fax.
A: I don't think they have one.
B: Well, in that case, I'll write him a letter before I leave the office.
A: Oh, come on, that will take far too long.
B: So, we'll fly out to see him!
A: Oh, that's a bit expensive …

1.26

A: S–A–G, can I help you?
B: Yes, could I speak to John Bird?
A: I'm afraid he's not in the office right now. Can I take a message?
B: Oh dear! It's an urgent order – we need five hydraulic pumps by 22 June.
A: Just a minute. Could you tell me your name, please?
B: Yes, I'm sorry. It's Elena Moretti from Stern Hydraulics in Switzerland.
A: Right, I'll **take down the details** and get John to contact you. Did you say five units?
B: Yes, the reference is SG 94321.
A: SG 94321 – five units.
B: Yes, that's right. But the important thing is the delivery date – 22 June.
A: I don't think that will be a problem.
B: Good, it's for a new customer.
A: I see. Right, when John comes in, I'll tell him immediately. Could you confirm the order by e-mail?
B: Yes, of course. Thanks very much.
A: You're welcome. Goodbye.
B: Goodbye.

1.27

A: Could I speak to Elena Moretti, please?
B: Speaking. Is that John?
A: Yes. Hello, Elena. I'm phoning back about your order.
B: Yes, it's quite urgent.
A: Don't worry. I've got all the details in your e-mail. No problem.
B: That's good. I was rather worried about it.
A: Well, can I help you with anything else?
B: No, but I hope we get more business from this customer.
A: Yes, of course. Okay, I'll be in touch. Bye for now.
B: Goodbye.

1.28

A: S-A-G, can I help you?
B: Yes, this is Elena Moretti from Stern Hydraulics. Could I speak to John Bird, please?
A: Oh, hello, Elena. I'm afraid John isn't here at the moment. Can I take a message?
B: Yes, he sent me an order confirmation – the reference is DH010601 – but the delivery date is wrong.
A: Oh, dear. Can you give me the details?
B: Yes, it says July 7th, but the agreed delivery date was June 22nd. It's really important.
A: I see. Well, I'll tell him as soon as he comes in.
B: Thank you. **I'm not at all happy about this.** A lot depends on this order.
A: Right, Elena, leave it with me. I'm terribly sorry about this.
B: No, it's not your fault. Just ask John to phone me.
A: All right, then. Bye for now.
B: Goodbye.

07 HOTELS

1.29

A: Hello. My connecting flight, IB621, was delayed so I've missed the flight to Caracas.
B: Yes, sir. I'm sorry about that. You're booked in on the next flight.
A: Right, but it's not until eleven tonight, right?
B: Yes. I'm afraid there's nothing before.
A: That's nearly eight hours to wait. Can you recommend a hotel I could try?
B: You could try the Travel Inn. It's not far from the terminal building.
A: Thanks. I really need somewhere to sleep.
B: Would you like me to phone for you, sir?
A: No, that's okay. I need to stretch my legs anyway. Thanks very much.

1.30

A: Good afternoon.
B: Good afternoon. Do you have any rooms available?
A: Yes sir. Is it just for tonight?
B: Yes. Well, actually **I have a flight** at eleven this evening so I'll check out in a few hours. I really need to get some sleep. Is it possible to pay for a room by the hour? I mean, do you have any reduced rates or something?
A: Err … no sir. I'm afraid not. I have to charge you for the whole night. I'm sorry, but that's the hotel policy.
B: Well, never mind. I'll take it anyway.
A: Okay, could I see your passport please? And I'll need a credit card.
B: Yes, of course. Here you are.
A: Would you like anything else sent up to your room?
B: Yes, please. I'd like a ham and egg sandwich and a diet coke. Oh, I need to send some e-mails. Is there Internet access available?
A: That's no problem. You can pick up the hotel wi-fi in every room.
B: Right, thank you.
A: You're welcome. Have a good stay.

1.31

A: Room service. My name is Johan. Can I help you?
B: Yes, this is room 301. Could I have an early morning call, please?
A: Certainly, sir. What time would you like the call?
B: At half past six.
A: 6.30. No problem. Would you like breakfast sent up to your room?
B: No, thanks. I'll have it in the dining room.
A: The dining room doesn't open for breakfast until 7.30.
B: Oh, in that case I will have it in my room. Just coffee and a croissant.
A: Coffee and a croissant. Anything else?
B: No, that's all.
A: Okay. Good night, sir.
B: Thank you. Good night.

08 DID I EVER TELL YOU …?

1.32

A: Look at that car!
B: Yes, very nice. It's a Porsche 911.
A: Did I ever tell you about the time I had a ride in a Porsche?
B: No, I don't think so.
A: It was when I was a student. I was hitch-hiking in Europe and a man in a Porsche stopped. He took me all the way across Austria. We went about 220 kilometres an hour all the way.
B: What about the police?
A: Well, they stopped us about four times, but this chap just showed some identity card and they waved us on.
B: Was he someone important, then?
A: I don't know, I didn't ask. I suppose he was some sort of high-ranking official. He didn't talk much, but he did drive well.

1.33

a Yes, that was a long time ago. It was while I was living in Italy. I had this apartment in the centre of Milan …

b I can remember what happened. It was before I started working here. I was working on a temporary basis …

c No, it wasn't until much later. It was after I left university. I'd got my degree …

d Oh, yes, that reminds me. It was when I was working at ICL. I was in the marketing department …

e I had more time in those days. It was before I got married. In fact, I hadn't even met Mary …

f The timing was awful. It was just after my children were born. And there I was without …

g I'd just arrived in London. I was looking for a job. I bought the paper every day …

h Yes, I was still studying at the time. I was doing my Masters in the States. At the Harvard Business School, in fact …

i I was nineteen. I was studying at Cambridge. Things weren't going very well …

j No, it was with a different set-up. I was working for a small company north of here. One day the boss walked into …

k I was having a gap year after university. I was travelling through Asia. I'd just arrived in Saigon and …

l It happened last March. I was staying at the Continental Hotel in Prague. Lovely hotel, I recommend it.

1.34

a We had a good time, but it did cost a fortune!

b He got the job, but he did have to marry the boss's daughter!

c We got there in the end, but we did sit on a bus all day.

d I got a good job, but I did have to leave the country to find one.

e She made a success of her business, but her husband did leave her.

f He sold more than anyone else, but he did have a heart attack.

CASE STUDY: CRISTAL MALVERN

1.35

R: Mr Jones, this is obviously a tremendous blow to Cristal Malvern. Is there anything you can tell us about the future of the company?

J: It's a bit early to say but obviously the fact that the whole plant has been destroyed is a total disaster. We are still waiting to see if anything can be salvaged but it doesn't look like we will be able to start production for a very long time.

R: What about the workforce?

J: That's our major concern at the moment. As I say, we haven't made any decisions yet but I'm afraid some sort of adjustment plan will be necessary. We will of course do what we can to protect as many jobs as possible.

R: Are you worried about the future of the brand?

J: Of course. Unfortunately, because of the nature of our product, we can't just move to another location, because this is where the water comes from. We will have to look at our options.

R: Thank you Mr Jones. I also have with me Ron White, who represents the main union active at the plant. Mr White, how are people feeling?

W: We are all shattered by what has happened. The livelihood of dozens of people has gone up in flames. It's not just the people who work in the plant but also the local community. I don't know what's going to happen. I think the company has a responsibility to do what it can to keep people employed while a new plant is built.

R: There is a rumour the company may have to close.

W: That would be totally unacceptable. After all, we all know that there will be an insurance payout. Cristal Malvern is a company with years of tradition behind it. Our water has some exceptional qualities and it would not make any business sense at all for the brand to disappear. We are all prepared to co-operate but the company must take the initiative and it must do it quickly.

R: Thank you Mr White. And good luck. Now back to the studio …

09 SPIRIT OF ENTERPRISE

1.36

A: … next on today's programme we talk to David O'Brian about his new book on entrepreneurial success "The Sky is the Limit". So David, are entrepreneurs born or created?

B: Well, I think they're basically born, but obviously for an enterprise to be a success there are certain key business skills which have to be learnt. Business studies courses provide an opportunity for the potential entrepreneur to get the skills without taking any risks while they do it. In other words, they can learn from the mistakes and experience of others.

A: So you don't think the classic MBA course does any harm?

B: No, not at all, but on the other hand an MBA is probably more important when you want to get a job working for someone else and not set up your own business.

A: Tell us about some of the people you feature in the book.

B: Well, Mike Clare, the founder of the bed shop chain Dreams, and Michael Welch, the entrepreneur behind car tyre distributor Blackcircles.com, are both good examples of people who started work when they left school. **They first picked up knowledge and skills** while they worked for someone else, but each knew that his real mission in life was to be an entrepreneur - **to set up a business, take risks and make a lot of money.**

A: Apart from their first names, do they have anything else in common?

B: Well, Welch started his business when he was a lot younger, but actually they do have certain things in common. For example, **both have made customer service a major selling point**. This sounds obvious but bad customer service is often the reason why businesses fail. Both businesses rely on efficient distribution and they've been successful at building up their networks.

A: Surely there is more to it than that.

B: Well yes, of course. They both saw an opportunity in a market where they felt they could do something better than the competition and had the confidence to take a risk. There is always a certain amount of luck involved but **the other thing I think they have in common is capacity for hard work**. They have worked incredibly hard to get where they are today.

10 STRESSED TO THE LIMIT

1.37

Interview 1

A: According to statistics, around 75% of all visits to the doctor are the result of work-related stress. Do you think you suffer from stress? That's the question we're asking in the streets of Edinburgh. Excuse me, I'm from the radio programme *Work Today*. We're doing a survey on stress. Would you mind answering some questions?

B: Eh, well, actually, I'm in a bit of a hurry, but … em … go on, then.

A: Thank you. What's your job?

B: I'm an accountant.

A: Do you suffer from stress in your work?

B: Eh, yes, I do, I think.

A: **What symptoms do you notice?**

B: Em, **I get a lot of headaches and I sleep very badly.**

A: And what causes your stress?

B: It's my boss. He's a real … well, let's just say he doesn't exactly make life easy. He always wants things done for yesterday.

A: Thank you very much.

1.38

Interview 2

A: … and what do you do?

C: I work in a shop.

A: Do you suffer from stress?

C: No, not at work, I don't. I find being at home more stressful.

A: Why's that?

C: Well, I've got three children and my mother's ill. She lives with us. And my husband … well, he doesn't help much.

A: And do you have any physical symptoms?

C: Well, **I get a bit on edge at times** and then **I get this horrible rash on my neck**.

A: So, stress is a problem in your life.

C: Yes, definitely.

1.39

Interview 3

A: … and you, sir. Do you suffer from stress?

D: Well, to tell the truth, I'm off work at the moment because of it.
A: Really, what do you do?
D: I'm a teacher. I work with teenagers and I don't know why but every year they seem to get worse.
A: Yes, that does sound stressful.
D: Everyone thinks teaching's an easy option because of the holidays, but you get to a point where you just can't handle it any longer. You lose control.
A: Well, I hope things get better for you.
D: Thanks, but I think that basically the solution is probably to change jobs. Fortunately, I'm still young enough to do that.
A: Right. Good luck, then.

1.40

Interview 4
A: Can I ask you if you suffer from stress?
E: Who? Me? No, not at all. I don't really understand what it is, really.
A: And what do you do for a living?
E: I'm a self-employed architect. I work for myself.
A: I see, and what's your secret?
E: I'm sorry?
A: I mean, how do you avoid getting stressed?
E: I think it's all down to a philosophy of life. I just take each day as it comes. I don't worry about things. What I say is that if you've got a problem, solve it. And if you can't because there's no solution, there's no point in worrying because that won't help.
A: So, you think avoiding stress is to do with mental attitude, not what you do?
E: Yes, that's basically it.
A: Well, thanks very much.
E: Not at all.

11 TOP JOBS

1.41

Jawed Karim is a college student with a difference. For a start, he is not worried about the $100,000 cost of his masters program at Stanford University because **he is already a millionaire. He first hit the Internet jackpot** in 2002 when eBay bought the online payment company he was working for. Then in November 2006 he got lucky again when Google agreed to buy YouTube for $1.65 billion.

When the deal was signed everybody was talking about two of YouTube's co-founders - Chad Hurley and Steve Chen. After all, they were the public face of YouTube. Most people didn't know that there was also a third co-founder of YouTube, Jawed Karim. In fact, he was the person who actually first proposed the idea.

Karim grew up in West Germany, but has lived in the USA since his family emigrated there when Karim started high school. His Bangladeshi father is a chemist at 3M, and his German mother is a professor at the University of Minnesota. Karim obtained his degree in computer science and engineering in 2004 at the University of Illinois.

Hurley, Chen and Karim have known each other since they met as employees at PayPal, the payment service. When eBay bought PayPal for $1.5 billion in 2002, they all received substantial payments. Now rich, the three men often met late at night for brainstorming sessions at Max's Opera Café near Stanford, and discussed possible ventures. Karim said he originally pitched the concept of a video-sharing website to his friends because at the time it was difficult to download videos off the net.

The three agreed to divide up the work based on their different skills. Hurley designed the site's interface and logo while Chen and Karim shared responsibility for technical aspects. At a later stage, when it was necessary to take on management roles, **Hurley became CEO** and Chen the chief technology officer. However, Karim really wanted to return to his computer studies, so he chose not to be part of the management team. As a result **he agreed to take a smaller stake** than the other two founders, and not to take a salary or even a formal title because in his own words, he was "focused on school." Although, since then, he has continued in an informal advisory role, he admits it was the other two who actually turned the basic idea into reality.

Jawed Karim is not the first entrepreneur to lose his place in history. Popular wisdom, for example, says that Bill Gates started Microsoft and Sam Walton founded Wal-Mart on their own, but they too had co-founders. In any case, it is not likely that Karim has too many regrets. While his former colleagues continue to run YouTube, his dream is to teach and become a university professor. Whatever he does, money is not likely to be a problem.

1.42

A: Good morning. Could I speak to Peter Davis, please?
B: Speaking.
A: Oh, hello, Mr Davis. My name is John Lindsay.
B: What can I do for you, Mr Lindsay?
A: It's more a case of what I can do for you … Em, how long have you worked for Blueprint International, Mr Davis?
B: For about six years. Why do you ask?
A: And before that you worked for Navigate for three years.
B: Yes, I joined them as a trainee manager when I left university. But … what is this about?
A: And you were made head of the International Division a year ago. How is it going?
B: Very well, thank you. Now, could you tell me what you want, Mr Lindsay?
A: I'd like to talk to you about an extremely interesting career opportunity. I work for People Search, the management consultants. We've been approached by a client who's looking for someone with just your professional profile.
B: Oh, I see. So that's what it's about. Listen, Mr Lindsay, I'm really quite busy and …
A: Yes, I understand that but you should know I'm talking about a considerable salary increase. You've been married for a couple of years now and recently became a father, I believe.
B: What's that got to do with it?
A: Well, think about your family and the financial possibilities of an advantageous career move at this moment in your life. I think you should at least talk to me.
B: Em, well, I suppose so. What's the name of the company?
A: I'd rather not say over the phone. Perhaps we could meet to discuss things further?
B: I'm not sure I'm that interested … Blueprint International have been very good to me.
A: Oh, come on, Peter! What are the real prospects in your present post? You've got as far as you can in Blueprint. Do you want to be in the same place ten years from now? At least find the time to talk to us.
B: I'd like to think about it. Can I phone you back?
A: No, I'd prefer to phone you back myself in a couple of days. In the meantime, think about what I've said. A more stimulating work situation, not to mention a considerable rise in salary … Talk it over with your wife.
B: Fair enough.
A: Oh, and one more thing, Peter. I'd appreciate it if you didn't mention this call to anyone in your company, okay?
B: Yes, yes, all right. So, you'll call me, then?
A: That's right. In a couple of days. We'll arrange a meeting somewhere. Bye for now, then.
B: Bye.

12 CONVERSATION GAMBITS

2.01

1 A: Excuse me, are you here for the ITM conference?
B: Yes, that's right.
A: Me too. Do you know where to register?
B: I think it's over there.
A: Oh, yes. Right, I'm Paulo, by the way.
B: Hello, Paulo, I'm Kate. Let's go and register.

2.02

2 C: Phew! Is it me, or is it boiling in here?
D: Yes, they always seem to have the heating on full.
C: So, it's not your first time.
D: No, it's my fourth time here.
C: Oh, right, so you're an old hand. I'm Boris.
D: David. Pleased to meet you.

2.03

3 E: Is it my mobile phone, or is there some problem with coverage here?
F: Oh, hang on. No, mine seems to be working okay.
E: Typical, flat batteries and nowhere to charge up.

F: Can I lend you mine?
E: Oh, that's very kind, but I was expecting a call on this number.
F: I see.
E: My name's Nadine, by the way. From Xanadu Electronics.
F: Pleased to meet you. I'm Miko.

2.04

4 G: Excuse me, do you know anything about this speaker?
H: No, I'm sorry, I don't.
G: I can't find my programme notes.
H: Oh, here. Borrow mine.
G: Thanks. By the way, I'm Bill Smart from Silicon Technologies.
H: Right, how do you do? I'm Kazuo Yamada from Lexico.

2.05

A: Excuse me. Would you mind if I had a quick look at your newspaper?
B: Er, no, go ahead. I've finished with it.
A: There's just something I want to check out.
B: No problem. Take your time.
A: Thanks. By the way, my name's Allan. I'm here on a business trip.
B: Oh, right.

2.06

A: Here's your paper then. Thanks very much.
B: Don't mention it.
A: I'm afraid my team didn't win.
B: Sorry?
A: The football results.
B: Oh, I see.
A: Can I buy you a drink? If you don't have anything else to do, that is.
B: I was just about to go, actually, but … yes, why not, … Al, I think you said your name was.
A: Allan, Allan Vilkas.

2.07

B: I'm Sean, Sean O'Malley.
A: Pleased to meet you, Sean. What would you like to drink?
B: A beer, please.
A: Right. Two beers, please.
C: Right, sir.
B: So, Allan, where are you from?
A: Well, I was born in Lithuania, but I've lived in Germany most of my life. Are you from here?
B: Yes, what do you think of Dublin?
A: Well, I've only just arrived today and it's my first visit, but it seems very nice. Lots of character.
B: Are you here on business?
A: Yes, that's right. I have a meeting tomorrow. I'm a bit nervous about it.
B: I'm sure it'll go all right. How long are you staying?
A: Just a couple of days. I go back on Thursday morning. I was just looking at your paper to see how Bayern Munich did yesterday. Do you like football?
B: If it's a good match, but I'm not that keen. Actually, I prefer golf myself.
A: Do you mean you play golf?
B: That's right.
A: I play myself. What's your handicap?

2.08

B: Oh, well, Allan, it's getting late. I have to be off. Thanks for the drink, and good luck with your meeting.
A: Right, it was nice talking to you.
B: It was nice to meet you too. Cheerio, then.
A: Bye.

CASE STUDY: STAFF APPRAISAL

2.09

Presenter: Anglesey Sea Zoo is Wales' largest marine aquarium, attracting over 75,000 visitors per year. Director and partner Alison Lea-Wilson describes how the company introduced an appraisal system that has proved to be a key motivator for its 25 staff.

Alison Lea-Wilson: When we started our appraisals a few years ago they were more of an informal chat. As we grew, we decided to introduce twice-yearly formal appraisals. We wanted to ensure that employees' work matched the goals of the business. We also wanted to provide a chance to recognise good performance and deal with any issues. We based the performance objectives on each employee's job description. We talked to staff so that the objectives could be agreed in advance and they knew what to expect. That was very important because the majority of our performance objectives aren't things which are easy to measure like sales, for example, so we use a scoring system. Each objective is rated on a scale of one to four and both managers and employees fill in the form. Comparing the two sets of ratings can be very useful for identifying differences in expectations and perceptions.

The process is formal. We invite staff to their appraisals in writing, and they get a copy of the appraisal form to fill in before the interview. The completed form is then discussed during the appraisal itself. There is an emphasis on constructive feedback, but as well as talking about performance, we discuss what kind of training might help employees achieve their goals. After the appraisal, team leaders write a report of the discussion and put action points and timescales against each item before giving a copy to the employee.

We have found that a system where staff can express their views and have issues and problems addressed is definitely good for motivation. It's also good to have a formal way of telling people when they've done a good job. We know this because we conduct anonymous staff surveys to assess the effectiveness of our appraisals.

13 AIR TRAVEL

2.10

Conversation 1

A: Good morning. **Is this where I check in for flight RA 264?**
B: Yes. Can you give me your reference number, please?
A: I'm afraid I've lost the paper I had it on, but here's my passport.
B: I'm sorry, but if you haven't got the reference number, I can't check you in. You'll have to go to the main desk over there. They'll give it to you.
A: But can't you look it up? You've got my name.
B: I'm not allowed to.
A: Do I have to queue up again?
B: No. Just come to the front.
A: Okay.
B: Next, please.

2.11

Conversation 2

A: Can I have your reference number and passport please?
B: Here you are.
A: You've just got one suitcase to check in.
B: Yes, this one.
A: I'm afraid it's over fifteen kilos. You'll have to pay excess baggage.
B: It's only just over.
A: Actually it's seventeen kilos.
B: Are you sure? How much will it cost me?
A: It will be ten pounds, but you have to pay over there at the main desk.
B: What, over there? There's a really long queue. Can't I pay here?
A: No, I'm sorry. But come straight to the front when you come back.
B: Okay. Thanks.

2.12

Book as early as possible – within three weeks of the flight. With an early booking you can choose the seat you want. However, if you book months in advance, you'll be too early for a seat assignment.

If you use a travel agent, make sure they have a record of your seating preferences – aisle or window. Tell them you want to sit close to the front. If you sit at the front, you'll get on and off the plane faster.

When you receive your ticket and boarding pass or e-ticket confirmation, check the seat assignment. Mistakes happen. If you have time, cross reference with the airline seating chart.

If you are unable to confirm a seat, be sure to get to the airport early – at least 45 to 60 minutes before the flight.

If you do have an assignment for your preferred seat, don't check in too late. Those few minutes reading magazines in the newsstand can translate into hours of discomfort in the air.

Finally, the gate check-in attendant can be your best friend. Ask politely if there is a better seat available. Saying that you are claustrophobic might not hurt, but don't feign an illness or say you're pregnant if you're not. There's no point in feeling guilty the entire flight.

If, in spite of your best efforts, you end up with the middle seat, here are some tips to cope:

If you are late boarding and have your choice of middle seats, go for the one up front near the exit.

Check out the aisle and window passengers. Do they look like they will be self-contained and give you plenty of room? Observe their body language and trust your instincts.

Capture as much personal space as you can right away. Dominate the two armrests. This will force your seatmates to give you more space. Be polite, but establish your territory. After all, they have 'personal space' on either side.

Don't work on the laptop during the flight. A cramped space becomes even more claustrophobic when you bring out the hardware. And don't try to read a newspaper. Stick to small paperbacks.

Although it is important to keep hydrated in the air, don't drink water by the gallon. If you climb over seatmates repeatedly to get to the bathroom, they'll get annoyed.

Get up once during the flight to stretch your legs, even if you don't have to use the restroom. This time away will allow your companions to move around as well and refresh the whole row.

2.13

A: If I order 100 units, will you give me a price of 5.5 euros?
B: No, I'm sorry. I can't do that. On 150 units I'll give you a price of six euros.
A: Six euros. And what about payment?
B: Payment is within 60 days.
A: If we pay within 30 days, will you lower the price?
B: I'll go down to 5.5 euros if you order 200 units or more. That's my best offer.
A: Well, what about the guarantee?

14 HIRING AND FIRING

2.14

Speaker 1

I think that these days you have to really sell yourself. Certainly this is what employers expect in the US. You should show them how great and self-confident you are. Modesty isn't going to get you anywhere and no one is going to mind if you exaggerate a bit and dress things up to sound more impressive. Make the potential employer feel that, although this is the job you always wanted and of course you are the ideal person for it, if they don't snap you up, someone else will. So, they had better hire you before they lose the chance.

2.15

Speaker 2

It's not often that qualifications and experience totally match up to an advertised post, so it's preferable to emphasise other qualities like your willingness to learn and the fact that you work hard. In fact, you should be careful not to give the impression you are over-qualified for the job. I think that employers are often more interested in things like loyalty and ability to fit in. A high-flier who knows too much can create a bad working atmosphere and break a team. Personally, I want the employer to think that I am going to be easy to work with and won't create too many waves.

2.16

Speaker 3

No one likes a 'big head' but, on the other hand, don't be falsely modest either. Basically, your qualifications and experience tell their own story so you're not going to impress anyone by adding a lot of adjectives like 'excellent' and 'outstanding' to your CV. Usually this will make an experienced recruitment officer suspicious. It doesn't hurt to acknowledge one or two weaknesses either – areas that you would like to improve and you want a chance to develop. Above all, be honest, because if you exaggerate or lie, in the end someone is going to catch you out and you'll end up looking stupid.

2.17

Speaker 4

People's motivations interest employers. If you want to work for a specific company, tell them why, especially if you are changing jobs. Valid reasons would be that you are frustrated by the limitations of your present post, or that you can't fulfil the potential of your background and education. Don't whine, though, and don't blame your current employers: you've learnt a lot with them, but it's time to move on. Tell potential employers that you have a lot to offer, and all you need is an opportunity to show it. If someone gives you a break, they won't be disappointed.

2.18

A: Right, shall we make a start? My name is Philip Rickett. I work in the human resources department and I'm responsible for recruitment.
B: Right, pleased to meet you.
A: Did you find us all right?
B: Yes, the map you sent me was very clear.
A: Good. **Now, this is just a preliminary interview to check out some details.** If you're successful, you'll go on to a more in-depth interview this afternoon. Is that all right?
B: Yes, I don't have to be back at work until tomorrow morning so as long as I have time to drive back this evening, that's fine.
A: Do your present employers know where you are?
B: No. I asked for a day's unpaid leave for personal reasons. I didn't say why.
A: What don't you like about your current position?
B: Actually, there are a lot of things I do like about it, but no job is perfect. I think I am ready for more responsibility and when I saw your advert, I thought I should apply.
A: You know this job is a managerial position. How much managerial experience do you have? It's not very clear from your CV.
B: Well, in my present job I'm a management team coordinator.
A: Yes. **Does that mean** you're the leader of the team?
B: Not exactly. I assist the general manager in running the department.
A: Oh, I see. Are you a kind of personal assistant?
B: No, I think it's a bit more than that …
A: **But are you a manager?**
B: I suppose not.
A: **It says in your CV that** in your previous position you were 'an SPC professional'. **What exactly does that mean?** Is Sales Productivity Centre basically a sales department?
B: Yes, we provided backup for twenty salesmen from different sectors of the company.
A: Are you saying you were directly involved in sales?
B: No, it was more about providing support to help drive sales and increase productivity.
A: I see. So, **what sort of work did the job involve?**
B: I'd say it was a position that required a lot of time management skills and prioritising of tasks. It gave me a lot of insight into the sales process.
A: **Can you be a bit more specific please?**
B: Well, to be honest, some of the work was secretarial but I am applying for your post because I'm capable of doing far more. I'd like more responsibility and to be able to use my studies and my languages.
A: Yes, your English is obviously excellent and you speak Spanish. Is your Spanish as good as your English?
B: Yes, it's not bad.
A: Could you tell me about your degree course … in Spanish?
B: I'm sorry? Oh, I beg your pardon … Well, I need a little time to think … Let's see …

15 TIME

2.19

A: Hello.
B: Hello, is that Domingo?
A: Yes, speaking.
B: Hi, this is Joe. Look, I need you to tell me something about the new database. We're worried because **it's behind schedule. What is the situation?**
A: Well yes, **I'm sorry about the delay but there have been some problems** with the application.
B: I appreciate that, but the system was supposed to be online last October. You didn't meet the deadline and it's now February. My boss is getting a bit nervous. And so am I.
A: Okay, okay. But you modified the requirements and the old system is not

compatible with the new design. That means we have a different timeframe.
B: What do you mean? **How long is it going to take?**
A: We need to make sure that migrating the data from the old database is going to go smoothly. We don't want to lose anything important. And then there are the security issues, but **I think we should be ready by October.**
B: I don't understand. Are you saying that the schedule for all this is now next October?
A: Yeah. **It shouldn't take longer than that.**
B: You're joking.
A: No, I'm not actually. It really is much more complicated than anyone anticipated.
B: Can you guarantee that you're giving us priority on this? **Will it be on time?**
A: Yeah, sure, you're at the top of the list.
B: Okay. Listen, is Jorgen there. I'd like to speak to him.
A: Hang on, I'll see if he's available.

2.20

Good afternoon. The subject of my presentation today is 'The Myth of Time Management'. Why is it a myth? Well, there are thousands of books and Internet courses on the market which are designed to help people be better managers of their time. They all suggest techniques for using our time more efficiently. They recommend making 'to do' lists, prioritising, and not answering the phone as ways to make us more time efficient. But do these techniques really work?

Well, they say that time is money. That may be true but time is certainly not like other resources which we manage such as materials and machines. It is much more complex than that because use of time depends to a big extent on personality and attitude. Sometimes we can change our own behaviour, but time management really depends on changing the behaviour of other people around us and the demands they make on our time. At best this is difficult, but more often than not it is beyond your control. As a result, you can be a very efficient user of your time - disciplined, organised and choosing the right moment to do vital tasks - yet still feel stressed and overworked. To be honest, in many cases this is simply because you are being asked to do more than is possible in the time available.

This leads me on to the next point because in fact, time management is frequently about making choices that in reality we don't have. One of the recommended techniques is to close your door at certain times, or leave your voice box to deal with calls. That's fine, but if interruptions and dealing with unpredictable human problems are part of your work, then those techniques don't help very much.

Another time management technique is to analyse what you are doing and decide if it is important or not. Well, I think most people of average intelligence can normally distinguish between activity which is useful and activity which is a waste of time. Unless they dislike their job or their employer, they will do useful things in their work time. In fact, often the problem is feeling guilty about using time to think or acquire skills and ideas which are not immediately productive. What apparently is a waste of time, is actually extremely useful because in the long run it will make you more efficient.

Time management may work with jobs with very defined tasks, where procedures and processes are very clear. Machine operators, for example, don't have to worry much about managing their time because the pace of work is imposed from outside. On the other hand, if you are faced with a task which involves creativity or problem solving, how to go about performing the task may not be clear. It could also be that you are in a job where you lack either the necessary skills or appropriate training to carry out your duties.

I will go on to look at these different aspects of time-use in more detail, but we have to remember that there will always be more work than time. This is what keeps us employed. How effectively you use your time is to some extent a question of ability, training and proper planning. But above all, it is about having a positive attitude towards your work combined with reasonable expectations about how much you can do.

Okay, that's a brief summary of the points I'd like to cover. Now let's go back to look at the question of how we can change …

2.21

Conversation 1

A: Where are you going?
B: Well, I've finished everything I had to do so I'm going to leave early.
A: What about the sales predictions for next month?
B: Oh, I'd forgotten about that. I'll start on them tomorrow first thing. I've arranged to meet someone at five.

2.22

Conversation 2

C: Have you planned Mr Logan's visit? What about lunch tomorrow?
D: I'm going to take him to The Redwing.
C: I seem to remember he's a vegetarian.
D: Is he? In that case I'll phone to check they have a vegetarian menu.

2.23

Conversation 3

E: Is everything confirmed for your trip to San Sebastian?
F: Yes, the plane goes to Bilbao. I'm going to take the train from there.
E: No, don't do that – it takes forever. The bus is much faster.
F: Is it? Well, I'll take the bus, then.

16 GETTING THINGS DONE

2.24

Conversation 1

A: Oh, look outside!
B: What's up?
A: I've got to go to the Post Office to pick something up and it's raining. Could you lend me your umbrella?
B: Of course. As long as you don't lose it.
A: Oh, right. Don't worry, I won't.

2.25

Conversation 2

C: Gert, I have a meeting with an agent this afternoon, and they're decorating my office.
D: Lucky you.
C: The thing is that I need somewhere quiet where we won't be interrupted. Could I use your office?
D: All right, as long as it's free by four. I've got a meeting myself.
C: Don't worry, it won't take that long.

2.26

A: Richard, I wonder if I could ask you a favour?
B: Depends what it is.
A: I've got to go over to the warehouse to do something, and I haven't got my car. Would you lend me yours?
B: No way!
A: What?
B: I never lend my car! In any case, where's your car?
A: It's in the garage. Eh, I had a little accident.
B: And you expect me to trust you with mine?
A: It's just a minor scratch. Oh, don't worry. I'll think of something else.

2.27

A: Sandra, we need someone to answer the phone from 2.00 till 4.00 while Julia is off sick. Could you do it?
B: From 2.00 to 4.00? It's not my hours.
A: I know, but you can take the time later on.
B: It's not the time. I'll have to get someone to pick the kids up from school. Isn't there anyone else?
A: No, there isn't. Look, I know it's inconvenient, but I can't think of any other solution.
B: Well, can't we just put the answer phone on for a couple of hours?
A: Not really. It creates such a bad impression. Listen, I'd do it myself but I've got to be somewhere else.
B: I'm sure you would, but it's not my problem, is it?
A: No, it isn't, and obviously I can't force you to do it, but …
B: But?
A: … but on the other hand, if you do it, I'll see it as a personal favour.
B: I see. I don't really have much choice, do I? I hope it's just this time …
A: Yes, in principle, yes. But you never know. Your contract is up for renewal next month. Enough said?
B: Yeah, enough said.

2.28

Conversation 1

A: Good afternoon, sir.

B: Hello. I'm on flight IB 603. I was wondering if there's any chance of an upgrade to business class.
A: Well, I don't know. It depends how crowded the flight is.
B: Yes, I quite understand, but I'd really appreciate it if you could have a look. I don't mind paying the extra. It's just that I've had a really hard day and it'd be really nice to have a bit more space and comfort.
A: Just a minute, sir.
B: I'm sorry to put you to any trouble.
A: No, that's okay. Oh, yes, there's lots of space in business class. I think we can do it.
B: Oh, fantastic. How much is that?
A: That's all right, sir. Don't worry.
B: Oh, thank you ever so much.
A: You're welcome. Have a good flight.

2.29

Conversation 2
A: Good evening, sir.
B: Look, I'm not at all happy with the room you've given me. It's on the wrong side of the hotel. It faces on to the road and it's far too noisy.
A: I'm sorry, sir. No one has ever said anything before.
B: I can't believe that. Are you going to change it?
A: I don't think I can, sir. We're a bit full tonight.
B: Look, I'm really tired, and the last thing I want to do is argue about my room. If you don't change it, I'll tell my company not to use this hotel again.
A: I'm sorry. There's no other room available.
B: Oh, come on.
A: There's nothing I can do.
B: What about some sort of discount, then?
A: I'm afraid I'm not authorised to offer a discount on your room.
B: So, I have to pay the full price for a noisy room. Brilliant!
A: Sir, if you want, I can call you a taxi …

17 OFFICE GOSSIP

2.30

A: Hi Quin. **How's it going?**
B: Trixy! **Where have you been?**
A: I had a few days' holiday owing to me.
B: Go anywhere interesting?
A: I wish! No, I went up north to stay with my parents.
B: So, you haven't have **heard the news**.
A: **What news?**
B: About the 'restructuring'.
A: What restructuring?
B: They want to reorganise marketing and sales.
A: No! **Really? Is it official?**
B: No, but somebody overheard Prescott talking to one of the management consultants.
A: What did he say?
B: Apparently he said that we were overstaffed in some areas.
A: Never!
B: Yes, this consultant chap told him they would have to let some people go.
A: But **that's awful**.
B: Yes, Prescott asked him how many people it involved.
A: And what did he say?
B: He said it depended on individual performance and attitude.
A: Does that include Maureen?
B: What do you mean?
A: Well, you know what they say about her and Prescott.
B: Go on …
A: I'm not saying who, but someone told me he often sees them in The Green Man together.
B: That little pub on the Oxford Road?
A: That's right.
B: Well I never! The other day he asked her if she would stay behind to work on something together. I heard him.
A: There you are, then. There's no smoke without fire.
B: Listen, don't tell anyone I told you.
A: Now, come on, Quin, you know me better than that.
B: Back to work, then.
A: Right. **Catch you later.**
B: Bye.

2.31

Conversation 1
A: Jeff, have you finished last month's production figures?
B: No, Jane, I'm sorry. Can I give them to you this afternoon?
A: It's no good being sorry. There's always some excuse. If they're not on my desk by 4 o'clock, I'll have to speak to Mr Bradley.
B: Yes, Jane. I'll start straight away.

2.32

Conversation 2
C: David, have you got a minute? There's something I want to discuss with you … in my office.
D: What's it about?
C: Oh, well, we're missing a laptop computer from the store.
D: What has that got to do with me?
C: Well, you are the only other person with a key to the store and …

2.33

Conversation 3
E: Marie, the figures you need are ready.
F: Thanks, Pedro. Is everything okay?
E: Yes, no problems. Would you like to look at them with me?
F: Yes, but I'm a bit busy this afternoon.
E: Me too. Er, do you know that new café they've just opened? It's nice and quiet. We can go through them there after work.
F: Oh, I suppose so, but I won't be able to stay for long.
E: Great. **See you there at about six,** then?
F: Yes, all right. See you there.

2.34

Conversation 4
G: Hi, Monica.
H: Oh, hello Jim. How are things going?
G: Great. In fact, you can be the first to congratulate me.
H: Yes, you look very pleased with yourself. What's up?
G: I'm the new head of the eastern sales team.
H: Oh, really? What salary are you on now, then?
G: Sixty grand a year.
H: **I can't believe it.** Sixty thousand!
G: And they're giving me a new company car.
H: Oh really? **Congratulations**, then. The drinks are on you. See you later.
G: Yes. Bye.

2.35

A: In this week's Business Today, we talk to Karina Schmidt. Karina is the author of a report by the Industrial Society which looks at workplace relations, and how they've changed over the years. Karina, first of all, welcome to the programme.
B: Thank you, it's a pleasure to be here.
A: In your report, you say that many companies nowadays have abandoned some useful institutions which allowed for social interaction.
B: Yes, these days there's less opportunity to gossip and socialise. For example, often the tea trolley has been scrapped, and having a chat in the tea break was an important part of the working day. The drink after work at the pub around the corner is another example.
A: And why do you think these things have disappeared?
B: I think it's all part of the revolution in human resources. Some of these traditions have become unfashionable. Talking about things not connected to work is now seen as bad and as wasting time. There are even theories about removing chairs from meeting rooms, so that the meetings are more efficient and finish quickly.
A: And are we more efficient now, then?
B: Well, that's a good question, but in any case, something has been lost from the workplace which is very important. And perhaps in the long term, with these drives for efficiency, companies are making false economies.
A: In what way?
B: The difference between a good job and a bad job are the human, emotional elements. In other words, happy employees are productive employees. People enjoy the social aspects of work, the personal interaction with colleagues, the friendships …
A: And the gossip!
B: And the gossip. Yes, in some ways gossip is the glue that holds the organisation together. Providing communal space such as coffee areas or lunch rooms allows employees to share information and

build relationships that benefit both the company and the employees.

A: Are you saying that gossip should be encouraged?

B: Not exactly, it's obviously a question of balance. All gossip and chatting doesn't make for an efficient company, but neither does no gossip or chat. All I'm saying is that I think companies would do well to remember this when trying to improve efficiency and bring down costs.

A: Karina, I'm afraid that's all we've got time for. Thank you very much for talking to us. It's been very interesting.

B: Thank you for inviting me.

A: That's all for now from Business Today. So, until next week, goodbye.

18 E-COMMERCE

2.36

I: For most listeners, Amazon, eBay and PayPal will of course be household names, and bring to mind books, music and shopping on the world wide web. According to latest surveys three out of five Europeans have at sometime bought goods on the Internet and online sales have doubled annually over the last five years. But will this growth continue? And what will the state of online trading and shopping be 10 years from now? Our guests today - Paul Bradley and Johan Webb - are both well-known commentators and bloggers on business and online technology. Paul, how do you see the future? **What are the pros and cons?**

P: It's difficult to say because things move so fast but I think the future is quite bright. I am pretty sure that e-commerce will become the normal way to buy and trade, not in all products, but in a fairly wide range of goods. **The advantages for the customer are obvious**: access to products that may not be available locally, in online shops open twenty-four hours a day, seven days a week and three hundred and sixty-five days a year with delivery to your doorstep.

J: **Yes, for the customer the benefits are clear** - convenience and lower prices. You can also compare the products and prices of different shops without leaving home. On the other hand, the seller can do business with anyone in the world connected to the Internet. In fact, the only limitation is when transport and delivery costs get too high to make it viable.

P: **That's absolutely right, but there are other drawbacks as well**. In the traditional scenario a customer can visit a bookshop and leave with a book. But when you buy online you inevitably have to wait for the goods to arrive. Some of us quite like waiting for the postman to arrive with a package, but a lot of us just don't have the patience. There is also the possibility the goods won't arrive as expected and when there are problems they can be difficult to sort out. For example, if things arrive damaged or you find they aren't what you really want, returning goods is not easy. If someone just takes your money and disappears, there is no-one to complain to. This stops a lot of people from buying online, and retailers have to find solutions. With a product like a computer or high definition TV for example, people like to have a shop where they can take it back to be repaired if something goes wrong. **After-sales service is still a negative factor.**

J: On the plus side the seller can deal directly with the manufacturer and offer a cheaper price as a result. There's no wholesaler in the middle taking a cut. You can take advantage of more competitive prices. For the customer the price difference has to be enough to make it worth taking the risk, if it exists.

I: Is payment a problem?

J: Not really - once people get over the initial worries about using credit cards.

P: For me **security is still the big issue** in people's minds. They're scared of identity theft and what happens to the information they give online. For the moment it's something which is slowing down growth.

J: There are solutions out there. The success of eBay is that the payment system offers guarantees and security. Also, they have a voting system which is good for potential buyers because they benefit from the experience of previous customers.

I: Is that where customers and sellers give each other positive or negative votes when the transaction has been completed?

J: Yes, it's a very effective system.

P: I agree but it's difficult to apply to other e-commerce situations because eBay is not the seller, it works as a market place for others and takes a commission.

I: What about the type of products that can be sold?

J: Well, I don't think buying food is ever going to take off except for perhaps making your order at the local supermarket via a webpage. **Books and DVDs are one thing, but fruit and vegetables are another.**

P: Yes, buying online will inevitably make groceries more expensive, so what's the point? Actually, this highlights another limitation. You can see pictures, read text and hear sounds on the Internet, but you can't smell a flower or feel the quality of cloth online. There will always be some products that people will want to touch and feel before they buy.

J: Not only that, but when you go to a shop and pick something up, you choose what to look at and how to look at it. On the Internet, you only see what the seller wants you to see. That's why people are more comfortable buying standard, generic products like DVDs, books and electronic gadgets. Often you've seen them in a shop before and you're just looking for a better price. Personally for example, I won't buy clothes online unless I know it's something I want because I've been able to try it on to see if it fits.

I: Can we go back to the use of credit cards? Apart from security, are there any other issues?

P: Well, yes. Credit cards are an added cost for the seller but you can't pay cash over the Internet. Credit companies charge big commissions on each purchase.

J: **There's another point here.** Because payment is by credit card, very small or very large transactions tend not to be conducted online.

P: That brings us back to what e-commerce is all about: buying and selling products which are suitable for package delivery, where compared to traditional retail, the costs of selling, payment and transport make it worth doing business online for both buyer and seller.

I: Well, Paul, Johan, thank you both very much. If you would like to comment on anything you've heard, don't forget you can e-mail us at …

2.37

a **The right qualifications for a job are one thing, but having experience is another.**

b **A high turnover is one thing, but making good profits is another.**

c **Having a good idea is one thing, but putting it into practice is another.**

d **High productivity is one thing, but improving staff motivation is another.**

e **Creating a good product is one thing, but selling it is another.**

19 E-WORK

2.38

A: Have you seen this?

B: What?

A: "Make money while you work at home. No skill required."

B: Oh, **it's not really about working at home**. You sign up to a scheme where they say they will pay you to reply to e-mails or visit pages on the Internet. **Then you are supposed to persuade your friends** and family to do it.

A: Oh, so it's like pyramid selling.

B: Yes, the more people you get to do it, the more money you make. **The idea is to** show potential advertisers that they have an audience. **I doubt it really works.** If it was so easy, everyone would do it.

A: That's a shame. I wouldn't mind working at home if I had the opportunity.

B: I'm not so sure. I wouldn't miss travelling in to work everyday but if I was at home, I'd miss the contact with people here.

A: That's true, but if you could just come in a couple of days a week it would be okay. On the other hand, unless you had somewhere quiet to work, it would be difficult to get anything done.

B: Do you think you'd be disciplined enough?

A: I don't know. I would if it was my own

business but otherwise who knows? **It probably sounds more attractive than it would be in reality.**

B: They do talk about telework a lot these days. Some people say that if people stopped commuting, it would be much more ecological.

A: That's probably right but in the end, I think it depends on the type of job you have.

2.39

Interview 1

A: The Internet and other new technologies have changed the way we work and the titles of our jobs. For example, instead of the secretary, meet Jill Spencer, a 'virtual assistant'. Jill, what exactly is a virtual assistant?

B: Virtual assistants, or VAs, work from home. We offer services to businesses which don't have sufficient work to justify employing someone full-time.

A: Why did you decide to be a virtual assistant?

B: I retired from my job as a conference organiser, but I wanted to earn some extra money. I became a VA because it meant I didn't have to leave my country home down here in Cornwall.

A: Yes, it's a lovely place – I can understand why you didn't want to move away. So, how did you start?

B: I had a lot of contacts from my previous work. I began by providing things like bookkeeping but now I offer a range of services for clients all over the UK.

A: It's going well, then.

B: Yes, I wasn't looking to earn a fantastic amount of money. The biggest advantage is that **you can do as little or as much as you want**. If it's a lovely sunny day, I can sit out in the garden and do the work in the evening.

A: What do you need to get started?

B: **The basic tools are** a computer with an Internet connection, a fax machine and a mobile phone. Anyone with basic office skills could do the job. Apart from that it depends on the kind of services you're going to offer and what the clients want.

A: And what's in it for the companies?

B: Companies get a huge amount out of it because they only use a virtual assistant when they need one. Also, they can perhaps get someone with a higher professional level than they could get if they had to pay someone full-time. There's also no problem of office hours. A businessman can be out of the office all day, but his assistant is still available in the evening if he needs to discuss things. I think it could make a big difference to everyone's lifestyle.

2.40

Interview 2

A: Anna, what exactly do you do?

B: I'm a concierge at the Westin Hotel in Santa Clara, California.

A: What was life like before you became a teleworker?

B: I had to get up at three in the morning so I could shower and dress, take my kids to my mother's, and set off to work by 4.30.

A: 4.30!

B: Yes, there was a lot of traffic. On a good day I got there by 6.30. That gave me half an hour to relax before starting my shift at seven o'clock.

A: It sounds awful.

B: Yes, I was getting up in the dark and getting home in the dark. I never saw my husband or children. I like my job but my life was a nightmare.

A: And what is life like now?

B: Oh, I feel like the luckiest person alive. I now get up at 5.30. My mother still looks after the children but I don't have the 80-mile drive to work along Highway 101. We've set up my workplace in one of the bedrooms. I sit down in front of a camera, pin on a microphone and I'm ready for business.

A: How does it work at the hotel?

B: Guests still go up to the concierge desk, but instead of me in person, they see me on a giant TV screen. They can only see my head and shoulders, so I can wear my slippers while I work.

A: What do your employers think about it?

B: Oh, they're happy because they can't afford to lose me. In the hotel industry we don't have the high salaries of Cisco, Palm or Sun Micro, so there's a high turnover of staff. With unemployment around here so low it's hard to replace workers. It cost them $50,000 but they thought it was worth a try.

A: And the guests?

B: They're happy. Apart from anything else they don't have to leave a tip!

20 WORKING LUNCH

2.41

A: This looks like a very nice place, Satoshi.

B: Yes, I thought you would like it.

A: Yes, I really like the décor. Er, could you order for both of us, Satoshi?

B: Of course. I think we could have some miso soup to start with. They do it very well here.

A: Okay. Sounds good.

B: And then I think you should try some unagi.

A: What's that?

B: It's eel – grilled and served on a bed of rice. It's delicious.

A: Hm, I'm sure it is. Actually, do you think I could have a steak?

B: Well, I'm afraid they don't serve steak here.

A: I'll try the unagi, then.

B: Fine. Would you like some sake, or would you prefer some beer?

A: No, no, let's have some sake.

B: Right. Sake it is, then.

2.42

B: Neil, I met Jeff Segram earlier this year. What exactly is his job title?

A: He's the Managing Director.

B: Do you mean the CEO?

A: Yes, that's what the Americans say. He's the person on the board who is responsible for the day-to-day running of the company.

B: And what about you?

A: I'm the Product Development Director. I'm on the board as well, but I report to Jeff.

B: Right, I see.

2.43

C: So, any news from Tokyo, Neil?

A: No, I'm afraid not, Jeff. It looks like they're not interested.

C: How did it go with Mr Tanaka?

A: Oh, he was really nice. He took me to a great restaurant. Actually, everything went okay until we got down to business.

C: What happened?

A: I don't know. I thought the sale was a sure thing, but he seemed to lose interest. I don't know what I did wrong.

2.44

A: Mm, that was delicious.

B: I'm glad you enjoyed it. So, Neil, tell me about this digital control software. Why do you think we should be interested?

A: Because it's easily the best program for the job on the market.

B: The system we use at the moment works okay. Why should we change?

A: It's a question of costs. It could save you up to 30%. If you look at the competition, there's just no comparison.

B: Can you give me some information about your sales?

A: Er … about two million dollars' worth worldwide.

B: Could I see the documentation?

A: Well, I'm afraid that's confidential, but listen, if we can make a deal today, I can offer you an even better discount.

CASE STUDIES GLOSSARY

CASE STUDY 1
INTERNET ACCESS

(un)authorised /(ʌn)ˈɔːθəraɪzd/ adj. (not) having official permission for something

blame /bleɪm/ verb [T] to say or think that someone or something is responsible for an accident, problem or bad situation

colleague /ˈkɒliːg/ noun [count] someone who works in the same organization or department as you

dismiss /dɪsˈmɪs/ verb [T] to force someone to leave their job

enforce /ɪnˈfɔː(r)s/ verb [T] to make people obey a law, rule etc.

firewall /ˈfaɪə(r)ˌwɔːl/ noun [count] a computer program that prevents people from entering a computer system illegally

gambling /ˈgæmblɪŋ/ noun [uncount] risking money in the hope of winning more if you are lucky

guidelines /ˈgaɪdˌlaɪnz/ noun [plural] official instructions or advice about how to do something

hire /ˈhaɪə(r)/ verb [T] to pay someone to work for you

inappropriate /ˌɪnəˈprəʊpriət/ adj. not suitable in a particular situation

induction /ɪnˈdʌkʃ(ə)n/ noun [count] a period of training that introduces people into an organization or institution

issue /ˈɪʃuː/ noun [count] a subject or problem that people discuss or argue about

IT /ˌaɪ ˈtiː/ noun [uncount] Information Technology; the use of computers and other electronic equipment to store, process, and send information

logon /ˈlɒgɒn/ noun [count] a user name and password

monitor /ˈmɒnɪtə(r)/ verb [T] to regularly check something or watch someone in order to find out what is happening

policy /ˈpɒləsi/ noun [count] a set of plans or actions that are agreed on by a government, political party, business, or other organization

prohibit /prəʊˈhɪbɪt/ verb [T] to officially stop people from doing something

recruit /rɪˈkruːt/ verb [T] to get someone to join a company, or an organization

spy on someone /ˈspaɪ ɒn sʌmwʌn/ phrasal verb to watch someone secretly so that you know everything that they do

surf /sɜː(r)f/ verb [T] to look at various places one after another on the Internet or on television

union /ˈjuːnjən/ noun [count] an organization that represents the workers in a particular industry

virus /ˈvaɪrəs/ noun [count] a program that enters your computer and damages or destroys information that you have stored

voicemail /ˈvɔɪsmeɪl/ noun [uncount] an electronic system that records and stores phone messages

website /ˈwebˌsaɪt/ noun [count] a place on the Internet where information is available about a particular subject, company, university etc

welfare /ˈwelfeə(r)/ noun [uncount] the health, happiness, and safety of a person or group

CASE STUDY 2
CRISTAL MALVERN

ad (advertisement) /æd (ədˈvɜː(r)tɪsmənt)/ noun [count] an announcement in a newspaper, on television, on the Internet etc that is designed to persuade people to buy a product or service, go to an event, or apply for a job

agreement /əˈgriːmənt/ noun [count] an arrangement or decision about what to do, made by two or more people, groups, or organizations

benefit /ˈbenɪfɪt/ verb [I/T] to get an advantage, or to give someone an advantage

a blessing in disguise /ə ˈblesɪŋ ɪn dɪsˌgaɪz/ phrase something that seems to cause problems, but that you later realize is a good thing

blow /bləʊ/ noun [count] an event that makes you feel very sad, disappointed, or shocked

bottled /ˈbɒt(ə)ld/ adj. contained in bottles

brand /brænd/ noun [count] a product or group of products that has its own name and is made by one particular company

challenge /ˈtʃælɪndʒ/ noun [count] something that needs a lot of skill, energy, and determination to deal with or achieve

commercial /kəˈmɜː(r)ʃ(ə)l/ adj. relating to the business of buying and selling goods and services

consumer product /kənˌsjuːmə(r) ˈprɒdʌkt/ noun [count] something intended to be used by households as the ultimate consumer

demand /dɪˈmɑːnd/ noun [uncount] the amount of a product or service that people want, or the fact that they want it

distribute /dɪˈstrɪbjuːt/ verb [T] to supply goods from one central place

distribution /ˌdɪstrɪˈbjuːʃ(ə)n/ noun [uncount] the process of supplying goods from one central place

Definitions from Macmillan Essential Dictionary and Macmillan English Dictionary

estimated /ˈestɪmeɪtəd/ **adj.** calculated or guessed by using the information that is available

genuine /ˈdʒenjuɪn/ **adj.** real and not pretended or false

the initiative /ɪˈnɪʃətɪv/ **[singular]** the opportunity to take action before other people do

installation /ˌɪnstəˈleɪʃ(ə)n/ **noun [count]** building or place that provides a particular service or is used for a particular industry

insurance /ɪnˈʃʊərəns/ **adj.** relating to an arrangement in which you regularly pay a company an amount of money so that they will give you money if something that you own is damaged, lost, or stolen, or if you die or are ill or injured

investment /ɪnˈves(t)mənt/ **noun [uncount]** the process of spending money in order to improve something or make it more successful

livelihood /ˈlaɪvlihʊd/ **noun [uncount/count]** something such as your work that provides the money that you need to live

mission /ˈmɪʃ(ə)n/ **[singular]** an aim that is very important to a person or organization

modernise /ˈmɒdə(r)naɪz/ **verb [I/T]** to become less old-fashioned, or to make something become less old-fashioned, as a result of new methods, equipment, or ideas

negotiate /nɪˈgəʊʃieɪt/ **verb [I/T]** to try to reach an agreement by discussing something formally

owner /ˈəʊnə(r)/ **noun [count]** someone who owns something

payout /ˈpeɪaʊt/ **noun [count]** an amount of money that is paid to someone

plant /plɑːnt/ **noun [count]** a large factory

rebuild /ˌriːˈbɪld/ **verb [T]** to build something again after it has been damaged or destroyed

reconstruction /ˌriːkənˈstrʌkʃ(ə)n/ **noun [uncount]** the process of building something again

redundancy /rɪˈdʌndənsi/ **noun [count]** a situation in which someone is told to leave their job because they are no longer needed

redundant /rɪˈdʌndənt/ **adj.** if someone is made redundant, they have been told that they must leave their job because they are no longer needed

renew /rɪˈnjuː/ **verb [T]** to do something again after a pause

rumour /ˈruːmə(r)/ **noun [count]** something that people are saying that may, or may not be true

salvage /ˈsælvɪdʒ/ **verb [T]** to save things from a ship or building that has been damaged or destroyed

shareholder /ˈʃeə(r)ˌhəʊldə(r)/ **noun [count]** someone who owns shares in a company

site /saɪt/ **noun [count]** a place used for a particular purpose

spokesman /ˈspəʊksmən/ **noun [count]** someone whose job is to officially represent an organization and to speak to journalists

subsidy /ˈsʌbsədi/ **noun [count]** an amount of money that the government or another organization pays to help to reduce the cost of a product or service

triumph /ˈtraɪʌmf/ **noun [count]** an exciting victory or success

viable /ˈvaɪəb(ə)l/ **adj.** able to be done, or worth doing

workforce /ˈwɜː(r)kˌfɔː(r)s/ **noun [singular]** the total number of people who work in a particular company, industry, or country

CASE STUDY 3 STAFF APPRAISAL

anonymous /əˈnɒnɪməs/ **adj.** done or written by someone whose name is not known

assessment /əˈsesmənt/ **noun [count]** the process of thinking about something carefully and making a judgement about it

atmosphere /ˈætməsˌfɪə(r)/ **noun [singular]** the mood that exists in a place and affects the people there

attitude /ˈætɪˌtjuːd/ **noun [uncount]** opinions or feelings that you show by your behaviour

basis /ˈbeɪsɪs/ **noun [count]** a particular method or system that is used for doing or organizing something

behave /bɪˈheɪv/ **verb [I]** to do things in a particular way

conduct /kənˈdʌkt/ **verb [T]** to do something in an organized way

delegate /ˈdeləgət/ **noun [count]** someone who is chosen to represent a group of other people at a meeting

detest /dɪˈtest/ **verb [T]** to hate someone or something

disadvantages /ˌdɪsədˈvɑːntɪdʒəz/ **noun [count]** something that makes someone or something less effective, successful, or attractive

effectiveness /ɪˈfektɪvnəs/ **noun [uncount]** degree to which something works well and produces the effect that was intended

efficient /ɪˈfɪʃ(ə)nt/ **adj.** working well and producing good results, using the available time, money, supplies etc. in the most effective way

emphasis /ˈemfəsɪs/ **noun [count]** special importance or attention that is given to one thing in particular

evaluate /ɪˈvæljueɪt/ **verb [T]** to think carefully about something before you make a judgement about its value, importance, or quality

evaluation /ɪˌvæljuˈeɪʃ(ə)n/ **noun [count]** the process of making a careful judgement about something's value, importance, or quality.

excuse /ɪk'skjuːs/ **noun [count]** a reason for doing something that you want to do

exploit /ɪk'splɔɪt/ **verb [T]** to treat someone unfairly in order to get some benefit for yourself

foundation /faʊn'deɪʃ(ə)n/ **noun [count]** the most basic part of something from which the rest of it develops

goal /gəʊl/ **noun [count]** something that you hope to achieve

inaccurate /ɪn'ækjʊrət/ **adj.** not accurate or correct

inconsistent /ˌɪnkən'sɪstənt/ **adj.** not always behaving in the same way or producing the same results

informal /ɪn'fɔː(r)m(ə)l/ **adj.** relaxed, friendly, and not official

irritate /'ɪrɪteɪt/ **verb [T]** to make you feel annoyed or angry

measure /'meʒə(r)/ **verb [T]** to form an opinion about how good or bad something is

medium /'miːdiəm/ **adj.** between small and large in size or amount

motivate /'məʊtɪveɪt/ **verb [T]** to make someone feel enthusiastic about doing something or determined to do something

motivation /ˌməʊtɪ'veɪʃ(ə)n/ **noun [uncount]** a feeling of enthusiasm about something, or a determination to do something

nonsense /'nɒns(ə)ns/ **noun [uncount]** ideas, behaviour, or statements that are not true or sensible

outstanding /aʊt'stændɪŋ/ **adj.** extremely good or impressive

performance /pə(r)'fɔː(r)məns/ **noun [uncount]** the standard of success that someone or something achieves

perspective /pə(r)'spektɪv/ **noun [count]** a way of thinking about something

prejudice /'predʒʊdɪs/ **noun [uncount]** an unreasonable opinion or feeling, especially the feeling of not liking a particular group of people

prepared /prɪ'peə(r)d/ **adj.** ready and able to do something

rate /reɪt/ **verb [T]** to consider that someone or something has a particular quality or has achieved a particular standard or level

rating /'reɪtɪŋ/ **noun [count]** a measurement of how good or popular someone or something is

reinforce /ˌriːɪn'fɔː(r)s/ **verb [T]** to make an idea, belief, or feeling stronger

reward /rɪ'wɔː(r)d/ **verb [T]** to give someone something such as praise or money as a reward

scale /skeɪl/ **noun [count]** a range of numbers or amounts forming a system for separating things into different groups

scheme /skiːm/ **noun [count]** a plan that is developed by a government or a large organization in order to provide a particular service for people

scoring system /'skɔːrɪŋ sɪstəm/ **noun [count]** an organized way of deciding the number of points or amounts given for something

subjective /səb'dʒektɪv/ **adj.** based on your own feelings and ideas, and not on facts

subordinate /sə'bɔː(r)dɪnət/ **noun [count]** someone who has less power or authority than someone else

teamwork /'tiːmˌwɜː(r)k/ **noun [uncount]** work that you do together with other people

timescale /'taɪmˌskeɪl/ **noun [count]** the period of time in which something happens or should be done

trust /trʌst/ **noun [uncount]** a feeling that you trust someone or something

trust /trʌst/ **verb [T]** to believe that someone or something is good, honest, or reliable

uneconomic /ˌʌniːkə'nɒmɪk/ **adj.** not capable of making a profit

unfair /ʌn'feə(r)/ **adj.** not fair, just , or reasonable

unpopular /ʌn'pɒpjʊlə(r)/ **adj.** disliked by many people

useless /'juːsləs/ **adj.** not effective in achieving the purpose it was intended to achieve

values /'væljuːz/ **noun [plural]** the principles and beliefs that influence the behaviour and way of life of a particular group or community

waste /weɪst/ **noun [uncount]** the failure to use something that is valuable or useful in an effective way

CASE STUDY 4
COMPANY STRUCTURE

accountability /əˌkaʊntəˈbɪləti/ **noun [uncount]** responsibility for something that has happened

accountable /əˈkaʊntəb(ə)l/ **adj.** in a position where people can criticize you or ask you why something happened

advantage /ədˈvɑːntɪdʒ/ **noun [count]** a good feature or quality that something has; something that makes one person or thing more likely to succeed than others

advice /ədˈvaɪs/ **noun [uncount]** an opinion that someone gives you about the best thing to do in a particular situation

advise /ədˈvaɪz/ **verb [I/T]** to give your opinion to someone about the best thing to do in a particular situation

approach /əˈprəʊtʃ/ **noun [count]** a way of dealing with something

branch /brɑːntʃ/ **noun [count]** a shop or office representing a large company or organization in a particular area

centralise /ˈsentrəlaɪz/ **verb [T]** to give control of a country, organization, or industry to one central group of people

centralised /ˈsentrəlaɪzd/ **adj.** brought together under the control of one central group of people

chain /tʃeɪn/ **noun [count]** a group of businesses that all belong to the same company

delivery /dɪˈlɪv(ə)ri/ **noun [count]** the process of bringing goods or letters to a place

depot /ˈdepəʊ/ **noun [count]** a large building where things are stored until they are needed

diversify /daɪˈvɜː(r)sɪfaɪ/ **verb [I/T]** to develop additional products or activities

division /dɪˈvɪʒ(ə)n/ **noun [count]** one of the parts into which a large organization is divided

geographical /ˌdʒiːəˈɡræfɪk(ə)l/ **adj.** relating to an area or place, or to geography

growth /ɡrəʊθ/ **noun [uncount]** an increase in the number, size, or importance of something

hierarchy /ˈhaɪəˌrɑː(r)ki/ **noun [uncount]** a system for organizing people according to their status

HR /ˌeɪtʃ ˈɑː(r)/ **noun [uncount]** Human Resources - the department in an organization that is responsible for looking after all of the people who work there, and for choosing new workers

logistics /ləˈdʒɪstɪks/ **noun [plural]** the practical arrangements that are necessary in order to organize something successfully

lorry /ˈlɒri/ **noun [count]** a large road vehicle that is used for carrying goods = TRUCK

operating costs /ˈɒpəreɪtɪŋ kɒsts/ **noun [plural]** the day-to-day expenses incurred in running a business

operational /ˌɒpəˈreɪʃ(ə)nəl/ **adj.** relating to the way something works

policy /ˈpɒləsi/ **noun [count]** a set of plans or actions that are agreed on by a government, political party, business, or other organization

profit /ˈprɒfɪt/ **noun [uncount]** money that you get when you sell something for a price that is higher than the cost of making it or buying it

project /ˈprɒdʒekt/ **noun [count]** an organized attempt to achieve something

promote /prəˈməʊt/ **verb [T]** to support something or to help something to develop

retail /ˈriːteɪl/ **adj.** relating to the sale of goods directly to the public for their own use

role /rəʊl/ **noun [count]** the purpose or influence that someone or something has

sector /ˈsektə(r)/ **noun [count]** a part of a country's economic or business activity

segment /ˈsegmənt/ **noun [count]** a part of something

stock /stɒk/ **noun [uncount]** the goods that are available to buy in a shop

supply /səˈplaɪ/ **verb [T]** to provide someone or something with something that they need or want

talent /ˈtælənt/ **noun [uncount]** a natural ability for doing a particular activity well

team /tiːm/ **noun [count]** a group of people who work together

temporary /ˈtemp(ə)rəri/ **adj.** existing, done, or used for only a limited period of time

truck /trʌk/ **noun [count]** a large road vehicle that is used for carrying goods = LORRY

warehouse /ˈweə(r)ˌhaʊs/ **noun [count]** a big building where large amounts of goods are stored

CASE STUDY 5
LINUX

adapt /ə'dæpt/ **verb [T]** to make something more suitable for a new use or situation

afford /ə'fɔː(r)d/ **verb [T]** to have enough money to pay for something

billion /'bɪljən/ **number** the number 1,000,000,000

budget /'bʌdʒɪt/ **verb [I]** to carefully plan the way you will spend your money

compatible /kəm'pætəb(ə)l/ **adj.** able to be used together with another piece of computer equipment or software

consequence /'kɒnsɪkwəns/ **noun [count]** a result or effect of something

desktop computer /ˌdesktɒp kəm'pjuːtə(r)/ **noun [count]** a computer of a size designed to be used on a desk or table, as opposed to larger machines, such as mainframes, and smaller machines, such as laptops

effective /ɪ'fektɪv/ **adj.** working well and producing the result that was intended

efficiency /ɪ'fɪʃ(ə)nsi/ **noun [uncount]** the ability to work well and produce good results, using the available time, money, supplies etc. in the most effective way

effort /'efə(r)t/ **noun [uncount]** physical or mental energy needed to do something

evaluate /ɪ'væljueɪt/ **verb [T]** to think carefully about something before you make a a judgement about its value, importance, or quality

licensing fees /'laɪs(ə)nsɪŋ ˌfiːz/ **noun [plural]** money that you pay to an organization to be allowed to use their software

format /'fɔː(r)mæt/ **noun [uncount/ count]** the arrangement, size, or shape of something

gadget /'gædʒɪt/ **noun [count]** a small tool or piece of equipment that does something that is useful or impressive

a great deal of sth /ə 'greɪt ˌdiːl əv sʌmθɪŋ/ **phrase** a large amount of something

hardware /'hɑːd(r)ˌweə(r)/ **noun [uncount]** computer equipment

illegal /ɪ'liːg(ə)l/ **adj.** not allowed by the law

install /ɪn'stɔːl/ **verb [T]** to put a piece of equipment somewhere or a piece of software into a computer and make it ready for use

license /'laɪs(ə)ns/ **noun [count]** an official document that gives you permission to do or use something

margin /'mɑː(r)dʒɪn/ **noun [count]** an additional amount of time, space, money etc that you include to be certain that you will be safe or successful

monopoly /mə'nɒpəli/ **noun [uncount]** complete control over something by one organization or person

pirate version /ˌpaɪrət 'vɜː(r)ʃ(ə)n/ **adj.** illegal copy of computer program, book, video or CD

policy /'pɒləsi/ **noun [count]** a set of plans or actions that are agreed on by a government, political party, business, or other organization

pricing /'praɪsɪŋ/ **adj.** relating to the amount of money that is charged for something

secure /sɪ'kjʊə(r)/ **adj.** safe from attack, harm or damage

software /'sɒf(t)ˌweə(r)/ **noun [uncount]** the programs used by computers for doing particular jobs

stability /stə'bɪləti/ **noun [uncount]** a situation in which things continue without any major changes or problems

stable /'steɪb(ə)l/ **adj.** not changing frequently, and not likely to suddenly become worse

update /'ʌpdeɪt/ **noun [count]** a piece of software that contains recent improvements to a computer program

upgrade /'ʌpˌgreɪd/ **noun [count]** a piece of equipment or software that is designed to make a computer more powerful or effective

version /'vɜː(r)ʃ(ə)n/ **noun [count]** a form of something that is different from other forms or from the original

viability /ˌvaɪə'bɪləti/ **noun [uncount]** ability to work and succeed

Macmillan Education
Between Towns Road, Oxford OX4 3PP
A division of Macmillan Publishers Limited
Companies and representatives throughout the world

ISBN 978-0-230-71717-6

First published 2003
This edition 2009

Designed by Keith Shaw, Threefold Design Ltd
Illustrated by Julian Mosedale p108
Cover design by Keith Shaw, Threefold Design Ltd
Cover photographs by IMAGE SOURCE, PHOTOALTO

Authors' acknowledgements:
The first edition of In Company was commissioned by David Riley who is sadly no longer with us. I will be forever grateful to him for giving me a chance to get into print in the first place and he continues to be an important influence. His ideas and advice have remained as pertinent and valuable for subsequent projects as for the first edition of In Company Pre-Intermediate.
Many thanks to the team at Macmillan and especially to Darina Richter who has brought this second edition to fruition and made the process so pain-free. I am also grateful to Katherine Stannett who edited the manuscript, correcting my errors with tact and steering me through all the technical aspects of book production with great precision and efficiency. Finally I would like to thank my long-suffering family for their patience and support.

The publishers would like to thank Rob Ratto, Bryron, Rome; Angela Wright, British Council, Rome; Norman Cain, IH Rome; Fiona Campbell, Teach-In Rome; Sue Garton, Lois Clegg and Irene Frederick, University of Parma; Simon Hopson and Gordon Doyle, Intensive Business English, Milan; Dennis Marino, Bocconi University, Milan; Mike Cruikshank, Advanced Language Services, Milan; Christine Zambon, Person to Person, Milan; Fiona O'Connor, In-Company English, Milan; Peter Panton, Panton School, Milan; Colin Irving Bell, Novara; Marta Rodriguez Casal, Goal Rush Institute, Buenos Aires; Elizabeth Mangi and Silvia Ventura, NET New English Training, Buenos Aires; Graciela Yohma and Veronica Cenini, CABSI, Buenos Aires; Viviana Pisani, Asociación Ex Alumnos, Buenos Aires; Claudia Siciliano, LEA Institute, Buenos Aires; Cuca Martocq, AACI, Buenos Aires; Laura Lewin, ABS International, Buenos Aires; Charlie Lopez, Instituto Big Ben, Buenos Aires; Alice Elvira Machado; Patricia Blower; Valeria Siniscalchi; Carla Chaves; Virginia Garcia; Cultura Inglesa, Rio de Janeiro; Susan Dianne Mace, Britannia, Rio de Janeiro; John Paraskou, Diamond School, Sèvres; Dorothy Polley and Nadia Fairbrother, Executive Language Services, Paris; Claire MacMurray, Formalangues, Paris; Claire Oldmeadow, Franco British Chamber of Commerce, Paris; Ingrid Foussat and Anne James, IFG Langues, Paris; Karl Willems, Quai d'Orsay Language Centre, Paris; Louis Brazier, Clare Davis, Jacqueline Deubel, Siobhan Mlačak and Redge, Télélangue, Paris; John Morrison Milne, Ian Stride, Gareth East and Richard Marrison, IH Madrid; Gina Cuciniello; Helena Gomm; Paulette Dooler.

The publishers would like to thank the following schools and teachers for their help in developing the second edition: Sylvia Renaudon, Hannah Leloup, Sven Steph at Transfer, Paris; Nadia Fairbrother at Executive Language services, Paris; Fiona Delaney at Formalangues, Paris; Paul Chambers, Ruth Maslen at BPL, Paris; Moira Jansen and teachers at Anglo English School, Hamburg; Patrick Woulfe and John Ryde at International House, Hamburg; Charles Reid Dick, Christine Dlugokencky, Petra Mocklinghoff, Marie-Colette Dodd, Orla Mac Mahon at Eurospeak, Hamburg; Bill Cope at English School of Hamburg; Slavomir Gibarti, Slovakia; Sylvie Jeanloz, France.
Many thanks to all the teachers around the world who took the time to complete our In Company online questionnaire.

The authors and publishers would like to thank the following for permission to reproduce their photographs:
Alamy p64, Alamy/T.Tracy/Stock Connection Distribution p82, Alamy/Image 100 p90(b), Alamy/ImageState pp114 ,115; **Altrendo Images** p56; **Corbis** p33(t&b), Corbis/Bettmann p104, Corbis/Sygma/L.Bonaventure p92, Corbis/Comstock p120, Corbis/Hulton Deutsch p31, Corbis/Zefa/J.Feingersh p106, Corbis/A.Fox p115, A.Inden p15, Corbis/M. Kulka p19(l), Corbis/G. Mendel p83, Corbis/Zefa/V. Mo p103(b), Corbis/J.Noble p52, Corbis/Zefa/T.O'Leary p89, Corbis/Mango Productions p21(b), Corbis/Zefa/T.Roepke p116, **Getty Images** /J.Arbogast p85, Getty /C. Casariego p46(l), Getty/E. Dryer p122, Getty / Kobal Foundation p73, Getty/S.Gallup p 84, Getty / T.Hopkins p37, Getty/Asia Images/T.Metaxas p127(b), Getty/D.McNew p30, Getty/P.Nicklen p121, Getty/D.Noton p139, Getty/Blend Images/J.Luis Pelaez Inc p80, Getty/China Tourism Press p40(tr), Getty/T. Shioguchi p6(tb), Getty/K.Steele p10; **Hulton Archive** pp 48(r), 66, 97; **Iconica** pp 54,103(t); **Image Bank** pp13(b),21(t),27, 90(tm), 99, 114(t), 123(mt); **Image Source** p63(b); **Inditex** pp 59. 60; **Masterfile** MTPA Stock p6(t), Masterfile pp28, 90(mb); **Macmillan Publishers Ltd** / Rob Judges/ Des Dubber p63(bm); **PA/** AP/Empics/T.Avelar p72(b), PA/AP/V.Ghirda p70, PA/AP/D.Hoemann p72(t), PA/P.Sakuma p7, PA/APC. Stache p130, PA/C.Young p46(tr); **Photodisc** pp 63(tm), 65; **Photolibrary.com** pp 6(mb), 6(b), 9,20,29, 55, 57, 67, 96, 107, 117,123(b); **Photographer's Choice** p49; **Photonica** p95; **Riser** pp 16,33(m), 58, 123(t), 123(mb); **Stock4B** p77; **Stone** pp 19(m), 40(b), 79, 88, 91,108, 113, 124, 127(t); **Taxi** pp13(t),26,33(m),34, 44, 53, 63(tr), 74, 90(t), 129;**Topfoto/** AP p32, Topfoto/Photri p78; **Vin Mag Archive** p102; **Rose Tower Hotel** reproduced with permission of: **<https://community.emporis.com/il/ii/?lng=3&id=100043> Marshall Gerometta/ Emporis.com** p48(l)

Picture research: Sally Cole/Perseverance Works Ltd

The author and publishers are grateful for permission to reprint the following copyright material:
Extracts about Facebook taken from www.facebook.com; Adapted extracts from www.brendan.com.au, copyright © Brendan Walsh, reprinted by permission of the author; Extract from 'Do you have/use Internet access at work?' from http://forums.monster.co.uk; Extracts from 'Office staff lose their jobs after bosses catch them trading on e-bay' by Simon de Bruxelles taken from Times On Line 21.09.07 copyright © N I Syndication 2007, reprinted by permission of the publisher; Adapted extracts from 'Here's how I introduced an email and internet policy' by Caroline Wheeler Taken from www.businesslink.gov.uk; Extract from www.4hoteliers.com, copyright 4Hoteliers 2008, reprinted by permission of 4Hoteliers.com – The Global Hotel & Travel News Portal; Extract about 'Yotel at Gatwick, reprinted by permission of Yotel Limited; 'Entrepreneur' taken from www.freedictionary.com; Extract about Blackcircles 'www.blackcircles.com, reprinted by permission of Blackcircles.com Limited; Extract about Dreams Bed Store taken from www.startups.co.uk; Adapted extracts and photograph taken from Inditex.com; Adapted extract from 'Doing it for the kids' from www.bmgroup.co.uk; Extract from 'How to avoid the middle seat, How to cope if you get stuck' from businesstravel.about.com; Extract from 'Business Hiring and Firing' by Lou Carloni taken from The Industrial Physicist Vol. 9 (3) copyright © American Institute of Physics, reprinted by permission of the publisher; Short extract from www.sme-blog.com copyright © Stefan Töpfer, reprinted by permission of Winweb International Limited; Extract from 'Wasting Time at Work' by Galen Black taken from www.vgg.com copyright © Galen Black 2001, reprinted by permission of the publisher; Extract from 'How to ……Get things done' by Guy Browning copyright Guy Browning 2005, first published in The Guardian 04.06.05, reprinted by permission of the author; Extract from 'Work-life balance debates "over-simplistic" by Judith Doyle taken from www.peronneltoday.com, reprinted by permission of the publisher; Short extract from www.axa.co.uk; Extract from 'Global IT firm predicts Linux will have 20% desktop market share by 2008' by Chris Gulker, copyright © Chris Gulker 2003, taken from Linux.com 14.08.03; Extracts from www.elliott.org copyright © Chris Elliot, reprinted by permission of the author.

Printed in Thailand

2014 2013 2012
10 9 8 7 6